African American Leadership

An Empowerment Tradition in Social Welfare History

African American Leadership

An Empowerment Tradition in Social Welfare History

Edited by Iris B. Carlton-LaNey

NASW PRESS

National Association of Social Workers Washington, DC

Cheryl Y. Bradley, Director, Member Services and Publications
Paula L. Delo, Executive Editor
Susan Fisher, Editor
January Layman-Wood, Acquisitions Editor
Robin Bourjaily, Copy Editor
Gail Martin, Editorial Associates, Proofreader
Deborah E. Patton, Indexer
Mia Reese-Smith, Editorial Secretary

Library of Congress Cataloging-in-Publication Data

African American leadership: an empowerment tradition in social welfare history / edited by Iris B. Carlton-LaNey.

p. cm.

Includes bibliographical references and index.

ISBN 0-87101-317-7

1. African American social workers--Biography. 2. Social service--United States--History. I. Carlton-LaNey, Iris.

HV27 .A46 2001

361.3'2'08996073--dc21 00-068701

Contents

About the Editor vii

About the Contributors ix

Introduction and Overview xi
Iris B. Carlton-LaNey

1 Victoria Earle Matthews: Residence and Reform 1
Cheryl Waites

2 African Americans and Social Work in Philadelphia, Pennsylvania, 1900–1930 17
Tawana Ford Sabbath

3 Birdye Henrietta Haynes: A Pioneer Settlement House Worker 35
Iris B. Carlton-LaNey

4 Margaret Murray Washington: Organizer of Rural African American Women 55
Joyce G. Dickerson

5 Marcus Garvey and Community Development via the UNIA 75
Aminifu Harvey and Iris B. Carlton-LaNey

6 Ida B. Wells-Barnett: An Uncompromising Style 87
Tricia Bent-Goodley

7 Lawrence A. Oxley: Defining State Public Welfare among African Americans 99
N. Yolanda Burwell

8 George Edmund Haynes and Elizabeth Ross Haynes: Empowerment Practice among African American Social Welfare Pioneers 111
Iris B. Carlton-LaNey

9 Janie Porter Barrett and the Virginia Industrial School for Colored Girls: Community Response to the Needs of African American Children 123
Wilma Peebles-Wilkins

10 Eugene Kinckle Jones: A Statesman for the Times 137
Felix L. Armfield and Iris B. Carlton-LaNey

11 Mary Church Terrell and Her Mission: Giving Decades of Quiet Service 153
Sharon Warren Cook

12 Thyra J. Edwards: Internationalist Social Worker 163
Elmer P. Martin and Joanne M. Martin

13 Sarah Collins Fernandis and Her Hidden Work 179
Huguette A. Curah

14 E. Franklin Frazier and Social Work: Unity and Conflict 189
Susan Kerr Chandler

15 Historical Development of African American Child Welfare Services 203
Vanessa G. Hodges

16 Traditional Helping Roles of Older African American Women: The Concept of Self-Help 215
Dorothy S. Ruiz

Index 229

About the Editor

Iris B. Carlton-LaNey, PhD, is professor, School of Social Work, University of North Carolina at Chapel Hill. Her research interests include aging in rural communities and African American social welfare history. Dr. Carlton-LaNey has co-edited two books, *African American Community Practice Models: Historical and Contemporary Responses* and *Preserving and Strengthening Small Towns and Rural Communities*. She has authored a monograph entitled *Elderly Black Farm Women as Keepers of the Community and Culture* and has served as guest editor for special issues of the *Journal of Sociology and Social Welfare* and the *Journal of Community Practice*. She has also served on the editorial boards of several journals and has published articles in *Generations*, *Social Work*, *Social Service Review*, *Arete*, the *Journal of Community Practice*, and the *Journal of Sociology and Social Welfare*.

In memory of W. Galloway Carlton, my father,
and Willie E. Carlton, my brother.

The strength of their character continues to empower me.

About the Contributors

Felix L. Armfield, PhD, assistant professor of history, Department of History and Social Studies Education, Buffalo State College, Buffalo, New York. Armfield is presently completing a manuscript about Eugene Kinckle Jones and his role in early African American social work activity.

Tricia Bent-Goodley, PhD, LICSW-C, assistant professor, Howard University School of Social Work, Washington, DC. Bent-Goodley is the current chair of the National Association of Black Social Workers Academy for African-Centered Social Work.

N. Yolanda Burwell, PhD, associate professor, School of Social Work and Criminal Justice Studies, East Carolina University, Greenville, North Carolina. Burwell's major research area is uncovering early social work/social welfare leaders and activities in African American communities.

Susan Kerr Chandler, PhD, MSW, associate professor, School of Social Work, University of Nevada, Reno. Chandler's historical work focuses on the experience of African American social service professionals in the 20th century.

Sharon Warren Cook, MSW, assistant professor of social work and social welfare coordinator, Winston-Salem State University, Winston-Salem, North Carolina. Cook is currently completing a PhD in curriculum and instruction at the University of North Carolina, Greensboro.

Hugette A. Curah, MSW, social worker, Family Support Unit, Wake County Human Services, Raleigh, North Carolina. Curah has been practicing social work for 13 years and is committed to family support social work practice.

Joyce G. Dickerson, PhD, MSW, assistant professor, Department of Sociology and Social Work, North Carolina A&T State University, Greensboro. Dickerson is a licensed certified clinical social worker.

Aminifu Harvey, DSW, LCSW-C, associate professor of social work, University of Maryland, Baltimore. Harvey's special interests are the cultural/ethnic influences in the development of social work and the development and implementation of culturally competent social services. He has published in both areas.

Vanessa G. Hodges, PhD, MSW, associate professor in social work, University of North Carolina, Chapel Hill. Hodges serves as interim associate dean of the School of Social Work. Her teaching and research interests include social work practice with high-risk children and families, culturally sensitive child welfare and family based practice, intervention and design and development, and strengths-based social work practice.

Elmer P. Martin, PhD, professor, Department of Social Work and Mental Health, Morgan State University, Baltimore, Maryland. Since 1976, Martin has taught courses on Black families, the Black community, social work research, social policy, and the politics of social work. He is also the cofounder and president of The Great Blacks in Wax Museum, Inc.

Joanne M. Martin, PhD, cofounder, The Great Blacks in Wax Museum, Baltimore, Maryland. The museum is the nation's first and currently the only wax museum concentrating on Black history, life, and culture.

Wilma Peebles-Wilkins, PhD, dean and professor, Boston University School of Social Work, Boston, Massachusetts. One area of Peebles-Wilkins' research and scholarship has focused on the historical developments of the contribution of Black women to American social welfare. She is also interested in the delivery of health and mental health services.

Dorothy S. Ruiz, PhD, associate professor, Department of African American and African Studies, University of North Carolina, Charlotte. Ruiz's present research concerns the health and social indicators of stress among African American grandmother caregivers.

Tawana Ford Sabbath, MSS, PhD, social worker and funeral business co-owner, Philadelphia, Pennsylvania. Sabbath has been a faculty member at Bryn Mawr and Antioch College, Philadelphia. She consults with local agencies and institutions regarding staff and client empowerment, racial and ethnic diversity, spirituality, and grief.

Cheryl Waites, EdD, MSW, ACSW, associate professor, Social Work Program, North Carolina State University, Raleigh. Waites has extensive social work experience in child welfare.

Introduction and Overview

Iris B. Carlton-LaNey

This book presents a discussion of African American social work and social welfare pioneers who contributed to and influenced the African American social welfare movement that began in the late 1800s and continued into the early 1900s and beyond, a movement that paralleled social work and social welfare among White Americans. The individuals included here are identified as pioneers in social work and social welfare because they were. The social work profession, however, has never acknowledged some and only recently has included others among the ranks of pioneers. A close read of the biographies of the White pioneers who worked with African Americans at various times throughout their careers finds no mention of the prominent African Americans with whom they sometimes associated, an oversight that could be attributed to any number of variables, not the least of which is race. Nonetheless, the individuals discussed throughout this text were remarkable, indefatigable, and determined to improve the quality of life for "the race" and for any others in need of relief from human suffering.

Accurate and cogently written social work history can be of great benefit to contemporary social work practitioners. It can help to connect present problems and future solutions with their historical antecedents. In addition to filling gaps in our knowledge, history can also add dimensions of time to the practice of helping in the context of physical, socioeconomic, and cultural environments (Reisch, 1988). Contemporary social work neglects and marginalizes its history and often leaves it to be written by others outside the profession. To leave the history of social work and social welfare to historians outside the profession can limit the historical record and the insight that those who understand the profession would bring (Fisher & Dybicz, 1999).

Building on the historical record, this book arms it readers with a perspective from which to examine present day problems, analyze current policies, and develop contemporary practice models. The scholars whose works appear in this book have committed themselves to presenting an accurate, truthful, and inclusive picture of social welfare history from a social work perspective. Contributing to this book was, for most of us, a professional imperative. It was an opportunity to set the historical record straight and to bring out of obscurity some little known pioneers whose works have been relegated to historical footnotes.

As Allen-Meares and Burman (1995) and Johnson (1991) noted, the social work profession has maintained a discomforting silence when viewing inequalities and social conditions that affect African Americans. The exclusion of African American social welfare pioneers from our historical record is part of that conspiracy of silence. That silence has allowed us to ignore the important pioneers whose work not only influenced the development of the profession, but also enhanced the quality of life for a substantial portion of the world's population.

The pioneers selected for discussion in this book were not chosen through any organized or strategic formula. Rather, I identified these pioneers over several years of historical research that began with my accidental discovery of George Edmund Haynes, co-founder and first executive director of the National Urban League (NUL), who subsequently became the topic of my dissertation. My dissertation was the third one written about Dr. Haynes and the only one written by a social worker from a social work perspective. Through my extensive research on Dr. Haynes's social work career, I was introduced to many other Progressive Era pioneers who committed themselves to social betterment for the African American community. Many of these pioneers have been ignored in social work, while others have enjoyed some marginal notoriety. I also asked social welfare and social work historians to identify individuals for inclusion in this book, and I selfishly included people about whom I wanted to know more as well.

The historical record of African American social welfare leaders is spotty and sometimes has huge information gaps. Furthermore, manuscripts and personal papers are often not neatly housed and catalogued in public or private archives. Therefore, it is sometimes difficult to write a story that presents a complete picture of these individuals' lives and work. Partly for this reason, and partly because a total biographical oration is not needed to convey the empowerment roles that these leaders played in social welfare, the chapters here were not intended to be complete biographies or life histories. Instead, they are more aptly described as intellectual biographies. The intellectual biography is the life history of an individual preeminently guided by the intellectual as distinguished from experiential or emotional. Of the three types of life histories, the complete, the topical, and the edited, the intellectual biography can be defined as an edited topical life history (Carlton-LaNey, 1990; Denzin, 1970). That is, it presents one phase of the subject's life (topical) with the continual interspersing of comments, explanations, and questions by someone other the focal subject (edited). These intellectual biographies, with few exceptions, focus primarily on innovators who lived and worked during the Progressive Era.

There are also three chapters (2, 15, and 16) in this book that focus less on the individual and more on the work surrounding a particular problem area. The three chapters each generally focus on child welfare issues. Chapter 2 addresses child welfare issues from the perspective of organizational responses; chapter 15 traces the historical development of child welfare in the United States; and chapter 16 focuses on the roles that women, especially older women, have played and continue to play in child caregiving.

The Progressive Era (1898–1918) was a critical period that marked the professionalization of social work as well as the widespread development of private social welfare organizations and programs. It was also a time of great prosperity for America; however, many, including African Americans, did not share in the country's good fortune. Instead, between the 1890s and 1920s, there was a sudden outpouring of anti-African American literature that inundated the South and the nation. Scientists and social scientists with easy access to journals published voluminously of the racial inequality and inferiority of African Americans. Social segregation was advocated and the "Negro's personality and character traits" were considered "depraved, immoral, and repugnant to the sensibility and sensitivity of civilized white men" (Newby, 1965, p. 16). Partly in response to this institutionalized racism and discrimination, several major social welfare organizations became entrenched in African American life. The National Association of Colored Women (NACW), which had been established in 1896 with 200 clubs, boasted 1,500 affiliates by 1916 (White, 1999). The National League on Urban Conditions Among Negroes (NLUCAN), founded in 1911, became synonymous with social work in the African American community by 1916, and the American branch of the Universal Negro Improvement Association (UNIA), organized in 1916 to empower all peoples of African ancestry to develop a "fierce Afro-centric view of the world" (Martin, 1986, p. xvi), eventually grew to include over 1,000 branches throughout the world (Harvey, 1994). Essentially, these organizations, as well as other similar ones, and their charismatic leadership provided the foundation and framework for social welfare service delivery in the African American community.

The problems to which these groups responded included an array of life-threatening social ills. Clearly, racism and its attenuating grasp made life harsh and oppressive for African Americans. This institutionalized racism permeated American life, denying access for African Americans to opportunities and resources. The race lens through which nearly all of life's circumstances were viewed and significant decisions addressed was always in place. Furthermore, among African American social welfare leaders, life circumstances had produced a "profound distrust of white people" in spite of the fact that some were valued benefactors and others even carried the label "friend" (Carlton-LaNey, 2000; White, 1999, p. 98).

Sexism was also a destructive practice and one against which many rebelled. Disparaging comments about and violent acts against African American women kept the issue of sexism at the top of the agenda for women's clubs and organizations like Victoria Earle Matthews' White Rose Mission. Combating sexual exploitation was inextricably linked to race uplift. Unlike their White sisters, African American women faced the fact that both African American and White men perpetuated sexual exploitation and violence.

Politicizing sexual exploitation and harassment for African American women placed it squarely within the context of race (Carlton-LaNey, 1999; Gordon, 1991; Hine 1990).

Many other social problems existed among African Americans during the Progressive Era. African American poverty was omnipresent. Because of poverty, the quality of life for African Americans in both the South and nationwide was miserable. Hemingway (1980) noted that the typical African American Carolinian, for example, "lived in a weather-beaten, unpainted, poorly ventilated shack, subsisted on a thoroughly inadequate diet and was disease ridden. Hook worms, pellagra and a variety of exposure-induced aliments consistently plagued him, limiting his life expectancy rate" (p. 213). Their northern, urban counterparts did not fare much better. They, too, found life harsh and difficult; however, circumstances in the North offered some room for self-respect and the hope for a better future. Nonetheless, the road to overcoming poverty was plagued with discrimination in housing and employment; inadequate education, health care, and diet; and disproportionate rates of delinquency, crime, and death.

Social Welfare Pioneers

The social welfare pioneers discussed in this book, along with the varied child-focused services and programs, set out to combat many of the ills that confronted African Americans at the turn of the century. This group of pioneers had strength of conviction and tenacity that allowed them to continue their work in spite of the institutionalized forces that militated against their success. Some, such as outspoken and aggressive leaders like Marcus Garvey and Ida Bell Wells-Barnett, who held political ideologies that were in conflict with those of the power elite, were persecuted for their activism. Others who were somewhat more palatable, like E. Kinckle Jones, were embraced. Beginning with little more than intellectual will and veracity, these pioneers found the resources and human capital needed to establish and provide social welfare services; to train social workers via institutes and formal schools; to travail as womanists, orators, and anti-lynching crusaders; to struggle and strategize against social injustices; and to implement programs for social change and group empowerment.

Moreover, African American "empowerment" was at the heart of their work, although coinage of the term was to come more than 60 years later when Barbara Solomon published her seminal work *Black Empowerment* (1976). Solomon defines empowerment as "a process whereby persons who belong to a stigmatized social category throughout their lives can be assisted to develop and increase skills in the exercise of interpersonal influence and the performance of valued social roles" (p. 6).

Solomon further noted the importance of helping professionals involved in empowerment practice engage in a set of activities with the client that are aimed at reducing powerlessness, which stems from the experience of discrimination. The African American pioneers discussed in this book were themselves members of the same stigmatized social category as the people whom they served. They lived in the same communities and, because of the physical and social distance caused by housing discrimination and other common practices of segregation, were neighbors to the people whom they served. Many of these pioneers, however, were able to escape some of the negative valuations that accompany powerlessness because of their family relationships, cohesive group relationships, and in some cases financial resources that provided a protective barrier or at least a protective cushion against society's larger negative valuation. Such individuals were able to obtain and utilize a broad range of personal and interpersonal resources to obtain some modicum of success. Their empowerment work embraced what Martin and Martin (1995) called the extended family model. They generally targeted those individuals who had lost a sense of family and community, such as urban migrants, orphaned and delinquent youth, young children of working mothers who were without caregivers for extended periods, frail and abandoned elders, and convicts. Through an array of other services and programs such as settlement houses, old folks' homes, and organized leisure, (for example, literary clubs and newcomers' dances), these pioneers tried to recreate the communities that had been lost. They engaged in program development, service delivery, advocacy, role modeling, teaching, and mentoring as strategies for empowerment.

Contents of the Book

Chapter 1, by **Cheryl Waites**, profiles Victoria Earle Matthews and her legendary work via the White Rose Home. Waites highlights Matthews's work as a journalist, as a womanist with women's clubs, and as a national organizer. The various programs at the White Rose Home are discussed in detail as the author illustrates the empowerment bent of Matthews's work.

Tawana Ford Sabbath, in chapter 2, discusses three social service organizations in Philadelphia during the Progressive Era: the Armstrong Association of Philadelphia, the Women's Christian Alliance (WCA), and the Bureau for Colored Children (The Bureau). The author presents a clear picture of the WCA's work, even with the limitations caused by a paucity of consistent primary data. Sabbath also discusses how the Armstrong Association was engaged primarily in activities placing migrating African Americans into suitable work settings. She discusses several pioneer social work and social welfare leaders and argues for more research to firmly entrench these organizations in social work history.

In chapter 3, **Iris B. Carlton-LaNey** discusses the career of Birdye Henrietta Haynes, a prominent social settlement house matron and the first African American to graduate from the Chicago School of Civics and Philanthropy. Haynes practiced social work at two of the most prominent social settlements established to serve African American clients: Chicago's Wendell Phillips Settlement and New York's Lincoln House. Using primary data, Carlton-LaNey presents an analysis of Haynes's career.

In chapter 4, **Joyce G. Dickerson** provides an exhaustive summary of Margaret Murray Washington's life as an organizer of rural African American women. Washington was Booker T. Washington's third wife and created an impressive record as a prominent club woman, educator, and community organizer. Washington established the Tuskegee

Woman's Club, the Town Night School for farm wives, and the Elizabeth Russell Plantation Settlement, all in Tuskegee, Alabama. She was also a leader in prison reform and helped to establish the Mt. Meigs Reformatory for Juvenile Law-Breakers and the Mt. Meigs Home for Girls.

Aminifu Harvey and **Iris B. Carlton-LaNey**, in chapter 5, present a descriptive historical analysis of Marcus Garvey's Universal Negro Improvement Association and African Communities League (UNIA & ACL). Discussing the UNIA & ACL as a model of community building, Harvey and Carlton-LaNey describe the services, programs, training, and discipline that were inherent in the growth and germane to the development of this organization. The authors also cite and highlight some of the various subgroups within the organization, for example, the universal African Black Cross Nurses who functioned as a social service and social welfare arm of the organization, providing an array of professional services.

In chapter 6, **Tricia Bent-Goodley** addresses the Womanist Christian Ethic that guided Ida Bell Wells-Barnett's career. Wells-Barnett was an advocate for social justice for African Americans. She was a founding member of several major human rights and human services organizations, including the NAACP, the Alpha Suffrage Club, and the Negro Fellowship League and Reading Room. Throughout her career, Wells-Barnett owned three newspapers and used them to inform and encourage African Americans in their struggle to survive segregated oppressive communities.

N. Yolanda Burwell discusses the social work and social welfare activities of Lawrence A. Oxley in chapter 7. Burwell presents an edited topical life history of Oxley, concentrating on his role in training African American social workers and his contributions to the maturation of professional social work practice in North Carolina. Oxley oversaw state institutions that served African Americans and worked diligently with state and county agencies to improve the pressing social conditions facing African American citizens. Burwell concludes that what Oxley did in North Carolina was not unique. Rather, the archival records for similar good work need simply to be unearthed.

Chapter 8, by **Iris B. Carlton-LaNey**, discusses the empowerment practice that characterized the careers of George Edmund Haynes and his wife Elizabeth Ross Haynes during the first half of the twentieth century. Details of the careers of this dynamic couple are discussed from the empowerment perspective, focusing on the types of services in which they engaged and their attitudes toward the work and the people whom they served.

Wilma Peebles-Wilkins, in chapter 9, discusses the social ethos that evolved among African American women during the late nineteenth and early twentieth centuries that led to internal child welfare reform in legally segregated African American communities. Her chapter describes the nature of these child welfare developments and provides a historical example using Janie Porter Barrett's Virginia Industrial School for Colored Girls. Prevailing themes derived from the historical account are discussed in a contemporary context.

In chapter 10, **Felix L. Armfield** and **Iris B. Carlton-LaNey** present the career of Eugene Kinckle Jones, social work educator, NUL executive, and community activist.

Jones was active with the major social welfare organizations of the times. He was an elected officer of the National Association of Charities and Corrections and believed in an assimilationist practice of social work. He also espoused a strengths-based practice perspective and encouraged college-educated African Americans, both men and women, to become professionally trained in the social work profession.

In chapter 11, **Sharon Warren Cook** examines Mary Church Terrell's role in the women's club movement. She identifies Terrell as an educator, activist, and social reformer who prevented African American women from being relegated to a state of "near paralysis" in the midst of cultural chaos. According to Cook, Terrell worked as an advocate for African American women, contributing to their development and advancement as independent and powerful citizens.

Elmer P. Martin and **Joanne M. Martin**, devote chapter 12 to the career of Thyra J. Edwards, whose main area of interest was child welfare. She fulfilled a dream when she opened her own home for children in 1928—the Lake County Children's Home. Described as an internationalist social worker, Edwards traveled worldwide to examine the policies and programs that affected children. Martin and Martin chronicle Edwards's life as it operated on three major fronts: child welfare, women's struggles, and social justice for the darker people of the world.

In chapter 13, **Huguette A. Curah** discusses Sarah Collins Fernandis and her social settlement house work in Washington, D.C., along with the many other social services in which she was involved. Curah also elaborates on the social ethos that motivated Fernandis as she took on the role of "settler" in the neighborhoods in which her social settlements were located.

Chapter 14, by **Susan Kerr Chandler**, discusses E. Franklin Frazier and his involvement in the social work profession. Chandler skillfully examines social work's reluctance to embrace Frazier and his own reluctance to acquiesce or to compromise where neither would serve the best interest of the African American community. Chandler identifies three of Frazier's intellectual and social commitments—socialism, racial justice, and a controversial effort to use a combination of psychoanalysis and social justice to probe the internal operation of racial prejudice and oppression.

In chapter 15, **Vanessa G. Hodges** provides an overview of African American child welfare services. Beginning with a brief discussion of African American child welfare in the early twentieth century, Hodges describes the nature and types of services, including individuals and organizations that made significant contributions to child welfare development. She concludes with a discussion of current child welfare challenges to African American children and the lessons gleaned from the past that are applicable to future dilemmas.

Finally, in chapter 16, **Dorothy S. Ruiz** discusses the traditional roles of women, especially grandmothers, in the provision of social services to families and communities. Ruiz traces the grandmother role from the period of slavery to the present and concludes with a focus on contemporary helping roles, problems, and challenges that will confront social scientists in the twenty-first century.

References

Allen-Meares, P., & Burman, S. (1995). The endangerment of African American men: An appeal for social work action. *Social Work, 40*, 268–274.

Carlton-LaNey, I. B. (1990). The intellectual biography: A mechanism for integrating historical content. *Arete, 15*, 46–51.

Carlton-LaNey, I. B. (1999). African American social work pioneers' response to need. *Social Work, 44*, 311–321.

Carlton-LaNey, I. B. (2000). Women and interracial cooperation in establishing the Good Samaritan Hospital. *Affilia, 15*, 65–81.

Denzin, N. (1970). *The research act*. Chicago: Aldine Publishing Company.

Fisher, R., & Dybicz, P. (1999). The place of historical research in social work. *Journal of Sociology and Social Welfare, 26*, 105–124.

Gordon, L. (1991). Black and white visions of welfare: Women's welfare activism, 1890–1945. *Journal of American History, 78*, 559–590.

Harvey, A. (1994). A Black community development model: The Universal Negro Improvement Association and African Communities League, 1917–1940. *Journal of Sociology and Social Welfare, 21*, 113–124.

Hemingway, T. (1980). Prelude to change: Black Carolinas in the war years, 1914–1920. *Journal of Negro History, 65*, 212–227.

Hine, D. (1990). "We specialize in the wholly impossible": The philanthropic work of Black women. In K. McCarthy (Ed.), *Lady bountiful revisited: Women, philanthropy and power* (pp. 70–93). New Brunswick, NJ: Rutgers University Press.

Johnson, A. (1991). The sin of omission: African-American women in social work. *Journal of Multicultural Social Work, 1*, 1–15.

Martin, E., & Martin, J. (1995). *Social work and the Black experience*. Washington, DC: NASW Press.

Newby, I. (1965). *Jim Crow's defense: Anti-Negro thought in America, 1900–1930*. Baton Rouge: Louisiana State University Press.

Reisch, M. (1988). The uses of history in teaching social work. *Journal of Teaching in Social Work*, 2, 3–16.

Solomon, B. (1976). *Black empowerment: Social work in oppressed communities*. New York: Columbia University Press.

White, D. (1999). *Too heavy a load*. New York: W. W. Norton.

CHAPTER 1

Victoria Earle Matthews

Residence and Reform

Cheryl Waites

Victoria Earle Matthews devoted her life to the advancement of her race and gender. Although she had little formal education, by age 20 Matthews was a journalist of national repute. Through her writings and other social services activities, Matthews sought to bring African American women together to work for the welfare of the race. An advocate for preserving race history and for using practical means to facilitate the social uplift of African Americans, Matthews opened a settlement house, organized women's clubs, and pioneered travelers' aid services at the turn of the century. While not as well-known as some of her peers, Matthews's work helped to shape the social welfare movement of the United States.

Matthews was portrayed by a New York newspaper reporter as "a woman of virtue, a Salvation Army field officer, a college settlement worker, a missionary, a teacher, and a sister of mercy all in one without being the least conscious of it" (Brown, 1988, p. 215). As an ardent feminist and gifted lecturer (Cash, 1993; Smith, 1992), she charged other African American women with the responsibility of shaping the intellectual and moral foundations of the race (Williams, 1894). Matthews believed that the power of organization and unity of African American women could bring about needed social reform. A New York associate and *Woman's Era* correspondent identified Matthews as "one of the most enthusiastic women in town, earnest, and to a remarkable degree, a believer in her own sex, and a woman destined to succeed in what she sets out to do. She's a credit to her sex . . . She has stirred our best women as no other woman has done, in my time, at least" (Williams, 1894, p. 5).

A leader of the Progressive Era, Matthews was like many other African American women of her time whose contributions to the development of social welfare history and social welfare institutions in the African American and larger community have been ignored (Carlton-LaNey, 1997; Kogut, 1970; Waites, 1990).

Birth into Slavery

The journey begins in Fort Valley, Georgia, in 1861—one month after the Civil War began. During this very onerous period of American history, Victoria Earle Smith, the youngest of nine children, was born enslaved. Oral history reports that her White slave master, William Smith, sexually violated Caroline Smith, Victoria's mother. Victoria and her older sister Anna were believed to be the result of this victimization. William Smith was described as a man with a very cruel nature (Penn, 1969; Smith, 1992). Female house slaves were often vulnerable to sexual exploitation by the master. One can only imagine the degrading conditions that Caroline faced. Her ultimate resistance to this sexual violence was to escape. After several attempts, Caroline Smith escaped to New York during the Civil War, leaving Victoria and her siblings in the care of an old nurse.

Caroline returned to Georgia for her children after emancipation. However, she was able to find only four of them. The others were believed to be dead. Victoria and Anna were being reared in the master's house. After extensive legal struggles, Caroline gained custody of her two daughters and took them to Virginia, where they lived in Richmond and Norfolk for several years. In 1873, Caroline Smith and her daughters moved to New York City.

At age 12, Victoria was described as "wise beyond her years, a fair-skinned, tall, lank, straight haired girl, with large soulful eyes" (Brown, 1988, p. 209). She attended Grammar School 48, where her advanced reading abilities surpassed those of her classmates. At age 15, she was forced to quit school to support herself and her mother. Victoria became a domestic worker, the only position available to her as a woman of color. She worked in a wealthy home that housed an extensive library. The owners granted her permission to use the library in her spare time. Victoria read "whatever she could lay her hands on" (Brown, 1988, p. 209). Though she was not able to complete her formal education, she continued her instruction through reading and other self-taught means. Whenever possible, she attended lectures, undertook special studies, and consulted with professionals to broaden her knowledge (Schockley, 1988). She took advantage of every opportunity to improve herself intellectually and culturally. Although she was largely self-educated, she is often considered among the first generation of educated Black women of the South (Wade-Gayles, 1981).

In 1876, at the age of 15, Victoria married William Matthews, a carriage driver and native of Petersburg, Virginia. Unlike many of her African American women social activist contemporaries of the Progressive Era, she was not married to a wealthy or prominent man. Victoria did not come from a middle-class background, was not college educated, and came from a financially disadvantaged circumstance. She did not have the educational background of many of her contemporaries, like Mary Church Terrell, Josephine Turpin Washington, and A. E. Tilghman (Wade-Gayles, 1981). Yet she rose to become a noted journalist and an impressive organizer (Cash, 1993).

Matthews gave birth to her son, Larmartine Matthews, in 1879. Very little is known about her relationship with her husband and son. Her son died in 1895 at the age of 16.

This tragic event marked a change in Matthews's work. Her social reform agenda became more focused on community development and the social welfare of children and young women (Best, 1939; Keyser, 1907; Lewis, 1925).

Journalist Reformer

Becoming a journalist was one possible career choice for erudite African Americans. This was a time "when white women were imprisoned by the sexist notion of a 'woman's place,' [but] Black women moved beyond this 'place' into any arena where the struggle for Black freedom was being waged" (Wade-Gayles, 1981, p. 138). Black women used their skills and their talents at all levels of the Black struggle, including journalism. Of the 23 Black women in the nation who were journalists by 1891, 16 were native southerners. Wade-Gayles (1981) described these writers as "phenomenal women, impressive Sojourners wielding pens of political militancy and social concern" (p. 139). Essentially, journalism gave these writers an opportunity for employment that provided a platform for influencing thought, raising consciousness, and facilitating social change.

There were several publishing outlets for women writers like Matthews. The Black church was a prominent institution and a major outlet for educating the community on matters relevant to Black progress and achievement through its many regularly published papers. In addition to church-affiliated literary organs, the women's club movement that flourished during the late nineteenth century also produced a Black press. The *Woman's Era*, a prominent journal, was established in Boston in 1894. It was initially the official publication of the Woman's Era Club of Boston, but later became the literary journal of the National Federation of Afro-American Women (NFAAW), which became the National Association of Colored Women (NACW).

Victoria Earle, often considered the "Queen" of the southern-born writers, struck out on her own as a cub reporter for any paper, South or North, that would use her talents (Wade-Gayles, 1981). During the 1890s, she was a freelance reporter who published in leading newspapers such as *The New York Times*, *New York Herald*, and *Brooklyn Eagle*. She also published in such leading Black newspapers as the *New York Age*, *Advocate* (Boston), *Washington Bee*, *Richmond Planet*, *Cleveland Gazette*, and *New York Globe*. In 1893, Matthews's short story, "Aunt Lindy: A Story Founded on Real Life," was published in book form under her pen name Victoria Earle. Five years later, with the encouragement of the *New York Age* editor, T. Thomas Fortune, Matthews edited *Black Belt Diamonds: Gems from the Speeches, Addresses and Talks of B. T. Washington* (1898). In praise of Matthews's ability and highly sought after skill, Penn (1969), a Black press historian wrote, "No writer of the race was kept busier than Victoria Earle Matthews" (p. 398).

Club Women's Movement: Empowerment and Social Reform

As African Americans began to migrate to urban areas after the Civil War, they faced numerous economic and social problems (Carlton-LaNey, 1989; Jones, 1990; Osofsky,

1963). Racism, discrimination, and segregation resulted in inadequate employment, substandard housing, and a lack of sufficient transportation for urban African Americans. In response to these social conditions and in an attempt to advance the African American race, activists formed women's clubs and other self-help organizations (Carlton-LaNey, 1989; Jones, 1990; Waites, 1990). A new racial consciousness was rising among African Americans. That consciousness was based on the race pride and the importance of self-help or community empowerment. Matthews found herself among like-minded men and women as she urged African Americans to work and stand together for social justice.

Matthews was one of the founders of the African American women's club movement. She shares this legacy with a list of prominent African American club women including Mary Church Terrell, Ida B. Wells, and Josephine St. Pierre Ruffin. These community leaders took it upon themselves to organize and lead women's clubs, setting as their primary mission the improvement of African American women and their position in society. In part, this movement was in response to a social climate characterized by male superiority and limited employment opportunities for women (Jones, 1990). These organizations served as information clearinghouses, centers for dispersal of funds for reform work, and hubs for race work within the community. The women's club movement embodied networks of women who were united by their reform efforts.

Matthews was very involved in organizing and advancing the women's club movement. An important event that gave impetus to Matthews's social and political club reform work was Ida B. Wells's antilynching campaign. Matthews was sympathetic to this cause and wanted to support Wells's efforts. On October 5, 1892, Matthews spearheaded a campaign to support Wells. With the assistance of Maritcha Lyons, a noted local educator, Matthews organized a testimonial to honor Wells in New York City's Lyric Hall. Two hundred and fifty women attended, both African American and European American. They raised $700 to resume publication of Wells's newspaper and to publish a pamphlet entitled *Southern Horrors: Lynch Law in All Its Phases* (Smith, 1992). The testimonial not only displayed support for Wells's campaign, but also pushed European American women to examine racial injustice. Concerns about lynching brought into focus similarities between racial and gender inequality, helped pave the way for women to contemplate their own inequities, and raised questions that inspired the women's suffrage movement. This testimonial, for which Matthews is given organizational credit, has been called the beginning of the African American club women's movement (Salem, 1990).

Women's Loyal Union—The Local Club Movement

Immediately after this historic Lyric Hall meeting, Matthews met with Josephine St. Pierre Ruffin of Boston and Susan McKinney of Brooklyn. These three women made plans to form women's clubs in each of their respective cities (boroughs). Matthews and Maritcha Lyons founded the Women's Loyal Union of New York and Brooklyn in 1892.

Matthews was its first president. More than 70 women, including journalists, career women, artists, homemakers, and housekeepers, joined the Loyal Union (Smith, 1992). This was the first club for African American women in those cities (boroughs). The group emphasized better schools and employment. Their watchwords were "Vigilant, Patriotic and Steadfast" (Carmand, 1895). This declaration demonstrated their commitment to social uplift and to the collection and dissemination of accurate information on the civil and social status of African Americans.

Also in 1892, Ruffin organized the Woman's Era Club of Boston; Helen Cook, Mary Church Terrell, and others helped to establish the Colored Women's League (CWL) of Washington, DC; and the Ida B. Wells Club was formed in Chicago. CWL's mission was to promote the interest of African Americans through "moral, intellectual, and social growth" (Terrell, 1940, p. 315). Under a national umbrella, the CWL organized other clubs in Pittsburgh, Omaha, Knoxville, Jefferson City, Providence, and New Orleans.

National Organizer and Leader

As these local clubs emerged, a powerful energy was generated. African American women voiced their alarm about social and political conditions for African Americans; they were ready to organize. The national call to organize came in the June 1895 issue of the *Woman's Era* in which Josephine St. Pierre Ruffin wrote an editorial entitled "Let Us Confer Together." That editorial was in response to an inflammatory letter written by J. W. Jacks, president of the Missouri State Press Club, in which he disclosed his scathing view of the moral character of all "colored" women. Ruffin called for "all clubs, societies, associations, or circles to meet with us in conference in this city of Boston" (p. 4). She distributed a copy of the letter and in her editorial asked her readers to "decide if it be not time for us to stand before the world and declare ourselves and our principles" (p. 4). Matthews's comments followed in the July issue of *Woman's Era* where she called for courageous women to speak through *Woman's Era*, a journal of the Boston women's club, so "that the world may feel the power of the chaste mentality of the true Negro women" (1895, pp. 2–3). In collaboration with the women's clubs throughout the country, a national convention was planned.

As a delegate of the Women's Loyal Union, Matthews attended the first national conference of Black women from July 29–31, 1895, in Boston. On the second day of the conference, she addressed the body of club women on "The Value of Race Literature." She praised the creativity of Black men and women and the contributions that they had made. She emphasized the importance of collecting the writings of Black men and women, including histories, biographies, sermons, speeches, essays, and articles, to preserve the culture and contributions of people of African ancestry. Matthews understood that self-knowledge was empowering. To that end, she was strongly committed to presenting and preserving the history of people of African ancestry throughout the diaspora. Documenting and informing people of African Americans' contributions empowered African Americans and helped to dispel the myths that were promulgated about the group.

At the conference in Boston, Matthews emerged as a national leader. A *Woman's Era* commentary on the convention acknowledged Matthews's contributions and praised her work saying "To many minds Mrs. Matthews was the 'star' of the convention; so devoted was she to the interest of the conference that Boston saw comparatively little in a social way of this gifted women" (*Woman's Era*, 1895, p. 15). Clearly, Matthews was a highly visible and active participant at the conference. Furthermore, she was an astute politician and was appointed to a committee to establish a platform for the convention and to tie together the loose ends of the conference (Smith & Carter, 1895). Matthews's passion, commitment, journalistic skills, organizational skills, and willingness to serve made her invaluable to the new organization during its infancy.

The founding of the NFAAW was the culmination of the first national conference. It celebrated the remarkable feat of women coming together and uniting around a common agenda of empowerment and social uplift. Women were given a chance to develop organizational and leadership skills. Women leaders came to the forefront. Margaret Murray Washington was elected president, and Matthews was elected chair of the Executive Committee. The *Woman's Era* became the official journal of the NFAAW and Matthews would continue to be a major contributor throughout her life.

Matthews's influence and leadership continued to develop. In December 1895, she attended the National Colored Women's Congress in Atlanta, Georgia. Black club women from 25 states attended the women's congress called by the Women's Auxiliary to the Negro Department of Cotton States and International Exposition. Matthews was elected to serve on the committee of resolutions. Immediately after the congress, she toured the South and visited New Orleans and other southern cities. She was interested in the self-help efforts of African Americans and was disappointed by the red-light districts in New Orleans. Following this tour and her investigation, Matthews returned to New York determined to continue her "uplift" and social reform work.

In her powerful position on the executive board of the NFAAW, Matthews played a primary role in planning the NFAAW's 1896 convention in Washington, DC. Presiding over the second annual meeting of the NFAAW's first session, she informed the club women that the NFAAW "began its work in 1895 with approximately twenty-eight clubs in the United States . . . but one year later, in 1896, there are sixty-seven clubs represented at this second annual meeting" (Smith, 1992). The growth of the women's clubs throughout the country was impressive. Much of this was due to Matthews's extraordinary ability to excite and motivate others.

In July 1896, both the National Colored Women's League of Washington (NCWL) and the NFAAW were scheduled to meet in Washington, DC. This was a concern for both groups, but it also presented an opportunity. Matthews was appointed to a joint committee of seven women from both the NCWL and the NFAAW to consider uniting. The consensus of the committee was that the two women's organizations should consolidate under the name of the National Association of Colored Women (NACW). In the interest of their work for social reform and social uplift, they chose the motto "Lifting As We Climb." As these two organizations merged, Mary Church Terrell was elected president, and Matthews served as the first national organizer from 1897 to 1899. She was disappointed with the name of the new organization because she was firmly committed to the term "Afro-American" (Moses, 1990, p. 173). Some had rejected the hyphenation Afro-American (Moses, 1990), feeling it was best to be simply American. Matthews was committed to the organization's need to identify as Afro-Americans. This illustrates that Matthews placed value on connecting and identifying with the group's African and American ancestry.

In 1897, Matthews was invited to represent African American women at the World's Christian Endeavors Convention held in San Francisco. On July 11, in her address entitled "The Awakening of the Afro-American Woman," she stated that it was the responsibility of the Christian womanhood of the country to join in "elevating the head, the heart, and the soul of Afro-American womanhood" (Cash, 1993, p. 760). At this international event, she encouraged respect for African American women, their work, and accomplishments. Her presentation was well received by all (Keyser, 1907), and respect became a theme that permeated her organizational and community development efforts.

White Rose Home: A Model of Community Empowerment

Matthews's concern for the social welfare of her community took a direct service focus after the death of her 16-year-old son, Larmartine, in 1895. She began to concentrate her attention on children and young women. Matthews said that her heart immediately "went out to other people's boys and girls" and she "found that this was [her] field." She selected families that needed her most and began to visit them regularly, trying to become "a real friend to the mothers" (Brown, 1988, p. 212). Matthews's interest in the mothers was simply another dimension of her women's club work. Matthews described the evolution of her work this way:

> . . . Then I began to hold mothers' meetings at the various homes where I visited; and you may not believe this, but one day at one of these meetings we prayed especially for a permanent home where we might train boys and girls and make a social center for them where the only influence would be good and true and pure. Almost immediately Winthrop Phelps, who owns an apartment house, offered us one of its flats, rent-free for three months to make our experiment. We opened here on February 11, 1897. (Brown, 1988, pp. 211–212)

Another event that gave focus to Matthews's social services effort was the victimization of young African American women who migrated North. In the spring of 1898, Matthews received a letter from Miss Hattie Moorehouse, a European American teacher at Baylan Home for Colored Youth in Jacksonville, Florida. Moorehouse, a contributor to the mission, wrote Matthews saying that they were sending a young woman to New York to work and asked Matthews to meet her at the docks. The young woman was to be identified by a red ribbon pinned on her coat. "Although Matthews was at the dock promptly, one of the unprincipled men who haunted the wharves and preyed upon young women managed to seize the girl and lure her away" (Lewis, 1925, p. 158). The young woman was found three days later when she wandered back to the docks. She could not find the place to which she had been taken, but it was clear that her experience had been "sad and bitter" (Lewis, 1925). She was sent back home, and Matthews resolved to devote all her energies to preventing another such disastrous occurrence.

The victimization of this young African American woman alerted Matthews to the exploitation of unsuspecting young southern women who migrated to the city in search of work. Employment agents went into the rural districts of the South with convincing stories of opportunities in northern cities. In exchange for transportation and the guarantee of a job upon arrival, women were often pressured into signing contracts to work where the agent placed them. Subsequently, many young women were at the mercy of the agencies that had financed their trip to the North. They often found themselves working as prostitutes to pay off the employment bureaus for their passage. They were helpless to resolve their situations because they were not familiar with the city and had no resources.

More than anything else, these two events seem to have shaped the theme of Matthews's work for the remainder of her life. She moved from the role of national organizer of the women's club movement to the more local roles of social worker and community organizer. She focused her empowerment efforts on developing services and providing assistance to women and children in New York.

Settlement House

Matthews's efforts to organize the women in her community to provide social services began early in 1896 when a group of prominent African American women, members of various church denominations, began plans for the formation of a social service organization. Headed by Matthews, the group met and outlined the general program of the association. Matthews founded the White Rose Mission and Industrial Association in 1897 in the five-room apartment that Phelps had offered on the second floor of his building on 97th street. The facility was to become a "Christian Industrial non sectarian home for Afro-American and Negro working girls and women, where they may be educated and trained in the principles of practical self-help and right living" (Smith, 1992, p. 738). The White Rose Mission was a nondenominational settlement house that provided friendly visitors to service the neighborhood (Keyser, 1907; Osofsky, 1963). New services and programs were added as need arose, and by 1906, the annual report indicated that the following services were available at the settlement:

- Mothers' Club—a neighborhood club where the members gathered and received instruction in sewing, music, and reading and held helpful talks.
- Adult Classes—regular classes teaching domestic work and cooking for residents of the home and others in the community. This service provided training to help secure employment as a domestic.

- Home Lodging—temporary housing to shelter and protect young women who were new to the city.
- Service for "Home Girls"—headquarters for many women who did domestic work and had no place of their own or to go on their day off. They received their mail, met friends, came for help or advice, and shared their successes at the home.
- Travelers' Aid—assistance for young women who were stranded and had no place to go after arriving in the city.
- Kindergarten Classes—classes for young children (taught by Alice Ruth Moore, who later married Paul Laurence Dunbar).
- Social Club—activities for young women who lived in the home and those who returned to the settlement on their day off. They received instruction in music and enjoyed entertainment.
- The Victoria Earle Club—a club for girls with another for boys from ages 10 to 15. The girls were taught sewing and table manners and the boys learned cobbling and caning.
- Relief Assistance—free meals, lodging, carfare, and clothing provided to families.
- Library—books for self-study, including a rare book collection.

The home's library was unique and reflective of Matthews's race pride. She established a special library of books by and about African American people. The books, some of which were contributed by the Women's Loyal Union Club, were used in Matthews's teachings on race history. Educating others about the accomplishments of Africans and people of African ancestry was essential to Matthews (Frazier, 1894). She had gathered many rare books, and her collection was described as one of the most unique special libraries in New York (Schockley, 1988). The library included books on African and African American history with specific works by authors such as Booker T. Washington, Charles Chestnut, and the poet Phillis Wheatley. Matthews's library also included rare manuscripts. For example, a letter from George Washington to a slave woman was a part of the collection. The library further featured the best books on cooking, laundry, and other domestic sciences.

Travelers' Aid

The White Rose Home's mission was "the protection of self-supporting colored girls who were coming to New York for the first time" (Best, 1939, p. 1). A pioneer in travelers' aid work, Matthews and her assistant began as early as 1898 to meet the boats at the Old Dominion pier and help the young, inexperienced African American women from the South. The White Rose Home became a haven for working girls and was known as a place of refuge for women who needed assistance in adjusting to life in the city. The White Rose Travelers' Aid Society was established in 1905. The society kept agents at the piers to meet boats in New York and Norfolk, Virginia, to answer questions and to escort women to their places of employment or to the White Rose Home. Girls and women from all over the South and rural communities were assisted by the White Rose Travelers' Aid services.

There were many situations that affected the young women who received help from the White Rose Home. Some of the young women had left their homes on tickets given to them by an agent, and they had run out of money before they reached New York. Confused by the conditions of a large city, they were vulnerable to the first person who offered a kind word. There were also young women from respectable southern homes who wanted to improve their sewing or cooking skills, and there were others who wanted to earn money during the summer to support their educations in the winter. Travel times varied, steamers did not always arrive on time, and the young women traveling alone could not always be sure that family or friends would meet them at the pier. Anna Rich (1906), Matthews's sister, eventually assumed the role of New York dock agent and described one day's experience this way:

> We leave the Home, 7:45 with a young girl from Farmville, Va., en route to Lime Rock, Conn.; her steamer arrived too late for her to make railroad connections. After seeing her on the train we go to West 40th Street to see about a young girl from Rocky Mount, N. C., whose "friend" encouraged her coming and wrote her to be sure and go to this place. The "friend" failed to meet her according to promise or be at the 40th Street house when we took her there. The people in the house knew the friend but had no information regarding the young girl. We find her very unhappy, so we take her to the Home.
>
> After a hurried lunch we rush, for it is getting late, to the Old Dominion Pier. We find four girls in tears because they could not get berths on the outgoing steamer; they had come a long way; all were strangers to each other. We assured them that we would take care of them, and see that they got off the next day. A few minutes before five the steamer arrived, crowded. As soon as passengers began to land, dock men and others could be heard calling, 'White Rose! White Rose! Look after these people' or something similar." (Keyser, 1906, pp. 3–4). The White Rose Home provided lodging and meals for young women until they could find work. They were charged $1.25 a week for lodging, which included kitchen privileges.

Matthews led the way, but others later became aware of the plight of African American women. Frances Kellor, a European American social reformer, also recognized the plight and exploitation of immigrants, foreign and Black, by employment agencies (Parris & Brooks, 1971). In her investigation and report on racial problems entitled "Out of Work: A Study of Employment Agencies," published in 1904, Kellor found that African American women "are often threatened until they accept positions in questionable places and are frequently sent out without knowing the character of their destinations." In an effort to protect these young women, Kellor established the National League for the Protection of Colored Women in New York City and Philadelphia (Osofsky, 1966). Like the White Rose Home and sometimes in conjunction with it, Kellor's organization stationed workers at the major depots within the city and offered advice to young women who came to town for the first time. The White Rose Home for Working Girls, the National League for the Protection of Colored Women, and the YWCA supported each other in sponsoring travelers' aid services (Parris & Brooks, 1971; Smith, 1992).

Support for the Mission

The White Rose Home and Industrial Association for Working Girls received contributions from patrons who valued and supported their work. Matthews's social and political power served the White Rose Home well and attracted a loyal following. Funds came from some of New York's wealthiest families, as well as the local community. Young women who had previously used the home's services often came back to donate money and time. Many distinguished African American leaders participated in the work of the association by conducting lectures, offering advice, and affiliating themselves with the activities of the settlement. Among these leaders were Booker T. Washington, a noted writer, scholar, and founder of Tuskegee Institute, and Paul Laurence Dunbar, a famous Renaissance poet. Philanthropists and organizers such as Grace Dodge also supported the work.

Leadership and Legacy

In 1898, Matthews was named president of the White Rose Home; a position she held while continuing to establish a series of social services from Norfolk to New York until 1906. In 1903, Matthews contracted tuberculosis at the wharves while performing her mission work (Lewis, 1925). She spent four years fighting the disease in various sanitariums (Friend of the Negroes Dies, 1907). As Matthews's health gradually failed, the assistant superintendent, Frances Reynolds Keyser, assumed the duties of superintendent of the White Rose Home. Matthews's sister, Anna Rich, took over much of the travelers' aid work. Frail and weak from her struggle against tuberculosis, Matthews died at the age of 45 at her home on Poplar Street in Brooklyn Heights on March 20, 1907.

In the 10 years with Matthews at the helm, the travelers' aid workers met and assisted 50,000 young women and provided shelter to 5,000. Countless women received meals, carfare, intellectual stimulation, and other benefits. After Matthews's death, Mary L. Stone served as president of the White Rose Home from 1906 to 1920. During her tenure, the White Rose Home moved from 97th street to 136th street in Harlem. The African American population was moving uptown to Harlem and the mission moved with them. A plaque outside the brownstone distinguished "The White Rose Home" and a large photograph of Matthews dominated the hall entrance as memorials to her dedicated service and as inspiration to others. The White Rose Home remained a haven for African American women until it closed some time in the 1960s.

The Empowerment Tradition and Implications for Social Work Practice

Organizing by women within ethnic communities in the United States has a rich and diverse history (Gutierrez & Lewis, 1994). Like Matthews, many African Americans, Latinas, and others describe themselves as motivated to engage in activism because of their commitment to their communities and ethnic groups (Barrera, 1987; Collins, 1991; Gilkes, 1981, 1983; Lacayo, 1989). Moved by social injustice and lack of service, Matthews provided a model for organizing, protecting, and training African American women. Such activities by and on behalf of African American women during the Progressive Era offer some lessons for present day community women (O'Donnell, 1995) and social workers.

Gutierrez and Lewis (1994) identified eight practice principles for organizing with women of color. These principles are grounded in the worldviews of women of color and emphasize group process, leadership by women of color, and the organizer's role as a facilitator. The work and life of Matthews epitomized these principles.

1. Know about and participate in the ethnic community.
2. Recognize and build upon ways in which women of color have worked effectively within their own communities.
3. Involve women of color in leadership roles.
4. Serve as a facilitator and use the "lens" women of color.
5. Use the process of praxis to understand the historical, political, and social context of the organizing effort.
6. Begin with the formation of small groups.
7. Recognize and embrace the conflict that characterizes cross-cultural work.
8. Understand and support the need that women of color may have for their own separate programs and organizations.

The Community of African American Women

As an African American woman who was born in the South and migrated north like many of her generation, Matthews was familiar with the social conditions that her community faced. She was a member of a new generation of African American women who emerged from the cataclysm of slavery. As a domestic worker, she understood the plight of African American women and families, and, as an activist, she recognized what was needed to address the myriad social problems that burdened them. Matthews constantly worked to expand her knowledge through reading, writing, and research.

Building on the Strengths of the Community

Women of color have traditionally been involved in activities to benefit their community (Gutierrez & Lewis, 1994), and they have often organized community empowerment efforts. Matthews was a great organizer who called upon African American women across the country to come together to form a national organization. She understood the power of numbers and worked to unite African American women for the social and economic benefit of their communities.

African American Women in Leadership Roles

Matthews collaborated with other African American women. Working with local community women, she organized the first women's club for African Americans in New York. As a result of her involvement on the national scene, Matthews encouraged other women to take leadership roles. She was the epitome of competent and effective leadership, as well as a respected role model for her colleagues, who continued her efforts after her illness.

An African American Woman's Vision

Matthews was a visionary. She was able to expand the work at the White Rose Home so that it met demand, but she was also able to anticipate need. Perhaps her skill as a reporter contributed to her ability to focus on the future issues and problems with an emphasis on social action. Matthews's work was conducted through her "vision" as an African American woman. She delivered speeches directly addressing African American women, their work, and their place in society. As a journalist, she wrote to inform and correct misperceptions and to advocate for justice and social reform.

Praxis: Understanding the Historical, Political, and Social Context

The principle that "the organizing process as well as the outcome will inform both the organized community and 'community'" (Gutierrez & Lewis, 1994, p. 37) indicates the importance of reflection on process. In organizing the White Rose Home as a settlement house in the African American community, Matthews and her colleagues learned as they progressed. Programs were added, such as travelers' aid and social clubs, as the community needs changed. Matthews's role as a journalist also reflects her talent toward praxis. She was in touch with the pulse of her community.

Small Groups Group Building

Matthews's women's club leadership, mothers' meetings, and White Rose Home are all examples of the grass roots efforts. The White Rose Home for Working Girls began with a small group of women who laid the groundwork to establish the mission. This small band of women formed the backbone of the organization that fueled local community commitment that helped to keep the home operating for more than 50 years.

Recognizing Conflict That Is Characteristic of Racism

Matthews was a member of a community of African American women that sparked the cry for respect, dignity, education, and social reform for their community. Using newspapers and journals such as the *Woman's Era*, Matthews called women's attention to the danger and negative impact of racism. Meaningful dialogue and interaction between African Americans and European Americans was not common. Many fears, lack of information, and laws separated these communities. Matthews attempted to bridge that divide in her work. She fought with her pen to dispel myths and inform everyone about African American people, especially women. She was able to draw people in to support her mission.

Programs in Their Own Community

African Americans were migrating to New York in great numbers during the Progressive Era. Few settlement houses, however, were willing to serve the African American population. By 1911, the Lincoln Settlement House was the only settlement opened specifically for African Americans. Other organizations would often refer African Americans who came to their door to the White Rose Mission for services. The home provided a variety of services to the African American community in New York that they could not adequately access elsewhere. As a result of this development, Matthews created a place were African American women could not only receive help, but also provide help to others. Through this experience the women developed teaching, organizing, and leadership skills in a supportive, safe environment.

Conclusion

Victoria Earle Matthews was a woman who worked tirelessly for the advancement of her race, and for African American men, women, and children. She was a leader of the Progressive Era. Through her work with the White Rose Mission and the Home for Working Girls, she left her mark by establishing a tradition of self-help and community empowerment for women. Her vision and work were the forerunners to travelers' aid in New York and other cities. She lived a life that epitomized social uplift. Despite her deprived beginnings and personal losses, she moved on to serve others with zeal and determination. Ultimately, her real strength and goodness lay in her ability to strengthen others and to spark the flames of self-knowledge and empowerment.

References

Barrera, M. (1987). Chicano class structure. In R. Takaki (Ed.), *From different shores: Perspectives on race and ethnicity in America* (pp. 130–138). New York: Oxford University Press.

Best, L. (1939). *History of the White Rose Mission and Industrial Association.* WPA Research Paper. New York: Schromburg Center for Research in Black Culture.

Brown, H. (1988). *Homespun heroines and other women of distinction.* New York: Oxford University Press.

Carlton-LaNey, I. B. (1989). Old folk's home for Blacks during the Progressive Era. *Journal of Sociology & Social Welfare, 16,* 43–60.

Carlton-LaNey, I. B. (1997). Elizabeth Ross Haynes: An African American reformer of womanist consciousness, 1908–1940. *Social Work, 42,* 573–583.

Carmand, K. (1895, August). Report of the Women's Loyal Union of Brooklyn and New York. *Woman's Era,* 2, pp. 4–5, 19.

Cash, F. B. (1993). Victoria Earle Matthews. In D. C. Hines (Ed.), *Black women in America: A historical encyclopedia* (Vol. 2, pp. 759–761). Brooklyn, NY: Carlson Publishing.

Collins, P. (1991). *Black feminist thought: Knowledge, consciousness and the politics of empowerment.* New York: Routledge.

Frazier, S. E. (1894, May). Mrs. Wm. E. Matthews (Victoria Earle). *Woman's Era,* Vol. 1, 2, p. 1.

Friend of the Negroes dies. (1907, March 11). *The New York Times,* 7, 16.

Gilkes, C. (1981). Holding back the ocean with a broom: Black women and community work. In L. F. Rogers-Rose (Ed.), *The Black Woman* (pp. 217–233). Beverly Hills, CA: Sage.

Gilkes, C. (1983). Going up for the oppressed: The career mobility of Black women community workers. *Journal of Social Issues, 39* (3), 115–139.

Gutierrez, L., & Lewis, E. A. (1994). Community organizing with women of color: A feminist approach. *Journal of Community Practice, 1* (2), 23–43.

Jones, B. (1990). The woman's club movement. In D. Hine (Ed.), *Black women in United States history: Vol. 13. Quest for equality* (pp. 17–29). Brooklyn, NY: Carlson Publishing.

Keyser, F. (1906, September 27). *Report of the White Rose Home,* pp. 3–4.

Keyser, F. (1907, March 14). Victoria Earle Matthews: A tribute to life and good works. *The New York Age,* p. 1.

Kogut, A. (1970). The Negro and the charity organization society in the Progressive Era. *Social Service Review, 44,* 11–21.

Lacayo, R. (1989, September 11). On the Front Lines, *Time.*

Lewis, M. (1925, 7 April). The White Rose Industrial Association: The friend of the strange girl in New York. *Messenger,* p. 158.

Matthews, V. E. (1895). New York Victoria Earle editor. *Woman's Era,* Vol 2, 4, pp. 2–3.

Matthews, V. (1898). *Black belt diamonds: Gems from the speeches, addresses and talks of B. T. Washington.*

Moses, W. (1990). Domestic feminism conservatism in sex roles and Black women's clubs. In D. Hine (Ed.), *Black women in American history, Vol. 3. From Colonial times through the nineteeth century*. Brooklyn, NY: Carlson Publishing.

O'Donnell, S. (1995). Urban African American community development in the Progressive Era, *Journal of Community Practice*, 2, (4), 7–26.

Osofsky, G. (1963). *Harlem: The making of a ghetto*. New York: Harper & Row.

Parris, G., & Brooks, L. (1971). *Blacks in the city: A history of the National Urban League*. Boston: Little Brown.

Penn, G. I. (1969). *The Afro-American press and its editors*. New York: Columbia University.

Ruffin, J. (1895, June). Let us confer together. *Woman's Era*, Vol. 2, 3, p. 4.

Salem, D. (1990). Black women in organized reform, 1890–1920. In D. Hines, (Ed.), *Black women in United States history* (Vol. 14, pp. 261–357). Brooklyn, NY: Carlson Publishing.

Schockley, A. (1988). *Afro-American women writers*. Boston: G.K. Hall & Co.

Smith, H., & Carter, L. C. (1895, August). Minutes of the first national conference of colored women. *Woman's Era*, Vol. 2, 5, p. 3.

Smith, J. (Ed.). (1992). *Notable Black American women*. Detroit, MI: Gale Research.

Terrell, M. (1940). The history of the women's club movement. In D. Hines (Ed.). *Black women in United States history: Vol. 13. Quest for equity* (pp. 315–325). Brooklyn, NY: Carlson Publishing.

Untitled Comments. (1895). *Woman's Era*, Vol. 2, 5, p. 15.

Wade-Gayles, G. (1981). Black women journalist in the south, 1880–1905. In D. Hines (Ed.), *Black women in American history*: *Vol. 4. The twentieth century* (pp. 1409–1423). Brooklyn, NY: Carlson Publishing.

Waites, C. (1990). The tradition of group work and natural helping networks in the African American community. In D.Fike & B. Ritter, *Working from strengths: The essence of group work*, Miami: Center for Group Work Studies.

Williams, F. B. (1894, December). *Woman's Era*, Vol. 1, 2, p. 5.

CHAPTER 2

African Americans and Social Work in Philadelphia, Pennsylvania, 1900–1930

Tawana Ford Sabbath

The first third of the twentieth century in American history is particularly significant because it marks the period when the largest movement of a population group occurred within the country. African Americans began migrating in large numbers away from their long-standing southern and rural existence to urban centers in the North and West. The period also saw the development of a profession, social work, and the expansion of social welfare efforts to care for the needs of the less fortunate in American society. The dovetailing of those two events created opportunities for the establishment of social welfare as a professional pursuit by African Americans.

Early African Presence

Prior to the 20th century, the overwhelming majority of African Americans were residents of the rural South. In fact, in 1900, clearly 90 percent of African Americans were living in the rural South (Billingsley, 1968; Franklin, 1980; Frazier, 1948; Taeuber & Taeuber, 1969). That stands to reason, since the usual ports to receive Africans for enslavement were in the South from 1619, when Africans first entered the colonies as permanent residents, until 1808, when America officially withdrew from the slave trade (Curtin, 1969). The few Africans who lived outside rural southern communities were those who had never been enslaved, those who had been freed by their previous owners, and those slaves who worked in the cities and towns on contract from their owners (Franklin, 1980).

Because of a constant fear of slave uprisings and revolts by free and freed Africans, the colonies established a housing pattern that dispersed the group. According to Wilson (1980), the plan was that there would be no residential block in which more than one African resided. Such a pattern persisted until after the War for Independence when restrictions toward Africans, especially in the northern cities, were relaxed for a brief time (Aptheker, 1951; Franklin, 1980). There was an increase in the number of freed Africans, and there were opportunities for advancement (Bennett, 1982; Frazier, 1948). The expansion of civil rights to Africans continued until the period before the Civil War when an all-out campaign to save the institution of slavery included the wholesale dehumanizing of all Africans. By 1860, the idea of separation of the races was a significant part of the American fabric. Housing patterns changed such that the less desirable European immigrants and the Africans were relegated to particular sections of the cities and towns (Bennett, 1982). Self-help efforts abounded among the Africans and the immigrants (Franklin, 1980).

By the end of the Civil War and the failure of the Reconstruction period, Africans in the southern portions of America were restless. A slow stream of migration began about 1890, with the flow swelling by about 1910. Finally, the flood gates opened wide as three labor issues converged: (1) the Immigration Act of 1917 cut off the ready supply of western European immigrants to the northern industrialists, (2) the new African American citizens were in greater supply than the South would employ, and (3) the northern factories made aggressive efforts to recruit cheap laborers of all races. Some employers hired train cars to ship men and women from the South to the cities of the North and Midwest (Franklin, 1980; Johnson & Campbell, 1981; Leinwand, 1968). Added to the mix was the fact that the Black Codes in the South were being strictly enforced as Jim Crowism took hold of the culture of that region (Bennett, 1982).

The second largest population shift in the history of America, the Great Migration, occurred between 1910 and 1920; it accounted for the change of African Americans from an overwhelming southern and rural population to about 30 percent northern and urban. Given the already established pattern of residence in the northern cities, the migrating African Americans were ushered into the stable communities with their own (Meier & Rudwick, 1976). The onslaught of the newcomers set into motion a new pattern of problem solving: the development of systematic social welfare programs in African American communities (Aptheker, 1974).

The Philadelphia Scene

According to E. Digby Baltzell in his 1967 introduction to W. E. B. DuBois's *The Philadelphia Negro*, Philadelphia was home to the largest and oldest African American population of any northern city at the turn of the century. In 1634, prior to the establishment of the colony of Pennsylvania by Benjamin Franklin in 1682, the settlers of the area included the Swedes and the Dutch, who brought with them enslaved Africans (Blockson, 1975; DuBois, 1899/1967; Green, 1975; Higginbotham, 1978).

The Pennsylvania colony did not have legal codes that established slavery, but the practice of slaveholding became an integral part of the social and economic fabric (Higginbotham, 1978). The Africans who resided there, some free and others manumitted, established themselves as contributing citizens and advocates for the improvement of the quality of life for their people. Among them were Absalom Jones, Richard Allen, and James Forten (Blockson, 1975; DuBois, 1899/1967; Green, 1975). They and their counterparts worked independently and with White citizens to establish social settlements, medical facilities, schools, and child welfare agencies (Billingsley & Giovannoni, 1972; DuBois, 1899/1967; Hillman, 1960; *The Philadelphia Colored Directory*, 1910; Starr Centre, 1901).

Philadelphia was the first city to have a home for elderly African Americans, the Home for the Aged and Infirm Colored Persons, opened in 1864 by a wealthy African American lumber merchant, Stephen Smith (Stephen Smith Home, n.d.). The home and the various services, organizations, and agencies, some established as early as 1850, provided training for some African Americans in the field of social welfare. Three social welfare organizations in Philadelphia, initiated in the first quarter of the nineteenth century, played critical roles in the development of the emerging field.

The Armstrong Association of Philadelphia, established in 1907, was the result of joint efforts of African American and White citizens. The Women's Christian Alliance (WCA), instituted in 1919, resulted from the work of African American women and men. Those two social welfare–oriented efforts were conceived in direct response to the sudden influx of large numbers of African Americans from the South into the already established African American communities in Philadelphia. A third agency, the Bureau for Colored Children, answered the call for additional foster care services for African American children as the need became more critical.

Armstrong Association of Philadelphia

The Armstrong Association of Philadelphia was the result of the coming together of a man with a vision for his people and another man who was sympathetic to the cause. Richard R. Wright, Jr., an African American, wrote in his autobiography (1965) that he was a student at the University of Pennsylvania in the doctoral program. In his studies, he had discovered that many of the African American migrants from the South were skilled tradesmen who could gain employment only in domestic service. His advisor, knowing of his interest, referred him to someone with connections to Hampton and Tuskegee Institutes, two schools that emphasized training in the trades. Wright made contact with John T. Emlen, a man whom his advisor had described as a "young colored man from Hampton Institute" (p. 157). Wright was amazed to find that Emlen was a White man, a Quaker, and a banker with a degree in architecture from Haverford College, who had taught at Hampton Institute for a year from 1905 to 1906. Emlen had been impressed with the mission of Hampton to equip African Americans and Native Americans to work in the trades (Emlen to A. Kennedy, July 18, 1945).

When he returned to Philadelphia from Hampton, Emlen initiated the Armstrong Association, named after the founder of Hampton Institute, General Samuel Chapman Armstrong, an agent of the Freedmen's Bureau. Although Armstrong thought students should be trained to counter their tendencies to be lazy (Armstrong Association, 1904),

Emlen seemed to approach the plight of African Americans with more respect for the people. He began the equivalent of a "chapter" of the Armstrong Association, since William J. Schiefflin, a member of the Hampton Institute Board of Managers, had started another organization with the same name in New York City in 1902 (Emlen, n.d.). According to Wright (1965), the Armstrong Association to which Emlen introduced him was "organized . . . for the purpose of raising funds for Hampton and Tuskegee Institutes, [and was] a loose association of white Philadelphia philanthropists" (p. 158).

Expanded Philanthropy

Wright asked Emlen to appeal to his brethren to expand their focus to include improving conditions for African American skilled laborers in Philadelphia. Because of his commitment to the training of African Americans in the trades, Emlen was distressed by the prospect that duly trained tradesmen were unable to work in their specialty field because of rampant racial discrimination. Emlen consulted with Dr. N. B. Frisell, principal of Hampton, about the idea of augmenting the work of the association. He was advised that if he maintained the name of Armstrong, the supporters of Hampton might be attracted (Emlen to A. Kennedy, July 18, 1945). The members accepted the challenge and initiated a separate arm of the organization, to include African Americans, called the Armstrong Association of Philadelphia.

A paper related to the 50th anniversary of the Armstrong Association of Philadelphia (known most widely as the Armstrong Association) includes an account describing the initial meeting of a group of people with Emlen in the Brown Brothers Building at Fourth and Chestnut Streets "to draft the blueprint for a social experiment to be launched in early 1907 dedicated to the welfare of the Negro citizens of Philadelphia" (Armstrong Association, n.d. 1). The account identified the original members of the Armstrong Association of Philadelphia as Dr. C. E. Grammer, W. W. Frazier, Dr. Talcott Williams, Archdeacon Henry L. Phillips, Mrs. William F. Jenks, Dr. R. R. Wright, Jr., Rev. Levi J. Coppin, Rev. E. W. Moore, Rev. C. A. Tindley, J. Henry Scattergood, Rev. W. A. Creditt, James S. Hiatt, Samuel Scoville, Jr., J. Rodman Paul, J. Edward Dickerson, and Charles C. Binney.

Wright asserted that the organization's administrative structure was deliberately designed to guarantee African American leadership. The position of president was granted to a White man, Rev. Carl E. Grammer. Four vice presidents included two African Americans, Rev. Charles A. Tindley and Rev. W. A. Creditt, and two White men, W. W. Frazier and Dr. Talcott Williams (Wright, 1965). The other officers were Emlen, Secretary; Frazier, Treasurer; and Wright, Field Secretary. A photograph of the original members included two women (Armstrong Association, 1957).

The Armstrong Association of Philadelphia restated its purpose on the cover of its *Sixth Annual Report*. It was "working in a practical way for the Colored people of Philadelphia, and endeavoring from year to year to supplement some of the community needs which (were) not being met by other organizations" (1914). Another annual report from 1915 gave an additional purpose as helping "the colored people to self help in meeting the community needs in this their newly found problem of city life" (p. 1). Finally, in the historical account of the Armstrong Association, the organization was described as "developing greater opportunities for the satisfactory advancement of colored people along the economic and social lines" (Armstrong Association, n.d. 1). The objectives of the Association were broad and yet specific enough to allow it to serve many purposes. Some of its activities in the first eight years included investment counseling, developing athletic leagues, and encouraging the planting of neighborhood gardens. In addition to working in Philadelphia, the Armstrong Association made inroads in Swarthmore, New Jersey, and Media, Pennsylvania.

According to Wright, the founding group determined that African Americans would fill the offices of Field or Executive Secretary and Industrial Secretary. The official representative of the organization was the Executive Secretary, who worked with the board to develop and monitor relevant programs. The job of the Industrial Secretary was to establish work placements for African American skilled laborers (1965).

In following the initial plan, Wright and another African American, Alex L. Manly, worked in the positions of field and industrial secretaries, respectively. As a team, they were able to secure jobs for the migrants in areas that had not been open to African Americans previously (Wright, 1965). Once the migrants opened up the new areas, Manly made certain that they were replaced with their own kind, rather than letting the jobs revert to Whites (Armstrong Association, 1914).

The *Third Annual Report* from 1911, summarized in the 50th anniversary historical account of 1957, was full of details of the organization's accomplishments. Job opportunities for African American artisans were expanded with contracts. Additionally, the Armstrong Association evaluated the quality of the work done by the laborers whom they placed, in order to inform the broader community of their abilities and dependability. Wright is cited in that report as the person who contributed the format for the expansion of economic opportunities.

Despite this acknowledgment, Wright's efforts to document his position with and contribution to the organization were unsuccessful. Unfortunately, other than the brief reference made in the 50th anniversary brochure, where he is also listed as a staff member, the records of the Philadelphia Urban League, the organization that grew out of the Armstrong Association, do not contain correspondence, reports, or other documentation of Wright's activities with the earlier group. (Carter, 1959; Wright, 1959). He is cited as a founder and was given a Merit Award on January 31, 1957 (Armstrong Association, n.d. 2). However, Emlen identified himself as the most consistent leader of the Armstrong Association of Philadelphia, assuming the Executive Director position for the first 14 years. In a letter he stated, "I was in charge of the work, and afterwards, President of the Board of Managers for many years. At the present time the Executive Secretary and the President of the Board are Negroes, which I think is the best plan" (Emlen to A. Kennedy, July 18, 1945, p. 2).

Contributions to Social Work

The Armstrong Association also identified with the developing field of social work. In its *Tenth Annual Report* (1918), the organization documented a connection with the Philadelphia Training School for Social Workers. It also credited itself with placing one African American social worker in a job (Armstrong Association, 1918). While pursuing its main task of connecting skilled African American laborers with jobs, the organization served as a training ground for sociology students from Lincoln University, a historically Black university in Pennsylvania. Social work students from the University of Pennsylvania School of Social and Health Work had practicum experiences with the Association, as did social service students from Temple University. Over a period of five years, 11 Lincoln University graduates were awarded scholarships to attend the University of Pennsylvania School of Social and Health Work. The 1933 Social Work Yearbook cited the Armstrong Association for giving two fellowships annually for students attending the University of Pennsylvania School of Social and Health Work. Most of those students did field work with neighborhood and community clubs. Later, the organization incorporated volunteers from the Works Progress Administration and the National Youth Administration (Armstrong Association, 1938).

The Armstrong Association's leadership made important contributions to the theoretical base of the field of social work. Emlen is credited with advancing five principles that became the foundational steps in community organization. In the late 1930s, those who focused on community organization adopted a five-step systematic approach: (1) create a body of records, (2) investigate the need for activities, (3) develop interest among potential benefactors, (4) develop awareness among those in need, and (5) assume leadership in needed activities in which no agency had taken responsibility (Armstrong Association, 1957).

Innovation by the Armstrong Association was beneficial to the schools of Philadelphia. The Association initiated the position of home and school visitors at the Durham School, which had a totally African American student body. According to the 50th anniversary account, Abigail L. Richardson made the job a profession. She worked at the Durham School starting in 1912 and, by 1915, was visiting the Reynolds, Logan, and Stanton Schools. The Armstrong Association's *Sixth Annual Report* (1914) described her activities in detail. She would follow up on truants and children with discipline problems. She would visit homes to determine the whereabouts and the living conditions of the children. Because of racial discrimination, the children were excluded from area recreational centers, so Richardson established and conducted a recreation center program from the Durham School. She also supervised showers for the children at the school. She sponsored the Second Annual Working Women's Conference where the Girls' High School principal discussed occupations for women.

According to the 1914 annual report, Richardson worked closely with the parents in outreach efforts like the social club for women that she developed. The women learned to sew and to do needlepoint, among other activities. She also organized a Little Mother's

League at the Durham School that was designed to teach the little girls proper behavior. Her primary emphasis was keeping children in school and garnering home support for proper behavior and good scholarship.

The Association's newly formed Bureau of Information pursued issues on a case-by-case basis to provide documented evidence to agencies and institutions about the status of African Americans in the Philadelphia vicinity. One of the studies was conducted to determine the relationship of African Americans with trade unions. That information was crucial because Philadelphia became the site of some of the worst labor riots, resulting from conflict between the migrants and immigrants. Some employers were using the migrants as strikebreakers, causing violent disruptions on labor sites (Bennett, 1982; Wilson, 1980).

Another study conducted by the Armstrong Association, as reported in its 1914 annual report, documented the living and working conditions of African Americans in Philadelphia's suburbs and in New Jersey. Still another study reported on the number of children in Philadelphia who were poor, were being neglected, and needed vocational education, but who were not part of the social welfare services network. Also in the 1914 report, the Association documented its venture into housing as an area of programming. It joined with other groups to start the Remedial Loan Company that was designed to assist poor people in purchasing homes.

The Association for the Protection of Colored Women, another effort headed by a racially integrated group, was listed in the 1910 *Philadelphia Colored Directory* as an organization developed to protect young African American women who had migrated from the South. In 1914, the Armstrong Association of Philadelphia affiliated with the National League on Urban Conditions Among Negroes. Along with the Association for the Protection of Colored Women, the partnership formed the Philadelphia wing of the national organization.

Operating with limited funds provided by Emlen and his associates, the Armstrong Association gained new support in 1921 when it received an allocation from the newly formed Welfare Federation of Philadelphia (Armstrong Association, 1957). The new funding allowed the organization to hire a new executive director, Forrester B. Washington, in 1923. Washington, an African American, was a graduate of Tufts College. He had been a National Urban League Fellow at the Columbia University–affiliated New York School of Philanthropy from which he was graduated in 1916.

Previous experience as the director of the Detroit Urban League (DUL) had afforded Washington the opportunity to develop programs to help settle the African American migrants. The DUL had engaged in job searches, housing location, work habit training, crime prevention through collaboration with the police, and the provision of recreational activities for the migrants. Washington had also served as Supervisor of Negro Economics of the U.S. Department of Labor for the states of Michigan and Illinois from 1918 to 1920. His position immediately before he came to Philadelphia was Director of the Research Bureau of the Detroit Associated Charities from 1920 to 1923 (Burwell & Carlton-LaNey, 1985).

Washington took the initiative to change some of the programs in the Armstrong Association. He negotiated with the Philadelphia Public School Board to have the home and school function adopted by the system. Increased emphasis was placed on settling the African American migrants and addressing the ever-increasing delinquency rate. Through the Community Organization Secretary, Marcella Beckett, neighborhood clubs were re-instituted to ease tensions between the old established residents and the newcomers (Emlen to A. Kennedy, July 18, 1945). Such clubs had been included in the work of the Association, as reported in the 1913 *Annual Report*, but had been discontinued (Armstrong Association, 1957).

Striding toward Settlements

In keeping with the renewed focus on settling the migrants, according to an excerpt from the *Seventeenth Annual Report* (1925), under Washington the Association opened community houses similar to the social settlements. No such settlements had been established in Philadelphia with African Americans as heads of the houses. The houses were demonstration projects, since the Association did not have funds or staff to run them. Volunteers were used to show the city how effective such services could be, and it was hoped that the city would develop similar programs. One house was opened in West Philadelphia, and plans were laid for another in North Philadelphia. In fact, in 1931, the first African American settlement house with an African American director, Wharton Center, was finally opened in North Philadelphia. A graduate of Howard University and an African American, Claudia Grant, was appointed director (Grant, personal interview, 1988; Hillman, 1960).

Committed to professional education and training in social work, Washington was active at conferences and meetings. Representing the Armstrong Association, he made a presentation in 1924 at the second All-Philadelphia Conference on Social Work titled "Racial Adjustments Through Neighborhood Groups." In that paper, he described the actual setting up of the clubs in homes of old residents. Speakers visited the clubs to provide information about night schools, public health, preventive health care clinics, and home economics. He also explained that the Armstrong Association attempted not to duplicate services, but rather worked to convince existing agencies and services to include African Americans. If the agencies or organizations did not agree to include African Americans, the Association would provide the service to prove its need until such time as some other agency would take on the task of offering the needed service (Proceedings, 1924). At the third annual conference in 1925, Washington presented a paper titled "What Professional Training Means to the Social Worker." He advocated training so services would be systematic and scientific (Proceedings, 1925).

After four years of leading the Armstrong Association of Philadelphia, Washington became the second director of the School of Social Work at Atlanta University, succeeding E. Franklin Frazier (Platt & Chandler, 1988). The school, started in 1920, was steered quite successfully by Washington until 1954 (Yabura, 1970).

The Armstrong Association was identified as a social service agency. A report of its activities during the Depression years titled "The Armstrong Association Meets the Emergency" made reference to the Association as "the only colored organization of its kind in the city (Philadelphia) carrying on a highly diversified social service program . . . [serving as] a clearinghouse for social work among colored people to bring about better cooperation and more coordination" (Armstrong Association, n.d. 3).

For 50 years, the Armstrong Association maintained its overarching purpose "wherever possible to prevent duplication of work and the creation of new social agencies by having existing agencies take care of the problems arising from the increase in the Negro population. Where this is impossible, the Armstrong Association demonstrates the value of the work needed by actually carrying it on until an agency equipped for the purpose takes it over, or a new agency is created" (Armstrong Association, 1957). Under the able leadership of African Americans, Wayne L. Hopkins for 23 years and Lewis Carter for 15 years, the Armstrong Association of Philadelphia continued to make significant contributions to life in Philadelphia (Bunker, 1949). The name of the organization was changed to the Philadelphia Urban League in 1956 (Philadelphia Urban League, n.d.).

Women's Christian Alliance/Bureau for Colored Children

Philadelphia is home to the oldest child welfare agency started by African Americans specifically to serve African Americans. This account is a composite of information about the Women's Christian Alliance (WCA) gleaned from archival materials, agency brochures, and personal interviews. Unfortunately, the preservation of documents has not been as consistent for the WCA as for the Armstrong Association of Philadelphia. After World War I, the influx of African American females into Philadelphia was so great that Melissa E. Thompson Coppin saw the need to "aid young women migrating from the South who were in dire need of wholesome living quarters . . . and to offer charity to Black families in need of temporary care" (WCA, 1988). Women of the African Methodist Episcopal Church in Philadelphia were meeting at Allen A.M.E. Church in April 1919 to determine how to aid the working women who had migrated (Billingsley & Giovannoni, 1972). As a result of the first meeting, they agreed that they wanted to provide a safe dwelling place for the migrants. They formed the WCA with Coppin as the founder. Before the end of the year, the WCA had opened a shelter for African American women (WCA, 1988).

Coppin was a known and well-connected community leader. She was a graduate of the Women's Medical College, now the Medical College of Pennsylvania, and the tenth African American woman to earn a medical degree in America. She was also the wife of Bishop Levi J. Coppin, one of the most prominent ministers in the Philadelphia area (WCA, n.d.).

Opened in a house in South Philadelphia, the WCA shelter was ready for occupancy on December 26, 1919. In its first two years, the agency housed over 100 young women in the shelter. The house provided temporary shelter to homeless mothers and their children. It also served as a daycare center for the children of working mothers. Those who were seeking employment could depend upon the staff for help and support. In certain situations, the agency provided convalescent care (WCA, 1988).

At the end of the first two years, a judge of the Juvenile Division of the Municipal Court asked Coppin to consider expanding the services of the WCA. There was an increasing need for placements for dependent and neglected African American children (WCA, n.d.). The organizing group for the WCA agreed to enter into foster care placement. In May 1921, the first four children, a family group, were placed in a foster home. After 18 months in the new service arena, the WCA had placed 120 children in foster homes. In early 1926, the Commonwealth of Pennsylvania made the WCA a state-chartered agency. Expanding services raised additional needs, such that the agency added a nursery and a small shelter for the temporary care of children (WCA, 1988).

Coppin's sister, Syrene Elizabeth Thompson Benjamin, evidently was involved in the early life of the WCA. However, there is some disagreement as to how long and in what capacity she served. According to Ada B. Carter Harris, in a series of personal interviews, Coppin had sent for her sister to come from North Carolina to perform the social work duties in the agency. Harris described Benjamin as a petite and sickly woman who became the official representative of the WCA at court. She was well-known and respected by the judges (Harris, personal interviews, 1988, 1989, 1990). Further documentation of Benjamin's contribution to WCA is needed.

According to Harris, the sisters confronted a major impasse regarding the philosophy and future direction for the WCA. Harris sets the year as 1927 when Benjamin left the WCA and started her own agency, the Bureau for Colored Children (the Bureau). That start-up date is also recorded in the account by Billingsley and Giovannoni, but in that account Ada B. Carter is erroneously identified as Coppin's sister and the first director of the Bureau (1972). The only written source that documents Benjamin's presence in Philadelphia is a self-published family history that mistakenly sets the start of the Bureau in 1921 (Williams, 1990).

Harris explained that she became acquainted with Benjamin while she was still with the WCA. She was told by the older woman to call when she finished high school. When Harris graduated, Benjamin hired her as an assistant at the newly founded agency. According to Harris, only a few months after establishing the agency, Benjamin died. Harris, despite her youth and lack of experience, was seen as a viable candidate for replacing Benjamin. She developed the reports that were requested by the governing board after Benjamin's death. That so impressed the board members that she was appointed Executive Secretary and Director of the Bureau. She stated that Benjamin had used her influence with the Juvenile Court judges to make major inroads into the foster care arena. The Bureau was identified as the largest African American–operated child welfare agency in Philadelphia in the 1930s, far outstripping its predecessor, the WCA. By 1936, the Bureau was offering foster care services, a shelter, and a residential program for boys (Billingsley & Giovannoni, 1972; Carter, n.d.).

The Bureau for Colored Children operated from 1927 to 1967, with Harris serving as director for the majority of those years (Harris, personal interview, 1990). The WCA remained smaller than the Bureau, but survived through the years. Benjamin's successor at the WCA was Sarah Sinclair Collins who was hired to direct the social work department. She became the official spokesperson for the agency, representing the organization at gatherings and conferences. Through her efforts, the WCA had a staff of social workers that served hundreds of children and their families. Collins became Executive Director of the WCA in 1940 after the death of Coppin (WCA, 1988).

As was the case for many early practitioners of social work and initiators of agencies, Collins did not have a degree in social work. However, she was keenly aware of what was required for sound social casework. The WCA became a virtual training ground for African American social workers in child welfare. "Miss Collins," as she was called by staff, colleagues, and superiors, developed a reputation as a tough supervisor. In a personal interview, retired social worker Daisy Gordon recalls that Collins was the person who convinced her to pursue professional social work education. Gordon went on to complete graduate studies, earning an MSW at the University of Pennsylvania. She did not return to the WCA because of the lack of competitive salaries, but she attributed her foundation for practice to her positive experience at the WCA (personal interview, 1988).

A contemporary of Collins, Claudia Grant of Wharton Centre fame remembered that the encouragement that was given by the WCA director sometimes included paying portions of the workers' expenses. On occasion, according to Grant, Collins used her own funds to guarantee the workers' abilities to enroll in school (Grant, personal interview, 1988).

During the first third of the twentieth century, the WCA and the Bureau for Colored Children became the foremost agencies providing child welfare services for African American children in Philadelphia. The Bureau no longer exists, but it left a legacy in the names of African American social workers who staffed it and the many lessons that their work shares (Carter, n.d.; Coleman, 1988; Meek, 1988). The WCA continues to thrive and is comprised of a dedicated professional staff of African American social workers.

Practice Implications

Several important elements are common in the social service efforts highlighted here. Understanding these elements will enhance current social work practice in general and practice with African Americans in particular. The organizations were started by people who could see strengths among African Americans. Those strengths were recognized both in the professionals and in the clients. The organizations were also designed to correct racial injustice that had resulted in systematic exclusion. All three social service entities maintained enough flexibility in program planning to identify and address evolving needs. Finally, they established that social work and social welfare were viable options for African American professionals.

Strengths Model

In the case of the Armstrong Association, the founders established leadership guidelines that kept it from becoming another group of benevolent Whites seeking to help African Americans. So, there existed the understanding that there was capable leadership among African Americans. Of the four vice presidents, two had to be African American. In addition, having African Americans in the most visible staff positions, the Field and Industrial Secretariats, showed a commitment to empowerment and self-determination. That deliberate structure made the Armstrong Association decidedly different from other efforts and more successful.

The WCA was an outstanding example of African Americans identifying a problem critical to their community and developing a strategy to resolve it. There was the expectation on the part of the founding group that there were capable African Americans to staff the agency. The same understanding was manifested at the Bureau for Colored Children, where a concerted effort was made to staff the agency with African Americans.

In present day structures, social workers must begin to question any underrepresentation of a population in an area of employment or service. In the past, members of the profession may have erred on the side of accepting the status quo. When a program or agency is providing services to a certain population and there is no one on staff who can identify with the target population racially or ethnically, questions must be raised about the lack of representation. Ethnocentrism may lull a staff into believing there are no qualified persons who are members of the target population. Or they may think that their own racial or ethnic identity makes them more suited to the task. For whatever reason, though, social workers must become uncomfortable when working in racially and ethnically isolated settings, especially when the client base is obviously different from the staff.

Correction of Injustice

An important addition to social work education occurred in the 1970s. There was recognition that racism and ethnocentrism have worked together to establish a persistent system of discrimination in America. Recognizing that fact and addressing it, however, are not intrinsically linked. Many times, social workers and students have been excited about understanding diversity and oppression, but they have been stymied as to how to rectify problems of inequity (DeVore & Schlesinger, 1991; Martin & Martin, 1995; Pinderhughes, 1989). The Armstrong Association is a good example of a proactive approach to applying theoretical knowledge about diversity and empowerment.

The Association was willing to admit that there was an established pattern of racial discrimination in the trades that kept African Americans at a disadvantage. The evidence of the discrimination was documented through study. Data were gathered and analyzed to prove that the migrating African American artisans were being denied the right to work in their respective trades. Instead, they were being directed into domestic service that afforded them less pay and little respect.

The Armstrong Association of Philadelphia chose to tackle the systematic exclusion of the migrating tradesmen by creating opportunities for them to prove themselves. The Association staff campaigned for support of their effort by soliciting jobs on their clients' behalf. The staff then monitored the contracts for fairness, evaluated the workers' performance, and reported the quality of the work to the community and to prospective employers. Of great significance is the fact that the Association interrupted the usual hiring pattern by ensuring the replacement of African American tradesmen by their own, rather than letting the positions revert to White ethnics.

Another lesson we may glean from the Association's experience is to resist the temptation to locate the problem in the client when a systemic problem exists. For instance, the Association could have assumed that the migrating tradesmen were incompetent or ill-prepared to compete for jobs. In that case, they would have developed job training or skills development programs. They would have effectively insulted the artisans and never would have tackled the real problem of systematic exclusion. A parallel may be seen when a population that has been targeted for a service does not participate in that service as expected. Instead of assuming that there is something inherently wrong with the population, effort must be made to determine why the service does not fit the population. Instead of developing programs and projects to prepare the population to utilize the service, data collection and analysis are indicated to ask what is missing such that the services and the population can be connected.

Flexibility

In all three instances, the Armstrong Association, the WCA, and the Bureau for Colored Children identified additional services to be provided. As one service was offered, they discovered that parallel or complementary services were needed. For instance, once the women of the WCA opened the shelter for working women, they realized the need for a nursery and daycare to accommodate the women's children and the children of other working mothers. While the Armstrong Association aided tradesmen in acquiring gainful employment, workers there also realized the need to help them qualify for housing loans. The Bureau sought to provide foster care services as well so as to house troubled boys in a residential setting.

Program planners must adopt a broad vision when designing services. A holistic approach will ensure that needs will not be ignored as they arise. An agency or program may not be able to actually provide a particular service due to financial and staffing constraints, but if the posture is one of willingness to address multiple needs, there will be attention paid to identifying resources and contacts. No agency or program should assume that the clients will have only one problem or situation for solution.

Professional Empowerment

The Armstrong Association, the WCA, and the Bureau for Colored Children contributed mightily to the cadre of African American social workers in Philadelphia. Each one was committed to providing social work positions and student training. Today, agencies and programs must encourage African Americans to pursue professional education in social work. Where the target population is predominantly African American, agency heads should even request African American students so the students can work with their own kind prior to launching their professional careers. African American students have issues to address relative to their own experiences and those of other African Americans that should be confronted during their tenure in schools and practicums (Martin & Martin, 1995). The leaders of the three pioneering efforts highlighted in this chapter understood that being African American was not the only prerequisite for African American social workers to be able to provide effective service to their own.

The field of social work is indebted to efforts like the Armstrong Association of Philadelphia, the WCA, and the Bureau for Colored Children. Such pioneering interventions established the base for African American schools of social work. Additionally, they provided fruitful learning experiences for African Americans who went on to become agency heads, supervisors, and educators in the profession.

References

Aptheker, H. (Ed.). (1951). *A documentary history of the Negro people in the United States: From reconstruction to the founding of the N.A.A.C.P. in 1910.* New York: The Citadel Press.

Aptheker, H. (Ed.). (1974). *A documentary history of the Negro people in the United States, 1933–1945.* Secaucus, NJ: The Citadel Press.

Armstrong Association. (1904) *The work and influence of Hampton.* Proceedings of a meeting in New York City, February 12, 1904 at Madison Square Garden Concert Hall. Pamphlet. Canaday Library, Bryn Mawr College, Bryn Mawr, PA.

Armstrong Association of Philadelphia. (1914). *Sixth annual report.* Pamphlet. Van Pelt Library, University of Pennsylvania, Philadelphia, PA.

Armstrong Association of Philadelphia. (1915). *Seventh annual report.* Pamphlet. Canaday Library, Bryn Mawr College, Bryn Mawr, PA.

Armstrong Association of Philadelphia. (1918). *Tenth annual report.* Pamphlet. Canaday Library, Bryn Mawr College, Bryn Mawr, PA.

Armstrong Association of Philadelphia. (1938). 1938 Statistical record of service of the Armstrong Association. *Urban League Papers,* Box 1/7. Urban Archives, Temple University, Philadelphia, PA.

Armstrong Association of Philadelphia. (1957). *50th Anniversary of the Armstrong Association, 1907–1957.* Souvenir booklet. *Urban League Papers,* Box 3, 1/4. Urban Archives, Temple University.

Armstrong Association of Philadelphia. (n.d. 1). History of the Armstrong Association. Draft. *Urban League Papers,* Box 3, 1/4. Urban Archives, Paley Library, Temple University, Philadelphia, PA.

Armstrong Association of Philadelphia. (n.d. 2). The Armstrong Association of Philadelphia. Paper. *Urban League Papers,* Box 1/7. Urban Archives, Temple University, Philadelphia, PA.

Armstrong Association of Philadelphia. (n.d. 3). The Armstrong Association meets the emergency. *Urban League Papers,* Box 3, 1/4. Urban Archives, Temple University, Philadelphia, PA.

Armstrong Association of Philadelphia. (n.d. and untitled). Paper re: Armstrong Association's affiliation with the Welfare Federation. *Urban League Papers,* Box 3, 1/4. Urban Archives, Temple University, Philadelphia, PA.

Bennett, L. (1982). *Before the Mayflower: A history of Black America.* Chicago: Johnson Publishing.

Billingsley, A. (1968). *Black families in White America.* Englewood Cliffs, NJ: Prentice-Hall.

Billingsley, A., & Giovannoni, J. M. (1972). *Children of the storm: Black children and American child welfare.* New York: Harcourt Brace Jovanovich.

Blockson, C. (1975). *Pennsylvania's Black history.* Philadelphia: Portfolio Associates.

Bunker, W. L. H. (1949, January). These inalienable rights. *Philadelphia Magazine.*

Burwell, Y., & Carlton-LaNey, I. B. (1985, April). Black leadership: Unsung heroes and heroines of social welfare. Paper presented at the Conference of the National Association of Black Social Workers, Detroit, MI.

Carter, A. B. (n.d.). Bureau for Colored Children shelter and farm and vocational school at Pomeroy. *Urban League Papers*, Box PC-31. Urban Archives, Temple University, Philadelphia, PA.

Carter, L. (1959, February 17). Letter to Bishop R.R. Wright, Jr. *Urban League Papers*, Box 2, 1/22. Urban Archives, Temple University, Philadelphia, PA.

Curtin, P. D. (1969). *The Atlantic slave trade: A census*. Madison, WI: University of Wisconsin.

DeVore, W., & Schlesinger, E. G. (1991). *Ethnic-sensitive social work practice* (3rd ed.). New York: Macmillan.

DuBois, W. E. B. (1967). *The Philadelphia Negro: A social study*. New York: Schocken Books. (Original work published 1899)

Emlen, J. T.(n.d.) *Emlen Papers*, Vol. I. Home of Woodruff Emlen, son of John T. Emlen, Bryn Mawr, PA.

Emlen, J. T. (1945, July 18). Letter to Albert J. Kennedy of National Federation of Settlements, Inc. Emlen Papers, Vol. I.

Franklin, J. H. (1980). *From slavery to freedom* (5th ed.). New York: Knopf.

Frazier, E. F. (1948). *The Negro family in the United States* (Rev. & abridged ed.). Chicago: University of Chicago.

Green, W. C. (1975). *The history of Black people in Philadelphia*. Philadelphia: The Council of Independent Black Institutions.

Higginbotham, L. (1978). *In the matter of color: Race and the legal process—The colonial period*. New York: Oxford University.

Hillman, A. (1960). *Neighborhood centers today*. New York: National Federation of Settlements and Neighborhood Centers.

Johnson, D. M., & Campbell, L. B. (1981). *Black migration in America*. Durham, NC: Duke University.

Leinwand, G. (1968). *The Negro in the city*. New York: Washington Square.

Martin, E. P., & Martin, J. M. (1995). *Social work and the Black experience*. Washington, DC: NASW.

Meier, A., & Rudwick, E. (1976). *From plantation to ghetto*. New York: Hill and Wang.

The Philadelphia colored directory: A handbook of the religious, social, political, professional, business and other activities of the Negroes of Philadelphia. (1910). Philadelphia: Author.

Philadelphia Urban League. (n.d., Untitled). Paper: Armstrong Association's affiliation with National Urban League. Urban League Papers, Box 3, 1/4. Urban Archives, Temple University, Philadelphia, PA.

Pinderhughes, E. (1989). *Understanding race, ethnicity, and power: The key to efficacy in clinical practice*. New York: Free Press.

Platt, T., & Chandler, S. (1988). Constant struggle: E. Franklin Frazier and social work in the 1920s. *Social Work, 33* (4), 293–297.

Proceedings of the Second All-Philadelphia Conference on Social Work. (1924, September 1). *Urban League Papers*, Box 9. Urban Archives, Temple University, Philadelphia, PA.

Proceedings of the Third All-Philadelphia Conference on Social Work. (1925). Every child—How he fares. *Urban League Papers*, Box 9. Urban Archives, Temple University, Philadelphia, PA.

Starr Centre. (1901). *History of a street*. Brochure. Van Pelt Library, University of Pennsylvania, Philadelphia, PA.

Stephen Smith Home. (n.d.). Brochure. *Urban League Papers*, Box 3, 1/4. Urban Archives, Temple University, Philadelphia, PA.

Taeuber, K. E., & Taeuber, A. F. (1969). *Negroes in cities: Racial segregation and neighborhood change*. New York: Atheneum.

Williams, M. S. (1990). *A colloquial history of a Black South Carolina family named Simons*. Philadelphia: Minnie Simons Williams.

Wilson, W. J. (1980). *The declining significance of race: Blacks and changing American Institutions* (2nd ed). Chicago: University of Chicago.

Women's Christian Alliance (WCA). (1988). Brochure.

Women's Christian Alliance (WCA). (n.d.). Will you share our concern? Brochure. *Urban League Papers*, Box 9. Urban Archives, Temple University, Philadelphia, PA.

Wright, R. R., Jr. (1959, January 10). Letter to Mr. Shorter, Secretary of Philadelphia Urban League. *Urban League Papers*, Box 2, 1/22. Urban Archives, Temple University, Philadelphia, PA.

Wright, R. R., Jr. (1965). *87 years behind the black curtain*. Philadelphia: Rare Book.

Yabura, L. (1970). The legacy of Forrester B. Washington: Black social work educator and nation builder. In C. L. Sanders (Ed.), *Proceedings of 50th anniversary at Atlanta University School of Social Work* (pp. 28–40). Atlanta: AUSSW.

CHAPTER 3

Birdye Henrietta Haynes
A Pioneer Settlement House Worker

Iris B. Carlton-LaNey

Birdye Henrietta Haynes was the first African American to graduate from the Chicago School of Civics and Philanthropy, and she became the head worker at prominent social settlements in Chicago and New York—yet little is written about her. Unlike most of her contemporaries, Haynes was a professionally trained settlement house worker when she assumed the leadership role first at Chicago's Wendell Phillips Settlement and later at New York's Lincoln House.

As a "race woman," Haynes was never able, nor willing, to separate her racial identity from her practice of social work. Race was a significant variable in determining the direction and extent of her career path. Haynes's career was characterized by a search for a meaningful professional identity within a strictly segregated social system. Furthermore, according to Evelyn Higginbotham (1992), an essential part of writing and understanding the history of African American women requires bringing race more prominently into the analysis of power. It is, therefore, critical that Haynes's story be told within the context of the segregated and oppressive system that controlled and shaped her career.

An Overview of Haynes's Career

Haynes was born in Pine Bluff, Arkansas, on November 21, 1886. She was the younger of two children. Her older brother, George, a pioneer social work educator and cofounder of the National Urban League, became one of her strongest supporters and mentors. Little is known about their parents, particularly their father. The scarce documentation that exists about the early years of the Haynes children focuses on their mother, a fiercely religious woman who demanded strict obedience from her children and encouraged formal education as a means to escape the poverty that the family endured

(Carlton, 1981; Perlman, 1972). Haynes attended the inadequate segregated primary schools in Pine Bluff and Hot Springs, Arkansas. Because few public high schools existed for African American children during Reconstruction, Haynes, like her brother before her, left Arkansas to attend Fisk Preparatory School in Nashville, Tennessee. With financial support from her brother, who was then secretary of the Colored Branch of the Young Men's Christian Association (YMCA), Haynes enrolled in Fisk University and graduated with a bachelor of arts degree in 1909. While at Fisk University, she completed course work in domestic arts, scientific cooking, ventilation, and sanitation (Haynes Student Record Card, n.d.).

With the focus of African American women's education on "race uplift" and educating the race, Haynes moved into one of the few job opportunities available to educated African American women at that time. She taught domestic science at Pearl High School in Nashville during the winter term of 1908. From 1909 to 1911, Haynes taught high school in Corsicana, Texas. Motivated by the spirit of voluntarism from her studies at Fisk University and acting on Christian principles, Haynes did volunteer work for mothers' clubs, young people's societies, and the sick and poor (Haynes Student Record Card, n.d.).

Haynes left Texas for Chicago after accepting a Julius Rosenwald Fellowship to study social work at the Chicago School of Civics and Philanthropy. She moved into the Wendell Phillips Settlement that had been established four years earlier. Haynes assumed the role of head worker in June 1911 and remained in this position until July 1915. She entered the Chicago School during the winter term of 1911 to 1912. After receiving her diploma from the school on June 5, 1914, Haynes considered several possible employment opportunities, including remaining at the Wendell Phillips Settlement as head worker and supervisor of African American students from the Chicago School (Breckinridge to J. Rosenwald, May 31, 1913); working for the Illinois Children's Home and Aid Society, where she had done volunteer work (Breckinridge to W. Graves, July 1, 1913); or moving to New York to work at Lincoln House Settlement, which had a vacancy for a head worker. She assumed the position of head worker at the Lincoln House Settlement in August 1915. She held the position for nearly seven years, and her work was described by the board of directors as "faithful and enthusiastic service" (Report of Lincoln Settlement, 1922). In April 1922, Haynes resigned from Lincoln House, ostensibly to pursue a career with the New York 137th Street Branch of the YWCA as secretary of girls' work. However, in early June, she entered a local hospital for surgery to remove a tumor. A few weeks later, on June 30, 1922, she died of heart failure at the age of 35 ("Obituary Notes," 1922; "Operation Fatal," 1922).

Although Haynes's social work career was relatively short, spanning just over 13 years, it gave her the opportunity to work very closely with some of the major pioneers in social work during the Progressive Era. These leaders, who were Haynes's teachers and role models, included Edith Abbott, Sophonisba Breckinridge, Eugene K. Jones, Florence Kelley, Mary White Ovington, Graham Taylor, Lillian Wald, and, of course, her brother, George Edmund Haynes. With few exceptions, however, the social reformers of the early 20th century did not easily embrace Haynes with sisterhood and support, which further complicated a career already circumscribed by strict policies of segregation.

The Influence of Julius Rosenwald

Haynes's entry into the field of social work began with the benevolent acts of Julius Rosenwald. It is unlikely that Haynes ever met Rosenwald, yet his values, beliefs, and power greatly influenced her career development and opportunities. Rosenwald entered Haynes's life quite fortuitously, and he determined the direction of her life's work with little, if any, input from Haynes herself.

Rosenwald (1862–1936) amassed great wealth after merging his clothing company with Sears and Roebuck. His philanthropic work began long before he became wealthy, and, as his fortune grew, so did his contributions to social causes (Embree & Waxman, 1949; Stanfield, 1985). Noted African American sociologist Charles Johnson (1935), who himself benefited from Rosenwald's generosity toward Fisk University's social science research, described Rosenwald as a "prophet" who taught that "money was a social as well as an economic instrument . . . useful only as it was ultimately an instrument of social and cultural evolution" (p. 110).

Rosenwald adhered to the accommodationist philosophy of Booker T. Washington, and although he had a sincere concern for racial uplift, he was a segregationist. He advocated that educated African Americans should use their education and training to help others of their race. Hence, he believed his funding should not be used to equip African Americans to become competitive with Whites economically or politically (Stanfield, 1985). Furthermore, Rosenwald was amenable to funding certain projects for African Americans if the projects were supervised by Whites or right-thinking African Americans, such as Washington (Stanfield, 1982, 1985). Rosenwald was a well respected leader among philanthropists and worked with them on determining appropriate race relations strategies. His interest in funding African American students, which allowed them to attend the Chicago School of Civics and Philanthropy, was based on his sincere interest in racial uplift, his association with other philanthropists and social reformers of his day, and his segregationist philosophy.

Breckinridge, who at that time was research director of the Social Investigation Department of the Chicago School, approached Rosenwald at an informal gathering in the home of wealthy Hull House activist, Louise deKoven Bowen. Breckinridge asked Rosenwald about his varied interests in African American people. She discussed the interests of Ruth Baldwin in improving conditions for African Americans in New York. Baldwin, along with George Haynes, was a cofounder of the National League on Urban Conditions Among Negroes. In her discussion with Rosenwald, Breckinridge added that there was a "sore need [for] trained Negro workers to take positions among their own people," a practice vigorously advocated by the National League on Urban Conditions Among Negroes (Breckinridge to G. Taylor, October 11, 1912). Rosenwald expressed an interest and asked her how this could be facilitated. Breckinridge suggested that a beginning would be a "stipend for three colored students who would take the work at the School of Civics and do practice work under our direction at Wendell Phillips Settlement" (Breckinridge to G. Taylor, October 11, 1912). After further encouragement from Breckinridge, Rosenwald decided to fund two students initially. Breckinridge began the process of locating two female students to accept the Rosenwald scholarships. There was no policy or precedent for such recruiting, and it is not clear how she went about it; it, however, may be assumed, that she was able to locate two female students with the help of Baldwin, who solicited George Haynes's assistance.

The two student recipients of the Julius Rosenwald scholarships were Birdye Haynes and Sophia Boaz, both graduates of Fisk University (Haynes in 1909 and Boaz in 1911). Rosenwald paid Haynes's tuition regularly during her tenure at the school. In appreciation for his generosity, Breckinridge wrote Rosenwald that "using the Wendell Phillips settlement as we have done with the help of the people at Hull House and using every possible opportunity that could be obtained in the offices of the various societies, such as the United Charities, the Juvenile Protective Association, and other agencies, we have really wrought out of the situation a kind of training for these two young woman that puts them in quite a different position from any other colored young women certainly in this part of the country" (Breckinridge to J. Rosenwald, May 31, 1913). Breckinridge further reassured Rosenwald that the school had been "sufficiently successful with these two [students] to justify [his] going on with the experiment" (Breckinridge to J. Rosenwald, May 31, 1913). Haynes became the head resident at the Wendell Phillips Settlement, and Boaz was her assistant.

Haynes's work at both the settlement and the School of Civics and Philanthropy was quite time-consuming. Her acceptance by the school was considered an exceptional case, and special arrangements were made for her to reside at Wendell Phillips. The school acknowledged that "residence in a settlement involved a considerable burden of extra work [and was] recommended only for students who [had] firm health" (*Chicago School of Civics and Philanthropy Announcement*, 1913–1914). Work at the Chicago School also included volunteer activities at various social agencies, such as the Illinois Children's Home and Aid Society (Haynes Student Record Card, n.d.). Like all other students, Haynes was required to spend three hours a day, five days a week in one of the district offices of the United Charities. She completed courses in public care of children, principles of relief, health and housing, and social statistics. Abbott, Jane Addams, Breckinridge, Julia Lathrop, and Taylor were among her professors. Both Haynes and Boaz were listed in the school announcement as receiving their certificates during the 1913–1914 school year (*Chicago School of Civics and Philanthropy Bulletin*, No. 24).

As Breckinridge saw it, the school could benefit by keeping Haynes on at Wendell Phillips as both head worker and director of fieldwork. In that capacity, Haynes could supervise other students under the direction of faculty members Breckinridge and Abbott. Breckinridge, always solicitous in her correspondence with Rosenwald, said that she was not hopeful that the school could continue its work with African American students without his support. She wrote, "The thing that [she] would hate to have happen is to have done the work so well in the case of these two girls and to lose out any chance for doing it in the future" (Breckinridge to J. Rosenwald, May 31, 1913). Breckinridge asked Rosenwald to provide stipends of $50 a month for one or two students, as well as $65 per month for Haynes's salary as head worker at the settlement (Graves to J. Rosenwald, June 21, 1913).

As Breckinridge waited for Rosenwald's response, she wrote to George Haynes indicating that it was not likely that Rosenwald would respond favorably to the request to pay his sister's salary. She stated that they were "very well satisfied with [his] sister's training and feel that she and Miss Boaz established a very good precedent for future work" (Breckinridge to G. Haynes, June 23, 1913). George Haynes, in seeking to ensure his sister's professional career, suggested that the League pay at least a portion of the head worker's salary. He saw the activities in Chicago as very significant work that should not be sacrificed and feared that the work would be lost "if the worker who has helped to bring about results is removed and a time elapses before a new effort is made" (G. E. Haynes, personal communication, August 19, 1913). By the following October, the League executive committee had agreed to George Haynes's suggestion, and Baldwin, in her position as president of the League board, wrote a letter promising a contribution of $250 for the current year from the National Committee on Urban Conditions of Negroes (Minutes from the Wendell Phillips Board of Directors Meeting, October 27, 1913).

In the interim, Rosenwald instructed his personal secretary, William Graves, to visit the settlement and to make an assessment of the facility and its operations before any decision on funding could be made. Graves's initial memorandum to Rosenwald described the physical facility with apprehension and expressed concern that "Haynes had no literature showing the finances, the directors, donors, etc., of the Settlement, but said such data was in the hands of Dean Sumner" (Graves to J. Rosenwald, June 21, 1913). Graves recommended that Rosenwald pay Haynes's stipend in order for her to complete the requirements of her certificate and that he request additional information on the settlement's finances before he make any further decisions about its funding.

The Wendell Phillips Settlement

Haynes described the mission of the Wendell Phillips Settlement as "a place for wholesome recreation and congregation for the Colored people of the West Side [of Chicago]" (Wendell Phillips Settlement, n.d.). Under her direction, the settlement developed programs to meet the needs of the community. Between 1912 and 1913, the settlement enrolled 335 children in various activities, including classes in sewing, millinery, embroidery, crochet, cooking, dance, and music, as well as social and literary clubs. The materials needed in each class or club were provided at no cost to the children. Piano lessons were also available at payment of ten cents per lesson paid directly to the instructors. In an effort to provide what Haynes called "social enjoyment," she ensured that parties were often held for each class or club throughout the year with "a general merry making at the Christmas season" (Wendell Phillips Settlement, n.d.) In addition to the 29 classes and clubs organized at the settlement, 42 lectures and meetings sponsored by independent organizations were also held at the settlement. Haynes noted that the settlement was a center of the community where "large crowds [had] gathered upon occasion of lectures, social functions, [and] concerts" (Haynes, n.d.). Perhaps, Haynes's skill at working with divergent groups and helping each to feel welcomed and significant accounted for the array of activities at the settlement and for the reputation that she gained as a capable and well-liked settlement house worker. Described as having a special ability to work successfully "with all kinds of social agencies," Haynes had "untangled and smoothed out very complicated and very difficult situations" in her position as head worker (Breckinridge to E. Walton December 15, 1914).

While generally pleased with the work of the settlement, Haynes acknowledged the dearth of programs and services for boys and girls between the ages of 14 and 21 and conceded that these youth could also benefit from "some opportunity for recreation [and] for social enjoyment" (Haynes, n.d.). Haynes was interested in providing services to as many people as possible and believed that the young boys and men of the community were especially in need. She understood that the girls needed services as well, but believed that "there [were] more ways to draw and interest" girls through clubs and classes (Haynes, n.d.).

In her position as head worker, Haynes reported to and was accountable to the Wendell Phillips board of directors that owned and managed the settlement house. The board was composed of 20 members, 10 African American and 10 White, who were prominent social welfare leaders, social reformers, businessmen, and other professionals. The interracial board included Abbott; Addams; Bowen; Breckinridge; J. W. Lewis, the first African American physician to serve on the faculty of the University of Chicago School of Medicine; Frank Sadler, an attorney and former municipal court judge; and Dean Walter T. Sumner, superintendent of missions for the Cathedral Saints Peter and Paul. The board was the center of power for the settlement. It had the major fundraising responsibilities and determined policy. Its members were among the most powerful and influential leaders in Chicago during that time, but as Graves reported to Rosenwald, often they were not very diligent in their management of the Wendell Phillips Settlement.

In a four-page supplement memo entitled "Retention of Miss Haynes at Wendell Phillips, Stipend for Colored Girls School of Civics," Graves cited several serious problems that he observed on his visit with Haynes at the settlement. On the basis of his observations, Graves made the following recommendations to Rosenwald:

1. That you decline to assist in the payment of Miss Haynes' salary as Head Resident of Wendell Phillips Settlement.
2. That you consider paying annually for five years not to exceed 25% of the budget of Wendell Phillips Settlement. [And that you consider the following:]
   a. When the Directors hold regular meetings.
   b. When officers, other than Head Resident are elected and serving.

c. When the balance of the budget over income from rents, classes, clubs, etc., is subscribed by reliable individuals with a reasonable part of the total subscribed by colored people.
d. When the flat above stairs in the barn is cleaned and put into rentable condition by installing gas.
e. When the Settlement is endorsed by the Association of Commerce.

3. That you decline to provide stipends for one or two pupils year after year. (Graves to J. Rosenwald, July 10, 1913)

In summary, Graves found that the directors of the settlement had no officers and had held no meetings attended by a quorum for more than a year. He noted that informal arrangements were in place for Sumner to handle legal matters, for Sadler to handle financial matters, and for Breckinridge and Abbott to serve as overseers of the work of the settlement. He concluded that "there is no responsible head for the place as a whole" (Graves to J. Rosenwald, July 10, 1913). This was a rather scathing commentary on Haynes's ability and performance. This statement also reflected Rosenwald's belief that Whites should be in control of the organizations and agencies that he funded, even though these organizations existed to serve the African American community.

Furthermore, it is clear from Graves's assessment that the board of directors of Wendell Phillips Settlement had not been assiduous in the performance of its duties. As Graves noted, only two of the 20 board members had made monetary contributions to the settlement over the past year. Bowen had contributed $50 and Breckinridge had given $10. A board member, Mrs. T. W. Brophy, had purchased the property for the settlement some years earlier, but she was no longer contributing to the operating budget (Graves to J. Rosenwald, July 10, 1913).

Haynes's role as both student and as head worker, under Breckinridge's and Abbott's tutelage, must have put her in a very precarious position. Although Haynes was head worker, the overall management of the settlement was out of her hands. Several factors contributed to Haynes's lack of authority, including her role as student learner; the presumption by Rosenwald, her primary funding source, that someone other than Haynes should be "in charge"; and the lack of involvement of the board. Any ideas that she may have had about the needs of the community and programming had first to be approved by Breckinridge and Abbott, and eventually the entire board. Breckinridge and Abbott felt themselves ultimately in control of programs at the settlement and were informally given that charge. Breckinridge, ambivalent about this responsibility, recalled that these tasks were performed "with a great deal of sacrifice on the part of Miss Abbott and myself" (Breckinridge to J. Rosenwald, May 31, 1913). Haynes could not have been expected to work effectively with a board that did not share her regard for the settlement and its participants. The common criticism that settlement movement leaders' energies were focused on too many different projects for them to be effective could also apply to the Wendell Phillips Settlement board (Davis, 1986; Kraus, 1980).

Another issue was the attitude of White board members toward African American Chicagoans. White reformers seemed willing to deal with the problems of African Americans at a comfortable distance, but were unwilling to tackle the problems close at hand. For example, Addams and Kelley were both founding members of the National Association for the Advancement of Colored People, but these Hull House residents did not warmly welcome African Americans to the activities at Hull House; they indeed devoted a rather small amount of time to the situation of African American people (Bryan & Davis, 1990). With an awareness of these attitudes and practices, it is unlikely that Haynes felt able to be assertive with board members, who were very powerful and influential individuals capable of having a tremendous impact on her life's work. She was, nonetheless, very clear in her assessment and articulation of the settlement's needs. In one of her annual reports to the board, Haynes, writing in a characteristically delicate tone, stated that "more trained workers" and "better equipment" were needed for useful social work to take place (Haynes, n.d.).

Haynes had a good understanding of her community. Two of the major problems facing African Americans in Chicago were inadequate housing and the lack of employment opportunities. These problems forced African American families to live in crowded slum housing, where they paid rents much higher than those paid by immigrants, and to accept employment in low-paying, service jobs. Grossman (1989) noted that the number of African American servants in Chicago increased by 6,000, nearly one-half of the city's increase in African American population, between 1900 and 1910. Furthermore, two-thirds of all employed African American women in 1910 were either servants or hand laundresses. This obviously left little time for child rearing. Problems in family stability were further complicated by the fact that many of these families had to take in boarders in order to make their rent payments (Philpott, 1978). Haynes believed that the young men of the area spent their spare time in the evenings on the street corners and in the poolrooms and saloons, not because they would rather be there, but because there was "positively no other place to go [and] no one to guide." She further concluded that, contrary to the popular beliefs of the day, these youths did not come from "unfit" homes (Haynes, n.d.). Her assessment in her annual report disputed the commonly held belief that African American families could not provide good homes because the African American women were believed to be immoral scourges having all of the inferior qualities of White women, but none of their virtues (Giddings, 1984). Haynes's statement also strongly intimated that the victim was not the source of the problem: "There is not a club room or game room on the whole of the West Side where a colored boy may spend his evenings." Because of segregation, when "he leaves the public school he does not have an opportunity to see inside a gymnasium," but finds his recreation elsewhere (Haynes, n.d.). In sum, Haynes encouraged the board not to blame the victim, but rather to understand the problems within the context of a racist and segregated system that denied African Americans equal access to resources.

It seems evident that to a great extent Haynes shared Rosenwald's concerns about Wendell Phillips's instability. She was not, as Graves's report suggested, an irresponsible head. She was simply not entrusted with full authority for running the settlement, nor was she given the board support that she needed to be successful. Discouraged by the lack of support, underfunding, and inadequate programs, Haynes summarized her vision for Wendell Phillips by saying, "We hope for the time when the work will have sufficient backing to put it upon a permanent basis. When confidence of its existence can be assured so that the people for whom it stands will feel satisfied to take hold in a substantial way and our friends who have helped and will help shall be able to feel that it is surely worthwhile" (Haynes n.d.).

Unmoved by Haynes's entreaty, the board continued its peripheral involvement and failed to champion the causes of the settlement. Breckinridge made it clear on several occasions that her first loyalty was to the School of Civics and Philanthropy, not to the settlement. She was always quick to say in her request for funding from Rosenwald that giving to Wendell Phillips and giving to the school were "two separate things" and that they would be "grateful indeed" for stipends for students "even if Mr. Rosenwald did not feel that he wanted to make any contributions to the continued existence of the settlement" (Breckinridge to W. Graves, July 1, 1913). In a similar vein, when an outstanding bill came due at the settlement, Breckinridge stated that she "did not feel responsible in any way" for its payment (Breckinridge to W. Graves, July 1, 1913). Although the board failed to respond to Haynes's request, it reacted rapidly and methodically to Rosenwald's specific terms that were to be carried out as a prerequisite to his further association with the settlement.

On October 27, 1913, the board met to reorganize. The members decided to continue operating the settlement, elected officers, agreed to schedule quarterly meetings, reelected Haynes as head worker, accepted partial funding from the National Urban League, charged the treasurer with the responsibility of renting two apartments and a barn that were attached to the settlement, and established a budget for the next fiscal year (Abbott to J. Rosenwald, November 28, 1913). It is also important to note that the board decided to hold its regular meeting at the settlement. Previous meetings had been held elsewhere, further illustrating the estrangement of the board from the settlement's work.

Rosenwald continued to support the settlement with 25 percent of its annual budget as long as the remaining expenses could be raised from board members and African Americans in the Chicago area. On the basis of Graves's recommendations, Rosenwald declined to pay Haynes's salary or to provide stipends for students at the Chicago School on a continuing basis.

Haynes at Lincoln House in New York

In early 1915, Haynes began to actively seek other employment. For several months, she communicated with Wald about the position of head worker at the Lincoln House Settlement in New York. The Lincoln House board offered to pay one-half of Haynes's expenses to travel to New York for an interview (Minutes of Lincoln House Board of Directors, March 27, 1915). Haynes and her brother, George, then director of the National

League on Urban Conditions Among Negroes and professor of social work at Fisk University, discussed the various employment options. In April, Haynes traveled to New York to interview for the position at Lincoln House. Breckinridge wrote a glowing letter of reference for Haynes, noting that she not only was "very well trained . . . [but also] knows how to cooperate intelligently with all kinds of social agencies" (Breckinridge to E. Walton, December 15, 1914). Haynes's interview was successful, and the Lincoln House board, chaired by Mary White Ovington, a reformer, was sufficiently impressed to offer her the job. On August 28, 1915, Haynes assumed the position as head worker at the Lincoln House Settlement in the Columbus Hill community of New York City. The situation was quite different there.

The Lincoln House Settlement was much better organized than the Wendell Phillips Settlement. The 15-member board met on a monthly basis and operated under the auspices of the Henry Street Settlement board, although they were given complete autonomy (Holt to O. Harris, March 24, 1922). The board was composed of prominent leaders like James Hubert, director of the Brooklyn Urban League; Jones, who replaced George Haynes as the executive director of the National Urban League; George Sims, pastor of Union Baptist Church in Harlem; Wald, founder of the Henry Street Settlement; and Elizabeth Walton, a staunch Quaker and leader in social welfare for African Americans. The settlement had a day nursery, a kindergarten, and numerous boys', girls', and mothers' clubs. Haynes also had a full- and part-time staff (Minutes of the Lincoln Home Board of Directors, March 27, 1915). She replaced Verina Morton-Jones, an African American physician, who had given up her medical practice to become head worker in 1914. Morton-Jones had lived and worked for many years in the community and was well liked and respected by its residents. Haynes, new to the city, gained the confidence of the people in the community. One community leader described her as being held in "great personal esteem . . . by the neighborhood people" (Lincoln House Report, March 20, 1922). The *New York Age* stated that Haynes and her assistant had "succeeded in increasing the interest of the neighborhood and . . . broadened the scope of the work very largely" ("Remodeling a Neighborhood," 1915). Yet life in the African American slums differed little from that in Chicago. Haynes described the area around the settlement as a "great desert" where families must struggle to "rear their children in keeping with the standards of American family life" (Haynes, 1919, p. 124).

Haynes was eager to improve the quality of life of the community residents. Adhering to the same tenets that guided her work in Chicago, Haynes advocated for the welfare of the community residents, for more meaningful social work services, and for better trained workers to provide those services. She felt that her close contact with the community was necessary for successful work. In a report of summer activities at Lincoln House, Haynes concluded, "We have lived together in this outdoor life all during the long hot summer and we feel that we know and understand each other better and can better help and comfort one another during the days that lie before us" (Lincoln House Report, 1916–17). This statement suggests that Haynes identified with the residents of the

Columbus Hill community and that she did not separate her personal life from her professional agenda.

Haynes took her administrative duties very seriously, and she understood and respected the role of her board. Her reports to the board were well prepared, thorough, and detailed. She was always careful to have budgets and justifications available whenever she made requests for expenditures. Her reports sometimes specified changes that she wished to make in the house and sought board approval for any expenditure of funds, ranging from the installation of an electric light to the removal of a piano from one floor of the house to another (Lincoln House Committee Meeting, June 13, 1918). While she understood the importance of competent administration of the house, her overriding concern was to enhance the collective life of the neighborhood. Her brother, George, recalled some years later that "developments in improving neighborhood living marked her administration" (Press release, June 30, 1958).

In her contact with local residents, Haynes found that there was a constant need to reassure them. Her conciliatory style worked very well, as residents grew to love her and respect her professional wisdom. She was sensitive to the concerns of parents and knew that they were sometimes "rather doubtful as to the safety of their children—especially the younger ones" who were involved in long-term Lincoln House programs (Lincoln House Summer Work, June 15–September 30, 1917). In response to these apprehensions, Haynes knew that she must explain, in detail, each activity that the house had planned and reassure the parents that the scheduled programs were safe, well supervised, and beneficial to the children. She indicated that "the problem of persuading and convincing them that all will be well cared for means endless visiting in the neighborhood" (Lincoln House Summer Report, June 15–September 30, 1917). Moreover, as head worker, Haynes felt that she had "the duty of creating a recognized place for the work [of the settlement] in the minds and hearts of the people of the community and elsewhere," a task that consumed a great deal of her time and energy (Haynes to V. Conklin, March 21, 1917).

Skilled as a community advocate and acclaimed by Abbott as "the best social worker of her people" (Breckinridge to E. Walton, December 15, 1914), Haynes committed herself to work on behalf of the Columbus Hill residents. Shortly after her arrival at Lincoln House, she met a group of 15 boys, ages 14 to 15, who called themselves "the gang." The boys had been a "nuisance about the House and neighborhood" (Haynes, 1915). Haynes found that the neighbors were reluctant to participate with the House because of the presence of "the gang." She acknowledged that this group of boys had "energy [that] runs up to the savage point; they are as loyal to each other as Damon and Pythias and will fight the common foe like German soldiers" (Haynes, 1915). Haynes, however, was not willing to sacrifice this group of boys and rejected requests to "get rid of 'the gang'" (Haynes, 1915). Instead, she emphasized the need to "divert these forces" and encouraged the boys to take an active and constructive role in Lincoln House. Since it was her aim that the House should serve everyone in the community, Haynes said,

"We have determined to so polish and refine the dance and 'the gang' that others will say it is good for them to be here, and will come and cast in their lot with ours." Haynes felt that working closely with the boys, carefully planning their activities, and providing good role models for them would help to change their behavior. Haynes believed that she must constantly call on her "ability to see light and order through chaos" to fulfill her professional goals and the mission of the House (Haynes to V. Conklin, March 21, 1917).

Haynes furthermore believed that "breaking down prejudices and misconceptions" was part of her role (Haynes to V. Conklin, March 21, 1917). On one occasion, she felt it necessary to go before her board to seek support for a "young woman in the neighborhood, a teacher, who had become blind and had been obligated to give up her work" (Executive Committee of the Lincoln House, 1920). The woman had applied for instruction in reading at the Light House (of the New York Association for the Blind) and felt that she had been discriminated against because of her race. Haynes solicited advice from the Lincoln House board about the best way to intervene on this young woman's behalf. The board, at Wald's request, appointed another board member to "take this matter up with the Light House" (Executive Committee of the Lincoln House, 1920).

Haynes may have found such incidents frustrating, but she remained optimistic and maintained the conviction that change was inevitable. She firmly held to the belief that "a smile with a pleasant greeting for the tired mother or father, sympathy for and patience with the irritable child" were the things that helped to break down barriers between the individuals, organizations, and communities (Haynes, 1915). She found reward in small incremental change and positive acknowledgment of the work at Lincoln House. In reflecting on a discussion with a 17-year-old neighborhood boy, she recalled the teenager's pensive inquiry as to "what the boys and girls would do if they did not have [Lincoln House] to come to instead of being out on the street" (Lincoln House Report, 1916–17). For Haynes, such queries helped to ease "the task of rehabilitating" the House "and establishing it upon a more substantial basis" (Haynes, 1917). It is evident that Haynes found her work at the settlement useful, necessary, and rewarding.

As she recounted "A Day at Lincoln House, Wednesday, May 26, 1920," Haynes presented a picture of continuous activity and interaction. Her day began at 8:30 a.m. with 40 children ranging in ages from four to six arriving for kindergarten class. The class lasted until noon. During this period, Haynes was engaged in "communications, telephone calls received and answered, information giving, consultations and private conferences." That particular morning, a teenage immigrant from the British West Indies "was sent by his aunt to Miss Haynes to help him find a job." Also a mother stopped by to inquire about taking her 18-month-old baby on a field trip to the Henry Street Settlement, and a neighbor who served as chairman of the Lincoln House housing committee visited to make a report on his progress. The afternoon clubs began to meet at 3 p.m. On the House ground floor, boys aged 11 to 14 met for the City History Club. A gymnasium on the second floor was "alive with younger boys enjoying basketball, boxing, and games under the paid boys' worker." Both the Lincoln House Girl Scouts and the Sunshine

Club were meeting simultaneously in adjacent rooms. Children were arriving at the House to attend the meeting of a dramatic club held at the Ethical Culture School. A sewing class was meeting in the domestic science room. On the roof, neighborhood residents were tending gardens throughout the summer days. Children were constantly stopping in the office to make inquiries, and a policeman from the local precinct stopped in to ask if Haynes wanted to have the street blocked off as a "playstreet" during the summer months. By 6:30, the House was "deserted and generally quiet until 7:30 except for the occasional ring of a telephone or knock at the door." This quiet hour was interrupted on Wednesdays, however, because the Boy Scouts began their meeting at 7:00. Between 7:30 and 10:00, the Lincoln Senior Club met on the ground floor and the gymnasium was open for other boys to play pool. Haynes's office remained open until 10:00 p.m. On that day, a neighbor stopped in to remind Haynes that "the funeral services of one of our community council members will be held at the church down the block and 'you are expected to be there.'" After she returned from the church at 10:30, Haynes stopped in to visit the Stillman Mothers' Club's closing party. On that day she closed the house at midnight, when she, along with "three faithful mothers," cleared and put away the dishes. Haynes recalled that "with a few variations or slight changes from time to time, the weeks go by leaving the imprint or influence of the House's life stamped deeply upon the present and future life of the community and the individual" (Lincoln House Report, October 1, 1917).

Haynes felt that her professional obligations included not only the formal duties of administrator, but also the informal duties of nurturer. In an effort to promote Lincoln House, Haynes felt that "developing a spirit of cooperation and sympathy" was necessary (Haynes to V. Conklin, March 21, 1917). As she acknowledged her third year's appointment, Haynes told her board that the enormous work of the settlement had "called forth all the ambition, energy and resourcefulness of [her] mental and physical ability" (Haynes to V. Conklin, March 21, 1917). Haynes was both able and ambitious, but the pace and volume of her work at the settlement began to take its toll, by 1920, periods of illness claimed some of her energy (Conklin to B. Haynes, November 30, 1922).

Haynes resigned from the Lincoln House Settlement in 1922 under less than favorable circumstances. On April 13, 1922, the board, in executive session, decided to close the House, indicating that the "present staff of paid workers (all colored) will be discontinued" (Holt, 1922). The kindergarten and the mothers' clubs, however, would continue to function. The reason the board gave for discontinuing the settlement house programs was two-fold. First there was a "lack of funds." Second, board members chastised Haynes and asserted that she had not performed her duties adequately because of her "unpunctuality which reacted badly on the house" and "her indiscreet choice of workers" (Lincoln House Minutes, April 13, 1922). The criticism was apparently not unanimous. Sims, whose church was next door to the settlement, testified "to the great personal esteem in which Miss Haynes [was] held by the neighborhood people" (Holt, 1922). Wald and Jones "voiced the general feeling of gratitude to Miss Haynes for the splendid work which she had accomplished" (Holt, 1922). But other board members ignored the problems of budgetary constraints and complained that because of Haynes, Lincoln House had not been "rendering the best possible kind of service." They further noted that the house was far too small to fill the district's needs, "over-congestion" had created problems, and, contrary to the community's beliefs, they were not "a lot of rich people who would keep things going indefinitely." At the same meeting, Haynes "tendered her resignation as head worker" (O.C. Holt, personal communication, November 30, 1922). The resignation was to be effective on June 1, 1922, after one month's vacation with salary. The board minutes reflect no other discussion of Haynes's resignation.

Conclusion

Haynes was apparently very ill prior to her resignation from Lincoln House. The quality of her work had diminished, and her energy level had decreased. There seemed to have been little sensitivity to Haynes's health or to any other factors that may have decreased the quality of her work as head worker. Until April 1922, Haynes's work was described by the Lincoln House board as "efficient and skilled," marked by excellent abilities in "administering the house, and fine spirit . . . shown, not only with the neighbors, but with the members of the [Lincoln House] Committee" as well (Conklin to. B. Haynes, November 30, 1920). Wald and the other board members, usually attentive to their own and each other's health and spirit of well-being, failed to show Haynes the same compassion. One Lincoln House board member complained several months after Haynes's death that they would have understood why Haynes "slumped" if "the poor thing had only told us about the big tumor" (Holt to A. Leach, September 13, 1922).

Prior to Haynes's final board meeting, the secretary of the board, Olivia Holt, wrote to Haynes's assistant that, perhaps, Haynes needed to "get away," not for a respite, but so that she would "not appear to be the issue" when the board discussed the reorganization of the House. Holt further acknowledged that Haynes appeared at the board's last meeting "to particular disadvantage," which made her "feel sorry" for the head worker. In acknowledging her own needs to escape the confines and stress of the city, Holt apologized for not feeling well and looking very tired at the last meeting and spoke of her need to spend some time "out in the country . . . and let the wind and the cold blow some vigor into" her body (Holt to O. Harris, March 24, 1922).

Numerous other examples of the White reformers taking care of themselves and each other abound in the literature. Wald, for example, often attended parties given by her wealthy friends to relieve her of the stress associated with her various reformist activities. She called this time "playing hooky" from "serious matters," and she understood the importance of the distraction in order to live a "sane and balanced life" (Daniels, 1989, p. 62). Florence Kelley, another noted feminist reformer, who spoke often of the loving friendship and economic support that she received from sister reformers, presents further testimony to the concern and compassion that these women shared for one another (Sklar, 1985).

If these White feminist reformers could show such concern and caring for each other, why were they unable to recognize the stress under which Haynes labored and to embrace her similarly? Perhaps these reformers, ahead of their times in so many ways, were very much a part of their times in other ways. Adhering to the tenets of racial segregation that dictated both physical and social distance prevented these women from seeing the struggles of African American women. Perhaps the noted anti-lynching crusader and journalist Ida Wells-Barnett was correct in her accusation that White reformers had an inability to know the souls of Black women (Duster, 1972). While the efforts of these reformers toward social justice were admirable for the times, they were, nonetheless, inadequate and did little to challenge the social fissures of the sociopolitical structure. African American women, professional and nonprofessional alike, were left with what Cannon (1985) described as four basic struggles: the struggle for human dignity, the struggle against White hypocrisy, the struggle for justice, and the struggle for survival.

Haynes's career path, from her undergraduate study at Fisk University to her certification from the Chicago School of Civics and Philanthropy to her work at the Wendell Phillips and Lincoln House settlements, was narrowly shaped by the constraints of racial segregation, a notion reinforced and legitimized by all who surrounded her (Jones, 1971). The editors of *The Messenger*, unrelenting in their attacks on capitalist-controlled social welfare organizations, accused such groups of manipulating "promising young college men and woman" like Haynes by "stifling their independence, thwarting their energies and sapping their judgement" ("The Invisible Government," 1920, p. 175). Accordingly, in this environment, Haynes was required to be diplomatic, tactful, and reticent as she interacted with the professionals, educators, advisory boards, and clients who were all key players in demanding success, yet they expected failure. At the same time, as a middle-class professional, she was expected "to inspire and share training and experiences" (Haynes to V. Conklin, March 21, 1917).

Being assertive and outspoken could have nullified any positive changes that Haynes may have accomplished and could have spelled disaster for her career. Both the African American and White professional communities of reformers were relatively small. This was especially true of African American social workers, who, according to Elise McDougald (1925, p. 689), numbered only about "fifty-odd women" in New York City during Haynes's time. While the White community of reformers was considerably larger, communication flowed very freely among and between the groups, and there was general agreement about proper behavior. Philanthropists and funding organizations also adhered to this unwritten code of expected behavior. Any imprudent behavior on Haynes's part could have put her at odds with major fundraisers who would have simply withdrawn their support from the settlement's already scarce budgets.

While Haynes was required to be competent, she was also required to maintain complete self-control. That Haynes was better educated than most African American women during the Progressive Era provided her with greater options, yet she was not given that "uncritical acceptance" (Daniels, 1989, p. 136) that characterized the feminist sisterhood of reformers. Through this sisterhood, these reformers gained social power that enhanced their influence and allowed them to move more easily into the political arena and other areas dominated by men. That sisterhood, which acknowledged personal individuality through loving friendship and economic support, was closed to African American women (Terborg-Penn, 1978).

This discussion should not suggest that Haynes was completely without a social support system. She maintained a very close relationship with her brother and his wife, Elizabeth. They communicated regularly and worked together to ensure their aging mother's comfort. George Haynes's prominence in the field of social work was a powerful impetus to his sister's career. As cofounder and first executive director of the National Urban League, George Haynes was in a position to negotiate on his sister's behalf. However, his style of civility and conciliation prevented direct intervention and led him to distance himself from obvious influence (Carlton, 1981). It is, nonetheless, probable that Haynes's recruitment and enrollment at the Chicago School can be traced to her brother's role as a social work educator, to his relationship with league cofounder Ruth Standish Baldwin, and to his power and influence in the reformer community. It may also be assumed that Haynes's employment opportunity at New York's Lincoln House settlement was enhanced by the high visibility of Urban Leaguers who served on the Lincoln House board, such as Field Secretary E. Kinckle Jones and Lincoln House board president Mary White Ovington. But while a personal and professional support network existed for Haynes, its strength and power paled in comparison to that of other comparable social work reformers of her day.

In retrospect, the young reformer, Birdye Henrietta Haynes, entered and worked within an extremely complex system. The ability to conduct herself professionally and to maintain a sense of self-worth was in itself a worthy accomplishment. The fact that genuine support systems were virtually nonexistent further complicated her professional roles. Haynes recognized her isolation and described herself as "one who stood at the head of the firing line in the thickest of the fight to acquire territory" (Haynes to V. Conklin, March 21, 1917). Haynes's race, education, training, and skill as a settlement house worker placed her within a unique historical context in the emerging profession of social work. Among first-generation social workers, Haynes's work is worthy of historical note and stands as a powerful reminder of the barriers that African American women faced while trying to carve a place for themselves in a profession that welcomed them with guarded reluctance, at best.

(Reprinted by special permission of the University of Chicago Press from Social Service Review, *Vol. 68, No. 2, June 1994, pp. 254–273.)*

Partial funding for this research was provided by the National Endowment for the Humanities and the Southern Regional Educational Board Travel to Collections Grants.

References

Abbott, E. (1913, November 28). Letter to Julius Rosenwald. Julius Rosenwald Papers, Joseph Regenstein Library, University of Chicago.

Birdye Haynes Student Record Card, Joseph Regenstein Library, University of Chicago.

Breckinridge, S. (1912, October 11). Letter to Graham Taylor. Julius Rosenwald Papers, Joseph Regenstein Library, University of Chicago.

Breckinridge, S. (1913, May 31). Letter to Julius Rosenwald. Julius Rosenwald Papers, Joseph Regenstein Library, University of Chicago.

Breckinridge, S. (1913, June 23). Letter to George Haynes. George Edmund Haynes Papers, Fisk University.

Breckinridge, S. (1913, July 1). Letter to William Graves. Julius Rosenwald Papers, Joseph Regenstein Library, University of Chicago.

Breckinridge, S. (1914, December 15). Letter to E. Walton. Lillian Wald Papers, Butler Library, Columbia University.

Bryan, M., & Davis, A. (Eds.). (1990). *100 years at Hull House.* Bloomington, IN: University Press.

Cannon, K. (1985). The emergence of Black feminist consciousness. In L. M. Russell (Ed.), *Feminist interpretation of the Bible* (pp. 30–40). Philadelphia: Westminster.

Carlton, I. B. (1981). A pioneer social work educator: George Edmund Haynes. Unpublished dissertation.

Chicago School of Civics and Philanthropy Announcement, 1913–14. Joseph Regenstein Library, University of Chicago.

Chicago School of Civics and Philanthropy, Bulletin, No. 24. Joseph Regenstein Library, University of Chicago.

Conklin, V. (1917, March 21). Letter to B. Haynes. Lillian Wald Papers, Butler Library, Columbia University.

Conklin, V. (1922, November 30). Letter to B. Haynes. Lillian Wald Papers, Butler Library, Columbia University.

Daniels, D. (1989). *Always a sister: The feminism of Lillian D. Wald.* New York: The Feminist Press.

Davis, A. (1986). *Spearheads for reform.* New York: Oxford University Press.

Duster, A. (Ed.). (1972). *Crusade for justice: The autobiography of Ida B. Wells.* Chicago: University of Chicago Press.

Embree, E., & Waxman, J. (1949). *Investment in people: The story of the Julius Rosenwald Fund.* New York: Harper & Brothers.

Executive Committee of the Lincoln House. (1920, November 11). Lillian Wald Papers, Butler Library, Columbia University.

Giddings, P. (1984). *When and where I enter: The impact of Black women on race and sex in America.* New York: William Morrow.

Graves, W. (1913, June 21). Letter to Julius Rosenwald. Julius Rosenwald Papers, Joseph Regenstein Library, University of Chicago.

Graves, W. (1913, July 10). Letter to Julius Rosenwald. Julius Rosenwald Papers, Joseph Regenstein Library, University of Chicago.

Grossman, J. (1989). *Land of hope: Chicago, Black southerners, and the great migration*. Chicago: University of Chicago Press.

Haynes, B. H. (1915). Report for December for Directors' Meeting. Lillian Wald Papers, Butler Library, Columbia University.

Haynes, B. H. (1917, March 21). Letter to Viola Conklin. Lillian Wald Papers, Butler Library, Columbia University.

Haynes, B. H. (1919). Lincoln House: Its work for Colored Americans. *The Standard*, *6*, 122–124.

Haynes, G. to S. Breckinridge, August 19, 1913, George Edmund Haynes Papers, Fisk University.

Higginbotham, E. (1992). African-American women's history and the metalanguage of race. *Signs: Journal of Women in Culture and Society*, *17*, 251–274.

Holt, O. C. (1922, March 20). Report to Lincoln House Settlement. Lillian Wald Papers, Butler Library, Columbia University.

Holt, O. C. (1922, March 24). Letter to Olivia Harris. Lillian Wald Papers, Butler Library, Columbia University.

Holt, O. C. (1922, September 13). Letter to Agnes Leach. Lillian Wald Papers, Butler Library, Columbia University.

The invisible government of Negro social work, [Editorial]. (1920). *The Messenger*, *2*, 174–177.

Johnson, C. (1935). Julius Rosenwald. *Opportunity*, *13*, 110–111.

Jones, M. (1971). The responsibility of the Black college to the Black community: Then and now. *Daedalus*, *100*, 732–740.

Kraus, H. (1980). *The settlement house movement in New York City: 1886–1914*. New York: Arno Company.

Lincoln House Minutes. (1922, April 13). Lillian Wald Papers, Butler Library, Columbia University.

Lincoln House Report (Branch Henry Street Settlement), (1916–17). Lillian Wald Papers, Butler Library, Columbia University.

Lincoln House Summer Work. (1917, June 15–September 30). Lillian Wald Papers, Butler Library, Columbia University.

McDougald, E. (1925). The double task: The struggle of Negro women for sex and race emancipation. *Survey Graphics*, *103*, 688–691.

Minutes of the Lincoln House Board of Directors. (1915, March 27). Lillian Wald Papers, Butler Library, Columbia University.

Minutes from the Wendell Phillips Board of Directors Meeting. (1913, October 27). Lillian Wald Papers, Butler Library, Columbia University.

Obituary Notes. (1922, July 2). *The New York Times*.

Operation fatal for Miss Haynes, Y.W.C.A. Worker. (1922, July 8). *Chicago Defender*.

Perlman, D. (1972). Stirring the White conscience: The life of George Edmund Haynes. Unpublished dissertation.

Philpott, T. (1978). *The slum and the ghetto: Neighborhood deterioration and middle class reform. Chicago 1880–1930*. New York: Oxford University Press.

Press release, June 30, 1958. Lillian Wald Papers, Butler Library, Columbia University.

Remodeling a neighborhood. (1915, January 13). *New York Age* [Newspaper clipping]. Lillian Wald Papers, Butler Library, Columbia University.

Report of Lincoln Settlement. (1922, March 20). Lillian Wald Papers, Butler Library, Columbia University.

Sklar, K. (1985). Hull House in the 1890s: A community of women reformers. *Signs: Journal of Women in Cculture and Society*, *10*, 658–677.

Stanfield, J. (1982). The cracked back door: Foundations and Black social scientists between world wars. *American Sociologist*, *17*, 193–204.

Stanfield, J. (1985). *Philanthropy and Jim Crow in American social sciences*. Westport, CT: Greenwood Press.

Terborg-Penn, R. (1978). Discrimination against Afro-American women in the women's movement, 1830–1920. In S. Harley & R. Terborg-Penn (Eds.), *The Afro-American women: Struggles and images* (pp. 17–27). Port Washington, NY: Kennikat Press.

Wendell Phillips Settlement. (n.d.) 2009 Walnut Street, handwritten copy, signed by B. H. Haynes. Julius Rosenwald Papers, Joseph Regenstein Library, University of Chicago.

CHAPTER 4

Margaret Murray Washington
Organizer of Rural African American Women

Joyce G. Dickerson

The scholars who have made reference to the life and works of Margaret Murray Washington and her roles as educator, activist, and reformer have often characterized her as a "remarkable" woman. Careful and critical examination of her life's work makes it quite clear that Washington was more than just remarkable; she was an exceptional woman of distinction whose accomplishments included significant contributions to the development of American social welfare history as a community organizer of rural southern women.

In recent years, there has been a resurgence of interest among professionals concerned about increasing awareness of the historical contributions that African American women made to the development of social welfare history, programs, and services. As a result of the efforts of African American educators, researchers, social work practitioners, and others, there are several excellent resources now available that highlight the public and private lives of notable African American pioneer women. An examination of the extant literature that chronicles the struggles and accomplishments of African American women who made noteworthy contributions to social welfare during the Progressive Era (1898–1918) reveals frequent citations of Washington's name in the biographies and memoirs of prominent African American women associated with the women's movement. However, a complete picture of Washington herself does not emerge. Information about her life and social welfare achievements is scattered among letters and documents, and intermingled with the biographies of other prominent race leaders. For example, Smith (1996) included Washington's profile in the second volume of *Notable Black American Women* and made the following observation:

> From the frequency with which her name appears in print, there would seem to be no doubt that educator and clubwoman Margaret Murray Washington was a major

> figure in her time. This makes the fact that she has received little attention in recent studies all the more surprising. For example, there is no listing of her in the index to Darlene Clark Hine's sixteen-volume series of reprints, *Black Women in United States History* (Brooklyn: Carlson, 1990). With few exceptions, printed sources are panegyrics or brief mentions. Even if it is felt by some that her role was no more than that of a well-oiled cog in Booker T. Washington's Tuskegee machine, she did survive him by nearly a decade and continued to make an impression on the women's club movement and on Tuskegee. While there is nothing to suggest that she did not heartily support her husband's policies and programs, the scattered letters printed in the *Booker T. Washington Papers* do support the proposition that she is of considerable interest and importance in her own right. (p. 1217)

Indeed, Washington created an impressive record as a prominent club woman, educator, and community organizer whose career spanned more than 35 years. Because of the role that she played in organizing county and industrial schools and in empowering women, she became the fifth woman to be inducted into the Alabama Women's Hall of Fame in 1972 (Booker T. Washington Memorial Programme, 1922). The impact and significance of her work is reflected in part of the Hall of Fame biography:

> Called 'one of the greatest women of her century', Margaret Murray spoke to national audiences as first president of the Federation of Colored Women's Clubs. But her greatest service came as a graduate of Fisk University and teacher at Tuskegee, where she founded country schools, taught women how to live and attend to their homes, worked for the improvement of prisons, started the Mt. Meigs school for boys and an industrial school for girls, and constantly worked for the betterment of the poor and neglected.
>
> Born in Macon, Mississippi, married to Booker T. Washington in 1893, she stood steadfastly beside her husband in making his dream of a great institute come true. A woman of great compassion, intelligence and independence of judgment, she became one of the greatest forces at Tuskegee Institute and among African-American leaders and thinkers. (Judson College, 1999, p. 1)

When Washington died on June 4, 1925, there were many who mourned her death. The Tuskegee Institute (now Tuskegee University) was flooded with condolences from across the nation, with expressions of sympathy coming from friends, colleagues, former students, and admirers. Among the mourners was Calvin Coolidge, President of the United States. As a group, the mourners agreed that a giant in compassion, social service, education, reform, and race work had fallen. Washington was remembered for her commitment and devotion to her husband and the school, her leadership in club work among African American women, and her service as a woman who touched hundreds of lives with her spirit and grace (Rouse, 1996). Such remarks serve as indicators that Washington was a phenomenal social service worker who left behind a great legacy for the African American race.

In the realm of community leadership, Washington served as a role model for rural southern women and provided the inspiration for them to move toward self-empowerment. It was largely through her organizational efforts that African American women from all social and economic levels in Alabama, first in Tuskegee and then throughout the state, began to create their own social programs (Neverdon-Morton, 1989). Proficient in exercising many of the organizational and interpersonal skills utilized by current social workers, Washington developed intervention strategies that were highly successful in organizing communities and improving the plight of rural African American women. As an organizer working to educate and uplift rural African Americans, she assumed the roles of enabler, mobilizer, change agent, and advocate. She used a strengths-based approach to influence and organize others based on academic, religious, and moral principles. She mastered the art of community organizing and helped empower individuals, families, and communities so successfully that she rose to national prominence.

During a time when heavy migration to the northern states left behind disorganized communities, Washington used her intellect and skills to empower southern rural women by teaching them how not to migrate from the South and how to take care of their homes and families. She taught them how to take their natural resources and transform them into healthy, viable, and productive means of self-sufficiency, thereby benefiting themselves, their families, and their communities. She inspired middle-class African American women to organize for the purpose of rebuilding their communities and uplifting the race. Washington firmly believed that women could make a difference in the improvement of schools, the elimination of lynching, and women's suffrage issues. She considered these social issues to be "women's work now as always" (Lasch-Quinn, 1993, p. 119).

Personal Road to Rural Leadership

Margaret Murray Washington's intimate life portrait provides few clues about the inner psyche of the woman behind the name. She lived a life that can be viewed from many different perspectives. Few, if any, of her public photographs present a smiling face. Yet, the fruits of her labor clearly demonstrate that she was a caring, compassionate, and compelling woman who was committed to helping the poor and oppressed. Throughout her career, there were times when she was praised for the strength, initiative, energy, and ingenuity that contributed to the success of her projects, and there were times when she was highly criticized and accused of being too elitist or too conservative. Regardless of the personal opinions held about her, no one ever accused Washington of being indifferent to the needs of African Americans. Essentially, she was a complex individual whose talents and abilities far exceeded those of most women of her time.

By some standards, Washington was perceived as quite an attractive woman. During the era in which she lived, some people used light skin color and European features as definitive standards of beauty. A New York settlement worker present when Washington and her husband spoke at a dinner of the Social Reform Club in New York said,

"Mrs. Washington is lighter than he and has beautiful features, arched brows, blue (?) eyes, a Grecian nose, and a poise of the head like a Gibson girl. Her hands are white as mine and beautifully shaped. But her hair is kinky" (Harlan, 1972, p. 188).

Washington was one of possibly 10 siblings. She was born Margaret Murray on March 9, 1865, to Lucy Murray, a washerwoman, living in Macon, Mississippi. Depending on the source, however, her exact date of birth, birth state, and family history vary. It has been speculated that she may have been born as early as 1861, based on data secured from an 1880 census that listed one sister and two brothers living with Lucy Murray during this time (Harlan, 1972). Research conducted by others found that she was the third of five children (Hine, 1997; Link, 1996; Rouse, 1996). Nevertheless, in 1898 Washington revealed that her mother had 10 children, most of whom lived long enough to have children themselves (Washington, 1898). Not much information is available to document the life of James Murray, her father, although she indicated on several occasions that he was a White Irish immigrant who died when she was seven years old. Her mother later married an African American sharecropper named Henry Brown.

Upon her father's death, Murray went to live with Quakers who resided in the local community. Although their exact surname is unknown, the Sanders or Sandler family took her into their home and instructed her in the social and religious teachings of the Quakers, teaching her, by their example, piety and good works. After she turned 14, one of her Quaker benefactors suggested that she teach. The next morning, she borrowed a long skirt, tied up her hair, and appeared before a local magistrate, where she passed the teachers' examination. Reportedly, the judge knew her and her father and assigned her to a teaching position at the same school where she had previously been a pupil (Harlan, 1972; Hine, 1997; Scott, 1907).

Murray's thirst for education and self-improvement is evidenced by her enrollment in Fisk University's Preparatory School in 1881 where she attended school for eight years while working part-time. Described as a model student, she studied Latin, Greek, German, French, philosophy, science, and literature. She was associate editor of the student newspaper, *The Fisk Herald*, and president of the Young Ladies' Lyceum, one of the three literary societies on the campus. During her senior commencement dinner, she reminded Booker T. Washington, founder of the Tuskegee Institute and commencement speaker, that she had written to him about a month earlier regarding employment at Tuskegee. Although offered a position at Prairie View in Texas, she had, for some unknown reason, a strong preference for Tuskegee, even if it meant accepting less money. According to Harlan (1972), both Booker T. Washington and Margaret Murray were "up from slavery". Unlike some of her contemporaries—such as Elizabeth Ross Haynes, whose family acquired wealth, or Mary Church Terrell, who was born to wealth and ease—she did not come from a privileged background, nor did her family amass a fortune. Murray's background, temperament, and conservative outlook closely matched Booker T. Washington's. Impressed by her maturity and wit, he later hired her as an English teacher.

Murray had been highly recommended by the President and the Lady Principal of

Fisk University. They described her as a model student, excellent scholar, and good disciplinarian. Anna T. Ballentine, Lady Principal at Fisk for over 20 years, described her as being "of good mind, of conscientious religious convictions, of unusual power in gaining influence over those younger than herself, and of ability to direct them" (Harlan, Kaufman, & Smock, 1974, p. 3). With such leadership qualities, shortly after arriving at Tuskegee, Murray was quickly promoted to Lady Principal and Director of Women's Industries. The following year, she became engaged to Booker T. Washington and married him in Tuskegee on October 12, 1892.

Washington was unsure that she wanted marriage and children, particularly since her husband had three small children born from his previous two marriages. For example, Washington wrote to her husband and stated, "You do not have much sympathy with me because I feel as I do in regard to little folks. I get annoyed with myself but the feeling is there just the same" (Giddings, 1985). Also, Giddings noted that Washington and her stepdaughter Portia had a particular dislike for each other, but after the marriage they eventually learned to live with one another.

Seldom mentioned in the literature is the fact that Washington had many nurturing characteristics. Harlan (1972) observed that despite her distaste for taking care of young children and her unromantic view of marriage and family, she felt more responsibility for Washington's motherless children than those officially in charge of their care. She made their clothes, worried about their care during her absence, and helped prepare them academically until they enrolled in the Tuskegee Institute. Correspondence from her sister-in-law, Mary A. Elliott, and comments made by various friends and family members document that the Washington family was pleased with her care of the children and there were definite affectionate bonds established between Washington and the children, especially the young boys, Davidson and Baker (Harlan et al., 1974). The family grew larger still when a nephew and niece came to Tuskegee to live with the Washington family after the death of their parents. Washington's niece took the name of Laura Murray Washington, called her aunt "Mama," and later inherited property from Washington's estate (Smith, 1996). Similar to many other prominent and active club women, Washington married late—when she was 31. She was married to Booker T. Washington for 33 years: they had a loving and collegial relationship.

After marriage, Washington juggled many roles—wife, mother, educator, First Lady of Tuskegee, club woman, community activist, and organizer of African American women. As expected, the stress of handling both personal and professional responsibilities sometimes affected her emotional well-being. Obviously, managing these enormous responsibilities created stressful times. Some of her correspondence hinted of brief periods of sadness and depression, even before the marriage occurred. In July 1891 during her courtship with Booker T. Washington, she wrote to him, "I feel just as if I could sit down by you and have a good cry this morning" (Giddings, 1985, p. 112), and on another occasion she wrote, "Sunday was another blue day for me" (Harlan et al., 1974, p. 174). Sensitive to his wife's enormous responsibilities, in 1912 Booker T. Washington expressed interest in purchasing a few acres of land away from the main campus so Washington could have a place to occasionally seek solitude from the constant strain of her daily routine.

After being thrust into a blended and closely knit extended family, Washington was forced to deal with frequent and long periods of absence created by her husband's fundraising and speaking engagements. Similarly, she had to learn to adapt to the dual roles of wife and mother while establishing a career. Additionally, she had to manage the stress associated with her women's work and race work. All of these tasks were no doubt daunting, and Washington's occasional bouts of mild depression are not surprising. Yet, Washington was tenacious and not deterred from reaching out to help the oppressed in the fight for social and economic justice.

Washington was perceived by others as being a very strong woman who was unafraid to acknowledge that she had human faults such as a fiery temper. Nor was she afraid of criticism and demonstrated on various occasions that she was able to withstand pressure when her ideas and actions proved contrary to others. Perhaps Washington's greatest strengths lay in her ability to motivate, unite, and lead both rural and urban women of all races in their quest for equality.

Tuskegee's Third First Lady

Hine (1997) stated that "Booker T. Washington did not make colleagues of his wives. Instead, he made wives of his colleagues" (p. 13). Certainly, all three of Booker T. Washington's wives played a major role in the development of the Tuskegee Institute, but it was Margaret Washington, the third wife, who lived long enough to serve Tuskegee for 35 years.

After graduating from Fisk, Margaret Murray arrived in Tuskegee in the fall of 1889 and in 1890 became Lady Principal and Director of Domestic Services, which included a curriculum of laundering, cooking, dressmaking, plain sewing, millinery, and mattress making (Hine, 1997). Although her academic preparation at Fisk revolved around the study of Shakespeare and Hawthorne, the speculation is that Booker T. Washington convinced her to give up academic teaching to supervise the women's industries.

Tuskegee's third First Lady was more than a figurehead. In addition to fulfilling her academic and social responsibilities, she kept her husband apprised of events and situations on campus and was responsible for developing a set of rules for teachers, developing a code of conduct for the girls, and developing curricula. Often, she made recommendations, and her opinions were carefully considered when Booker T. Washington hired faculty. She also assisted her husband in developing many of his speeches. Washington's intense involvement in campus activities and her position on Tuskegee's 15-person executive committee provided ample opportunities to develop supervision and administration skills. She was able to engage in planning, budgeting, and program evaluation activities. These skills further enhanced her personal and political power, thereby increasing her ability to help make executive decisions and preparing her to become the Dean of Women.

Washington worked tirelessly for the school and its constituents. Harlan and colleagues (1974) quote Washington's description of a typical day in her life at Tuskegee as follows:

> My Dear Booker—It is Monday night and I am just faged out. Got up at seven—ate no breakfast—called the roll at 8:30—came over and visited the sick till 10—went to the faculty meeting till five minutes of eleven—taught a class the last hour before noon. Took dinner with Mrs. Logan and came pretty nearly being late—kept Mr. Hamilton's classes the three periods after dinner. Met the girls at 4:30 and finally ended by stopping by to see how Miss Lischy is getting on—and now I am in study with the girls but I am glad of this fact because I should imagine that I was too tired to write you if I had nothing to do. (p. 27)

Washington genuinely cared about the faculty, staff, and students. For example, her concern about fairness and equity for teachers became apparent in one instance when the school was losing good faculty because of the Institute's tardiness in granting significant raises. This incident led her to petition her husband strongly to reconsider the issue of teacher salaries. The students also felt her power and presence. They saw her as a nurturing mother figure, a mentor, and a friend. Washington firmly believed in traditions, values, and rituals, and she felt that appropriate behavior was an essential element in creating the renowned "Tuskegee Spirit" (Rouse, 1996). Washington had a reputation for keeping a close eye on female students, but she also found numerous ways to instruct them in self-improvement and engage them in wholesome youth activities.

Washington frequently accompanied her husband on trips to the North and often gave lectures to different groups and organizations. Considering the era in which she lived, Washington traveled extensively for a southern African American woman. She spoke at various club meetings and was entertained with celebrities such as Susan B. Anthony and Mark Twain. She traveled abroad to England and had tea with Queen Victoria. She also delivered speeches before the Women's Liberal Club of Bristol, the Royal College for the Blind at the Crystal Palace, and the Agricultural College for Women at Swanley (Harlan, 1972). Her leadership, fundraising, and community outreach efforts as Tuskegee's First Lady were so forceful that Booker T. Washington dedicated his famous autobiography, *Up from Slavery*, both to her and to his brother John H. Washington. According to Booker T. Washington, their patience, fidelity, and hard work were essential to Tuskegee's success (Washington, 1901/1989).

Organizing Southern Rural Women: Pathway to Social Services

Washington used her organizing skills to create a broad range of social service programs and institutions for the rural population. She always searched for new ways to uplift families and communities, and in addition to providing leadership on the campus, she also provided outreach opportunities to the local Black community and was the prime force behind social service programs (Hine, 1997). Her outreach efforts to the rural community and beyond became successful primarily because of three major projects: the development of the Tuskegee Woman's Club, establishment of the Town Night School, and settlement work with the Elizabeth Russell Plantation.

Tuskegee Woman's Club

Washington's community activism began with development of the Tuskegee Woman's Club, and her first organizing strategy was to find a way to link the campus with the community. On March 2, 1895, she organized 13 women at the first meeting of the Tuskegee Woman's Club for the purpose of promoting the "general intellectual development of women." Although the club's membership was exclusive, composed of only female faculty or spouses of faculty, she was able to influence the women to get involved in helping the less fortunate. Washington believed that it was the responsibility of the more fortunate members of the race to help the poor and oppressed. One class of people could not survive without the other because in her mind, "the [N]egroes of America have no superior class" (Link, 1996, p. 135), and everyone, particularly women, had a role to play in helping the less fortunate members of the race. She believed that an essential part of women's work was to "reach out to those who should be awakened to the necessity of proper home making and training for their children" (Link, 1996, p. 139) and the work must be practical.

Originally, the Tuskegee Woman's Club meetings were held twice monthly, but as the need for education and social services became more evident, the club women and the students who joined later found themselves involved in organizing and providing service on a weekly basis. By the end of 1895, membership had increased to the point that two other clubs, the Brooklyn Literary Group and the Women's League of Women, had requested branch affiliation (Neverdon-Morton, 1989).

One of the major activities of the club was a series of mothers' meetings that took place every Saturday in rented rooms above a Black-owned grocery store. While students entertained the children in one room, their mothers heard a lecture and participated in discussions on women's issues in another. By 1904, these meetings attracted almost 300 women every week. The club members instructed rural women on various subjects, ranging from child care and home management to how to buy land and build homes for their families (Rouse, 1996; Thompson, 1997).

For the rural African American, it was difficult to make social and economic progress. Washington recognized the magnitude of socioeconomic problems confronting the rural residents and devoted an inordinate amount of time to the preparation and facilitation of mothers' meetings. She was successful in encouraging club members and community residents to focus on individual change and community reform with the overall ambitious goal of racial uplift.

In addition to economic and gender issues, Washington also had a personal need to improve the quality of segregated public spaces designated for African Americans.

Although she did not openly attack the political ideology and humiliations associated with legal segregation, Washington and the Tuskegee Woman's Club thought that it was important that the segregated spaces provided be clean, comfortable, and pleasant. So, they cleaned segregated waiting rooms, hung curtains, secured modest furnishings, added reading materials on African Americans, and hung portraits and photographs of prominent African Americans and Native Americans (Rouse, 1996).

The Town Night School

In 1892, Tuskegee Institute began sponsoring conferences for farmers, but women were excluded until 1916. Washington continued to plan for rural women even though her husband did not include women's issues in the conferences offered at Tuskegee until much later. When women's issues became part of the conference format, she began to give lectures at the conferences. She viewed this endeavor as a vehicle that could help provide opportunities for the women of Alabama to learn important skills necessary for administering social service programs and to hear what others were doing to resolve social problems in their communities.

Washington seized this opportunity to teach skills to farm wives. In 1910, she selected 12 other women and met with them separately to establish the Town Night School. She convinced her husband to help finance the school through the Tuskegee Institute. The fact that Washington secured her pupils for the Town Night School by hiring a small boy to tell the women milling around town that "a woman upstairs" had something for them attests to her ability to influence others. Within a year, the Town Night School had eight teachers who taught reading, cooking, sewing, carpentry, bricklaying, painting, and tailoring to the people of the town of Tuskegee. To keep the children occupied while their mothers were in class, they were taught cooking. Also, these classes helped both men and women secure jobs as cooks, carpenters, seamstresses, and tailors.

Two years after the school opened, the Tuskegee Institute withdrew its financial support from the school, and the Woman's Club took over. They were able to keep the school open eight months of the year, supporting 103 night classes and 37 day classes, including cooking for the children. Eventually, academic courses were offered; the most successful of these was Negro history. Washington promoted the teaching of the subject in other schools around the country.

Once again focusing on practical training, Washington converted the space rented from a Black shopkeeper into a two-model room that included a dining room and a bedroom and used them as practicum space for housekeeping and instruction (Rouse, 1996). It is obvious that she understood the significance of integrating theory and practice, and without her foresight, many African Americans would not have had access to these educational opportunities.

To fully understand the significance of Washington's organizing abilities and the need for educational and social services requires a brief review of the historical forces operating in a post-emancipated South. The summary from a 1978 study on the roots of Black poverty in America concluded that the historical circumstances of Blacks and the role that they played in the southern economy relegated them to being the lowest income population in the poorest region of the country (Mandle, 1978). The inequities and social injustices were so oppressive that they created negative and long-lasting effects on an entire race of people. Forces such as segregation as an aftermath of slavery, sexual exploitation of African American women by White males and prison guards/inmates, random lynchings, illegitimacy, poverty, and illiteracy were only a few of the social ills that plagued the South. Thus, there was an obvious need for rural women in the South to organize, given the prevailing conditions under which they lived. From a grassroots perspective, Washington was quite cognizant of the needs of the rural population. She had observed and worked with the people and understood the importance of helping them to increase their self-esteem and to acquire education and other basic necessities missing from their lives.

Tuskegee, located in Macon County, was in the heart of the Black belt of the South and one of the most rural areas in Alabama. Eight years prior to Washington's arrival in Tuskegee, poverty was a central force in the remote county districts. Shanty houses, poorly dressed children, inadequate diets, and illiteracy confronted the rural population. Booker T. Washington commented on the state of affairs observed during his travels throughout the rural beats of Alabama in 1881 saying, "I went to the black belt of the South, inhabited almost exclusively by Negroes and mules" (Harlan, 1972, p. 118). Booker T. Washington almost never saw children decently dressed, reporting that when they wore any clothing at all, it was usually a single garment "and this was so greasy that it did not resemble cloth" (Harlan, 1972, p. 120). Also, in some cabin homes, he found incongruous extravagances side by side with poverty and cultural deprivation.

The routine of everyday life of most rural African Americans involved long work hours on the plantations and visits to town on Saturday for most of the day. It seemed that Saturday trips to town offered a much needed and eagerly anticipated respite from rural life. Washington (1901/1989) observed:

> The whole atmosphere of the town would change when the country people arrived, the men in overalls and wool hats, the women in bonnets and calico dresses, both usually barefooted, the men chewing and spitting, and the women either smoking corncob pipes or dipping snuff. For some reason that held true in every social class in the Southern rural culture, women never chewed. Dipping snuff, on the other hand, was widespread among both black and white rural women. (p. 115)

This graphic description of the people and how they were forced to live provides a strong rationale for establishing the Town Night School and other types of institutions. Washington believed the people deserved a quality life and was determined to give them more than hard work and poverty. Additionally, some Whites operated under the misconception that southern African Americans were happy with their circumstances. The mass exodus of African Americans from the rural South to urban centers served to belie that assumption.

Washington, a firm supporter of education, sought to use the knowledge, values, and skills of the Tuskegee Woman's Club to educate and organize rural women and help empower them to engage in planned change. She sought to teach them how to remain and survive in the South. For Washington, education was an empowerment tool, and she was confident that women were capable of learning how to improve their own circumstances, as well as the state of their communities. With two major successful community projects to her credit, Washington extended her organizing skills and social programs from the campus and town to the surrounding Black communities and began tackling the problems confronting rural women and their children on various plantation settlements.

Elizabeth Russell Plantation Settlement

In 1897, two years after founding the Tuskegee Woman's Club, Washington led the club toward community activities. The members organized a community project with the Elizabeth Russell Plantation Settlement located eight miles from Tuskegee. Under Washington's leadership, the group tackled illiteracy by helping rural residents establish a school and church. For 12 years, members of the Woman's Club spent their weekends working with the residents of the plantation. They taught Sunday school and organized boys' clubs, sewing classes for girls, mothers' clubs, and newspaper-reading clubs for men. Children were taught advanced farming methods and household industries in addition to basic literacy skills (Thompson, 1997).

The settlement's mothers' club provided the organizing structure for social service and reform activities. Hundreds of women attended meetings, walking or riding from miles around in the Alabama countryside. Members divided the work into committees devoted to particular projects such as temperance work, community work, Sunday schools, and mothers' meetings. Other programs included the current news and a music department. The Social Service Committee raised money by making and selling candy and other food, paid the dentist bills for 100 children one year, provided medical services, built a playground and park, and constructed a Reading Room and a Boys' Social and Literary Club. These club women were pioneers following in the tradition of the settlement house movement. In 1901, Washington also started a small public library by using her children's discarded books and staffing the library with members of the Woman's Club (Lasch-Quinn, 1993).

The settlement school opened in 1898 and was largely the result of the work of Ann Davis, a graduate of the Tuskegee Institute, but it was Washington who was responsible for securing county funds in the amount of $15 per month to supplement Davis's salary. Due to Washington's club's involvement and financial support, the school became part of the public system in 1906 (Neverdon-Morton, 1989). The fact that the tenants were able to maintain the programs without the assistance of club members provides concrete evidence that their work was successful. It was also a testament to Washington and the other club women's selflessness and their commitment to the growth and development of the African American community. The significant work being done by Washington and the Tuskegee Woman's Club was known throughout the South and eventually became a model for other clubs throughout the state and the nation.

Working the State and National Scene

Whenever there was interest in forming new organizations, it seems that Washington either took the initiative or was summoned to take a leadership role. When Josephine Ruffin called a meeting of African American women in Boston in July 1895, the National Federation of Afro-American Women (NFAAW) was established and Washington emerged as president. This organization united 36 women's clubs in 12 states. At the regional level, Washington founded the Southeastern Federation of Colored Women (White, 1999). She was also the principal organizer and first president of the Alabama State Federation of Colored Women's Clubs founded in 1898. Composed of approximately 30 clubs with a diverse membership of women from various service fields, the Alabama Federation embarked on a wide range of projects that focused on the needs of the most vulnerable members of the rural population—women, children, and the elderly. Projects included reforming prison systems, purchasing property to build institutions for boys and girls, creating libraries and reading rooms, distributing clothes, marketing foods, looking for and reporting cases of motherless children on isolated rural plantations, and providing shelters for the aged and infirm. Members organized statewide programs commemorating Negro history, predating by several decades Carter G. Woodson's "Negro History Week" celebrations, which did not begin until 1926 (Rouse, 1996). These projects were similar to those of the Tuskegee Woman's Club, but because of its larger membership and greater financial resources, support from Whites, and influence over the allocation of state funds, their Alabama State Federation's programs and services reached larger numbers of rural African Americans (Neverdon-Morton, 1989).

In an effort to protect and direct youth of the state, Washington led the group to work toward prison reform for African American youth by founding the Mt. Meigs Reformatory for Juvenile Law-Breakers and the Mt. Meigs Rescue Home for Girls. Previously, the state's policy was to mainstream delinquent boys and homeless youngsters into adult penal institutions. The Federation was successful in its attempt to have the young inmates transferred into the custody of the boys' school at Mt. Meigs. Under Washington's leadership, many young lives were saved from prison. The Mt. Meigs Reformatory became a state institution in 1911 (Litwack & Meier, 1988; Neverdon-Morton, 1989; Rouse, 1996).

The Mt. Meigs Rescue Home for Girls was established by the Federation to provide shelter and assistance to African American girls. Financial support for the home came from branch clubs, as well as public and private sources. Washington used her networking skills to secure funding from affluent Whites and African Americans such as Lucy C. Jefferson, club woman, philanthropist, and cofounder of the W. H. Jefferson Funeral Home in Mississippi (Smith, 1996).

From 1912 to 1918, Washington was president of a newly formed group known as the National Association of Colored Women (NACW). The national agenda of the NACW focused on such issues as women's suffrage, antilynching, and the improvement of schools. It is likely that Washington was largely responsible for the NACW, adding to the national agenda the establishment of more mothers' groups for rural women. Over 500 active groups affiliated with the NACW by 1913; the Tuskegee Woman's Club was used as a model by other groups.

NACW members asked Washington to write an article to provide simple instructions on how to establish mothers' meetings and clubs. This article was one of many that Washington penned on topics such as "Girls' Home Responsibilities," "An Ideal Home for a Girl," "When Shall a Girl Be Permitted to Receive Her First Company," and "Mother's Relation to the Teacher" (Lerner, 1972; Neverdon-Morton, 1989). These articles generated much interest among groups in the South and across the nation. Relevant, practical, and essential for rural girls and women, the topics piqued the interest of Anne M. Evans, a White woman who served as an investigator in the Women's Rural Organization for the U.S. Department of Agriculture. Washington and Evans developed a relationship and exchanged information that helped increase awareness about the service needs of rural populations.

Prior to serving as president of the NACW, Washington coordinated the membership committee, where "her work was apparent in the development of federations in Western states, including Colorado, California, Montana, and Idaho" (Rouse, 1996, p. 36). She also edited and subsidized the official newsletter of the NACW, *National Notes*. In spite of criticism from some members who felt the content was too conservative, she was able to maintain control of *National Notes* for many years because most members were comfortable with her philosophy and supported her work. In 1904, the NACW selected her as one of five women to attend the International Congress of Women in Germany, and in 1906, she presented a paper at the fifth biennial session at the Detroit convention. In addition to these conferences, Washington often spoke to groups on the social achievements of rural southern African Americans.

Washington and other women associated with the NACW also founded the International Council of Women of the Darker Races in 1920. Washington was chair of the education section and was elected as the first president in 1922. She shared the vision of other club women in helping the national women's organization become a significant link between women of color and international causes. These women were responsible for incorporating literature on Negro history and other groups of the darker races into the curriculam of various schools. Study groups were developed and the women pledged their support to improve the social, economic, and political welfare of the women of "dark races" (Smith, 1996). Washington's expertise at organizing was once again recognized as Janie Porter Barrett reported that the women in her study group modeled their discussions after the Tuskegee club.

Around 1920, Washington's extreme conservatism placed her in an uncomfortable position with some club women who were stronger advocates for political activism on issues such as women's suffrage. Her attempts to respond to the conflict with moderation were challenged, particularly when she attempted to get the group to maintain their support of White female allies in the spirit of interracial cooperation. Washington was skillful in cultivating friendships and learned much about multiculturalism. She held many interracial meetings in her home and was convinced that all races of people have unique cultures. She maintained that good people could be found among all races and classes.

By 1924, an increase in club membership combined with class, color, and regional differences to create a climate of discord. As the stories of prominent African American pioneer club women continued to unfold, it was clear that they worked collectively toward some goals, but sometimes allowed personal agendas to determine their priorities. These priorities were dictated to some extent by their own social environments. Social cliques, as well as different ideological leanings of the women in the various areas, often meant that they were loyal to their section of the country and its issues when electing officers or establishing program priorities (Davis, 1981; White, 1999). Washington refused to put the organization in jeopardy by participating in these struggles for power and control. Nonetheless, she continued to work diligently with the organization until her death.

Historically, the positions taken in political debates regarding the appropriate and effective means of assisting oppressed groups and communities usually have been characterized as either liberal or conservative. Tropman, Erlich, and Rothman (1995) noted that people of color have traditionally been caught between the polarized struggles of conservative and liberal theoretical forces. Consequently, many liberal community organizers have emphasized class issues and ignored racism and cultural diversity. From this perspective, history's comments on the final chapter of Washington's life can be misleading; some have implied that she failed the African American race because she was not a liberal political spokeswoman and her world view was extremely conservative. For example, Thompson (1997) summarized Washington's club activities and work with the NACW by stating:

> Washington was involved in the earliest parts of the process, as she often was. She offered her own resources to make things happen, as she so often did. She participated actively, but then came down firmly on the side of compromise and concession. It was the keynote of Washington's life that she could work fiercely and effectively for social improvement, never stinting herself in the service of her people, but that she could not or would not take the final step into political action. (p. 189)

Washington's role in race work was broader than her political philosophy. Much of the success of the women's club movement was based on the significant contributions made by Margaret Murray Washington, because she helped lay the foundation for the organization's education and social service programs.

Implications for Social Work Practice

Many times it is assumed that practitioners who provide direct services have no opportunities to promote large-scale progressive change (Longress, 1995). On the contrary, there are many opportunities for social workers to influence change within ethnically diverse communities. Since the Progressive Era, social workers have developed a plethora of orientations, strategies, and techniques that have proven useful in helping to empower people of color and their communities. In recent years, however, it appears as though there has been a de-emphasis on working in ethnic communities that has contributed to the deterioration of community spirit, social progress, and economic viability.

In some cases, organizers who have attempted to work with people of color have been unsuccessful in working with community residents. Their organizing and mobilizing techniques have often been met with resistance. This lack of response and connectedness may suggest a need to reassess the manner in which services are delivered in ethnically diverse communities. Specifically, practitioners must have not only tools and techniques designed for change, but also faith in their clients and a belief that change is possible. Washington and other African American pioneers maintained an unwavering faith in the African American race. She and other reformers rejected the idea that African Americans were a hopeless race of people.

Successful community organizers in ethnic communities are those who seriously believe in change and take action to eliminate the cultural and historical gaps that exist between workers and clients. Rivera and Erlich (1995) found the following 12 qualities to be ideal for organizing with people of color: (1) cultural and racial identification; (2) familiarity with customs and traditions, social networks, and values; (3) an intimate knowledge of language and subgroup slang; (4) leadership styles and development; (5) an analytical framework for political and economic analysis; (6) knowledge of past organizing strategies, their strengths and limitations; (7) skills in conscientization and empowerment;[1] (8) skills in assessing community psychology; (9) knowledge of organizational behavior; (10) skills in evaluative and participatory research; (11) skills in program planning and development and administration management; and (12) an awareness of self and personal strengths and limitations. Similarly, Washington believed that effective community organizing with people of color required workers to have cultural and racial identification with the group and according to Rivera and Erlich "there is no stronger identification with a community than truly being a part of it" (p. 208).

Washington, a strong advocate for racial pride, never attempted to distance herself from her race. Although she was the product of an interracial background, she once remarked that "we cannot separate ourselves from our people, no matter how much we try; for one, I have no desire to do so" (Washington, 1898, p. 865). She believed that regardless of class or gender, everyone was responsible for making a contribution toward the advancement of the race because "no nation or race has ever come up by entirely overlooking its members who are less fortunate, less ambitious, less sound in body and hence soul" (Washington, 1898, p. 864).

Since it is unrealistic to expect all practitioners to be people of color, it is incumbent upon workers from other ethnic groups to identify in different ways. To achieve racial and cultural identification, workers must develop a multicultural perspective that includes an Afrocentric paradigm that can be incorporated into their practice modalities. In order to achieve this end, social workers must increase their knowledge of African American clients and other ethnic groups and the communities in which they live. To do otherwise conveys indifference and misses opportunities for both the worker and the client to contribute something valuable to the helping process (Carlton-LaNey, 1999). Also, practitioners can attain cultural competence by making an assessment of their agency's staff training needs, strengths and deficits, and obstacles that impede serving culturally diverse clients (Kirst-Ashman & Hull, 1997).

Developing a leadership style is crucial to successful organizing. During a time when color was an issue between and within races, Washington was adept at organizing and leading diverse groups of women. The quality of her work was reflected in the progress made by low- and middle-income women from both rural and urban backgrounds. Organizing rural women was a special challenge because of the differences that existed among urban and rural women. Rural women were not as motivated to effect changes in the social structure because segregation was clearly defined and rigidly enforced in the South. There were few who challenged these customs for fear that they would endanger the lives, programs, services, and institutions available to the African American race (Neverdon-Morton, 1989). Washington put herself at risk to become a leader. As a leader, she was careful to treat the women with dignity and respect while acknowledging their level and pace of activity. Concurrently, the women put themselves at risk because they accepted the challenge and worked for individual change and community reform.

Washington led by example and taught others to lead. "The hallmark of macro social work is leadership" (Falck, 1988, p. 161), and a leader helps communities of people take risks and envision a better future for themselves. Competent leaders encourage commitment and help people move along a path to accomplish their goals. When social workers take leadership roles in African American communities and other ethnic communities, they share in the risk-taking that can help clients draw on the strengths of their community and attain self-empowerment by exercising self-determination and independence. Working together, the results can be tangible policy concessions, better laws, and guarantees of people's rights (Brueggemann, 1996).

A distinct and noticeable difference between settlement leaders and current social workers is in the area of service delivery. Settlement leaders firmly believed that their presence in the community made a significant difference in their ability to understand and meet the needs of the people and their communities. Today, heavy caseloads, managed care, and other organizational constraints can inadvertently distance practitioners from the community and hinder their effectiveness. Moreover, the economic, social, and political realities of ethnic groups and their communities can become foreign to practitioners. Social workers are trained to understand that these are the people on the "fringes of today's modern social systems who lack power, control, resources, and opportunities" (Brueggemann, 1996, p. 104). They also understand that these are "the people who are trapped in a dangerous environment and are at significant risk in the economic and social areas of their lives" (Devore, 1990, p. 83). These are the oppressed groups who need visual contact with professionals capable of providing culturally specific services.

Finally, a major task of the organizer in disenfranchised communities is that of empowering people through the process of developing critical consciousness (Rivera & Erlich, 1995). Social workers are challenged to learn from these pioneer club women who helped themselves and African American clients develop the type of racial consciousness that guided them on the path to empowerment and self-sufficiency.

Conclusion

Education and training for future social workers must include content that will help students embrace a multicultural perspective that includes an Afrocentric paradigm. They can learn much from African American social welfare pioneers like Margaret Murray Washington, whose example can guide them toward a deeper appreciation for human diversity and gender issues. Also, students may gain a new perspective about the significance of why their presence and skills are needed in ethnic communities.

Social workers who expand their realm of practice to include learning more about African Americans and other ethnic groups and their communities will be in an ideal position to be effective practitioners with people of color. These workers will be prepared to provide culturally specific services and will have the capacity to help improve the social functioning of individuals, groups, and communities. Practitioners can gain inspiration from Washington's persistence by recognizing that contemporary social problems are demanding, but not overwhelming enough to give in to feelings of hopelessness and despair. Social workers can continue to help young girls and women, as well as boys and men, to develop self-help skills that will assist them in providing clean and healthy homes free of poverty, neglect, and violence.

Finally, based on a systems perspective, individuals and groups are interdependent, and as long as one racial group is politically, socially, or economically enslaved, the entire nation can never experience authentic freedom. Hence, the social work profession is challenged not only to teach skills, but also to prepare others to "uplift a people."

Note

1. Rivera and Erlich (1995) elaborated further on the phrase "conscientization and empowerment". "A major task of the organizer in disenfranchised communities is that of empowering people through the process of developing critical consciousness. How the personal and political influence each other, and the local environment in which they are played out, is a key in this process. It is not enough to succeed in ameliorating or even solving community problems if there is little or no empowerment of the community" (p. 209).

References

Booker T. Washington Memorial Programme. (1922, April 5). Tuskegee AL: Tuskegee Institute Press.

Brueggemann, W. (1996). *The practice of macro social work.* Chicago: Nelson-Hall.

Carlton-LaNey, I. B. (1999). African American social work pioneers' response to need. *Social Work, 44,* 311–321.

Davis, A. (1981). *Women, race and class.* New York: Random House.

Devore, W. (1990). The African American community in 1990: The search for a practice method. In F. G. Rivera & J. L. Erlich (Eds.), *Community organizing in a diverse society* (p. 83). Boston: Allyn & Bacon.

Falck, H. (1988). *Social work: The membership perspective.* New York: Springer.

Giddings, P. (1985). *When and where I enter: The impact of Black women on race and sex in America.* New York: Bantam Books.

Harlan, L. R. (1972). *Booker T. Washington: The making of a Black leader, 1856–1901.* New York: Oxford University Press.

Harlan, L. R., Kaufman, S., & Smock, R. (Eds.). (1974). *The Booker T. Washington Papers* (Vol. 3). Urbana: University of Illinois Press.

Hine, D. (1997). *Facts on file encyclopedia of Black women in America: Education. The early days.* New York: Facts on File.

Judson College. (1999). Alabama Women's Hall of Fame. [Online]. Available: <http://home.judson.edu/extra/fame/washington.html>.

Kirst-Ashman, K., & Hull, G. (1997). *Generalist practice with organizations and communities.* Chicago: Nelson-Hall.

Lasch-Quinn, E. (1993). *Black neighbors: Race and the limits of reform in the American settlement house movement, 1890–1945.* Chapel Hill: University of North Carolina Press.

Lerner, G. (Ed.). (1972). *Black women in White America.* New York: Vintage Books.

Link, W. (1996). *The rebuilding of old commonwealths: And other documents of social reform in the Progressive Era South.* Boston: St. Martin's Press.

Litwack, L., & Meier, A. (Eds.). (1988). *Black leaders of the nineteenth century.* Chicago: University of Illinois Press.

Longress, J. (1995). *Human behavior in the social environment.* Itasca, IL: F. E. Peacock.

Mandle, J. (1978). *The roots of Black poverty: The southern plantation economy after the Civil War.* Durham, NC: Duke University Press.

Neverdon-Morton, C. (1989). *Afro-American women of the South and the advancement of the race, 1895–1925.* Knoxville TN: University of Tennessee Press.

Rivera, F., & Erlich, J. (1995). Organizing with people of color: A perspective. In J. Tropman, J. Erlich, & J. Rothman (Eds.), *Tactics and techniques of community intervention* (pp. 208–212). Itasca, IL: F. E. Peacock.

Rouse, J. (1996). Out of the shadow of Tuskegee: Margaret Murray Washington, social activism, and race vindication. *Journal of Negro History, 18,* 31–46.

Scott, E. (1907). Mrs. Booker T. Washington's part in her husband's work. *Ladies Home Journal*, *24*, 42.

Smith, J. (Ed.). (1996). *Notable Black American women (Book 2)*. Detroit: Gale Research.

Thompson, K. (1997). Margaret Murray Washington. In D. Hine (Ed.), *Facts on file: Encyclopedia of Black women in America. The early years, 1617–1899.* New York: Facts on File.

Tropman, J., Erlich, J., & Rothman, J. (Eds.). (1995). *Tactics and techniques of community intervention.* Itasca, IL: F. E. Peacock.

Washington, B. T. (1989). *Up from slavery: An autobiography*. New York: Carol Publishing. (Original work published 1901)

Washington, M. M. (1898). We must have a cleaner "social morality." In P. Foner & R. Branham (Eds.), *Lift every voice: African American oratory, 1787–1900* (pp. 863–868). Tuscaloosa: University of Alabama Press.

White, D. (1999). *Too heavy a load: Black women in defense of themselves, 1894–1994.* New York: W. W. Norton.

CHAPTER 5

Marcus Garvey and Community Development via the UNIA

Aminifu Harvey
Iris B. Carlton-LaNey

Many disenfranchised groups have historically found ways to solve their own problems without governmental intervention or support. Through local community approaches to problem solving, many marginal groups have been empowered to seek unique solutions that are specifically tailored to their needs, resources, and aims. Community building is critical to the success of such approaches.

Community building has been defined as "an ongoing comprehensive effort that strengthens the norms, supports, and problem-solving resources of the community" (Committee for Economic Development, 1995, p. 3). Weil (1996) defines community building as those "activities, practices, and policies that support and foster positive connections among individuals, groups, organizations, neighborhoods, and geographic and functional communities" (p. 482). Throughout history, individual leaders and social work professionals via the African American women's club movement, the Charity Organization Society, the settlement houses, and the National Urban League have been committed to community building. These social welfare–oriented organizations and individuals have employed community and economic development strategies to empower marginal and oppressed groups.

Marcus Garvey was among the social welfare leaders who engaged in community building at the turn of the century. Martin and Martin (1995) contend that Garvey's community building used "social work-type community organization and group work and social action techniques to recruit a huge following" (p. 148) of African Americans. Simon (1994), furthermore, notes that Garvey's preachings and teachings highlighted the "daily cost" that African Americans paid for an "integrationist strategy" (p. 90).

Using the principles of community building, Garvey created one of the most powerful organizations of the early twentieth century—the Universal Negro Improvement

Association and African Communities League (UNIA & ACL). The UNIA & ACL was one organization, divided in name only in order to separate the functions of the friendly and fraternal organization—UNIA—from those of the business organization—ACL—as required by New York state law. Designed to serve the African and African American community throughout the diaspora, Garvey's UNIA & ACL initiated community strategies that were multifold, connecting empowerment strategies with economic, political, and social development.

Close examination of Garvey and his UNIA reveals a remarkable persistence of what social workers now call an ecological perspective (Germain & Gitterman, 1987). For Garvey, the UNIA was a mechanism for improving the goodness-of-fit between needs and resources for African Americans and African people worldwide.

Since the emancipation of enslaved African people, African Americans have found themselves struggling within an environment damaged by discrimination, oppression, and capriciousness. Their ability to cope was challenged and hampered by the lack of available external resources. The experiences that had helped to shape their identity and self-esteem were experiences of race and gender oppression. Their internal resources—levels of motivation, self-esteem, and problem-solving skills—were well formed and had sustained them throughout enslavement, but these were greatly improved by the philosophy, opinions, and activities of the UNIA. The UNIA enhanced its members' sense of competence by allowing and encouraging them to have an effect on their social and physical environments. Moreover, the UNIA provided the social environment to sustain and nurture that competence, with a goal toward developing the needed physical environment to ensure a sense of place. Essentially, Garvey's consciousness raising and Pan-Africanism, together with a network of African American–owned businesses, unmistakably and consistently embraced the person-in-situation perspective. Furthermore, as Simon (1994) notes, Garvey and his work were an "important influence on social workers of an empowerment bent" (p. 90), who paid close attention to Garvey's message of cultural self-determination.

Marcus Mosiah Garvey lived from 1887 to 1940. Born in Jamaica, West Indies, he moved to New York in 1916. He was deported back to Jamaica as an undesirable in 1927 after his release from serving one year in prison for alleged mail fraud. The name Marcus Garvey is usually associated with flamboyance, and few could deny that his uniform of purple, green, and black with a white feather sticking from his cap struck a noble pose (White, 1999). Beyond his splendor and powerful physical appearance, Garvey's genius, oratorical eloquence, hard work, self-discipline, and single-minded commitment to the race are legendary (Martin, 1986). DuBois (1920/1971), scholar, civil rights leader, and editor of the National Association for the Advancement of Colored People journal, *Crisis*, acknowledged that Garvey was the central and dynamic force of the UNIA. Pickens (1921/1971), an early supporter of Garvey, felt that "nearly everyone who look[ed] in the face and listen[ed] to the words of Marcus Garvey [became] convinced of his honesty and his utter sincerity" (p. 328). Moreover, Garvey aroused the zeal and fervor of millions of Africans and African Americans during the UNIA's heyday.

Garvey engaged in functional community organizing. A functional community is defined as a community of interest. People share concern about common issues, but they may or may not live in close proximity. Weil and Gamble (1995) note that functional community organizing means engaging in internal capacity building, increasing knowledge about the shared issues, and developing leaders. Within a functional community, the group's ability to articulate and educate about its issues is of paramount importance. Garvey understood this critical component. His charisma and oratorical skill were essential to the UNIA's success. He understood that knowledge was power, and he encouraged his followers to educate themselves and to use every opportunity to educate people about the organization. He told them that the UNIA should be at the forefront of their every deed. He also cautioned his followers that because "the majority of the Negroes are ignorant," they should exercise a great amount of tolerance to educate others to "your point of view" (Martin, 1986, p. 176). Garvey urged his followers to make this task their "missionary work" (Martin, 1986, p. 176). Eventually, Garvey formalized his teaching via *The Course of African Philosophy* (Martin, 1986). This course was designed to train a cadre of UNIA leaders to carry the work forward after his death. Many of the lessons of the African philosophy course were unwritten and jealously guarded by his followers after his death. It was not until 1986 that Martin was granted permission to publish this work.

Garvey's work also embraced the social and economic development model of community practice. This model merges development and economic development in recognition of the fact that both must take place with low-power, marginalized communities in order for organization to be successful (Weil, 1996). With this model, Weil and Gamble (1995) identified a dual focus on "strengthening the capacity of citizens and communities to develop and implement plans for social and economic development and resources development and enlisting the resources available through city and county governments, banks, foundations, and external developers" (p. 585).

Garvey employed this approach in his work; he was able to balance investments in both the social and economic aspects of community development. A fundamental element of this model of organizing, according to Garvey's work, was a "fierce Afro-centric view of the world" (Martin, 1986), including a firm economic base for both individual African Americans and for the UNIA. Afrocentricity emphasizes a collective conceptualization of human beings and their group survival and rejects the idea that the individual can be understood separate from others in his or her social group (Ak'bar, 1984; Nobles, 1980). In order to facilitate Afrocentricity, Garvey supported capacity building and self-efficacy; he also emphasized self-reliance, nationhood, and race first whether in religion, history, literature, or the economy.

The terms *Garveyism* and the *Garvey Movement* describe the phenomena that identified Marcus Garvey from the organization's beginning, first in Jamaica in 1914 and two years later in Harlem, New York, in 1916. Today, this leader's name continues to receive recognition, but the social welfare activities that characterized his organization are not nearly as well-known. Most discussion of this organization has taken place primarily in the context of exploring Garvey's philosophies and opinions or of critiquing his economic development strategies, especially his Black Star Line Steamship Corporation (Crono, 1955; Garvey, 1970; Miller, 1927/1971; Nembhard, 1978). Whatever the realm of discussion, between 1916 and 1940, the world resounded with the ring of the name Marcus Garvey and of the UNIA, an organization that he hoped would be the instrument for people of African ancestry throughout the diaspora to gain their cultural, economic, political, and social freedom (Garvey, 1923; Harris, 1978).

The UNIA & ACL was organized to raise the status of the "Negro" to national expression and general freedom. The preamble of the UNIA (1921) identified it as "a social, friendly, humanitarian, charitable, educational, institutional, constructive and expansive society founded by persons subscribing to the utmost to work for the general uplift of the Negro peoples of the world" (p. 1). The organization's two slogans summarized Garveyism and the general aims of the organization: "Africa for the Africans" and "One God, One Aim, One Destiny." The slogans not only embraced aspects of the ecological perspective, but also touted the importance of a "sense of place" and the urgency of implementing the principle of self-determination for African people. For Garvey, a sense of place was both physical and spiritual. In addition to his advocacy of Pan-Africanism, he encouraged his followers to always look "beyond the present by calling upon their past experiences when looking at the future" (Martin, 1986, p. 156). The UNIA philosophy emphasized the fact that the "Negro" community was a global or functional community. Moreover, in identifying the primary constituency, Garvey said that the UNIA should "maintain an interest in every Negro, irrespective of his nationality or his condition, as long as he has not been proven a traitor to the race and outlawed as such" (Martin, 1986, p. 167). Essentially, Garvey felt that he was doing God's work and this work would speak for itself. He encouraged his followers to give of themselves, as well as to give charitable support to other African Americans. He said that "to give to help carry on social service work in the community or to help the poor of the community or to rescue the children of the community is giving to God" (Martin, 1986, p. 88). In this way, Garvey stressed community reinvestment as a critical aspect of successful practice.

Aims and Objectives

Garvey felt that the ultimate culmination of all of the UNIA's efforts was "Negro independent nationalism on the continent of Africa" (Martin, 1986, p. 33). The articulated aims and objectives of the UNIA were the necessary steps to facilitate reaching that goal. Article I (UNIA, 1921, p. 4) of the constitution lists 11 aims and objectives of the UNIA and the ACL:

1. To establish a universal confraternity among the race.
2. To prompt the spirit of pride and love.
3. To reclaim the fallen.
4. To administer and assist the needy.

5. To assist in civilizing the backward tribes of Africa.
6. To assist in the development of independent Negro nations and communities.
7. To establish commissionaries or agencies in the principal countries and cities of the world for the representation and protection of all Negroes, irrespective of nationality.
8. To promote a conscientious spiritual worship among the native tribes of Africa.
9. To establish universities, colleges, academies and schools for the racial education and culture of the people.
10. To conduct a world-wide commercial and industrial intercourse for the good of the people.
11. To work for the better conditions in all Negro communities.

The official organ of the UNIA, entitled *Garvey's Voice*, prominently displays the organization's motto, "One God, One Aim, One Destiny" (Martin, 1986). The newspaper carried several names after its inception, including *Negro World*, which was changed in 1933 to *World Peace Echo* and later to *Garvey's Voice*. For Garvey, the Negro press was inadequate and, in his opinion, had "no constructive policy nor ideal," which he felt was due to their emphasis on the profit motive. He thought that his publications, on the other hand, "rendered a wonderful service to Negro journalism in the United States" and had gradually changed the tone and makeup of some of the other papers (Martin, 1986, p. 79).

The *Negro World* included a women's page that Amy Jacques Garvey, Garvey's second wife, edited. On this page, which ran from 1924 to 1928, Jacques Garvey urged women to fight for their rights as African Americans and as women. She also kept women abreast of issues that were important to women in other countries, summarily promoting a sense of place and community that was global. Through this publication, she taught women about feminism, revolutionary thought, and political economy (White, 1999, p. 139.)

Membership and Dues

All persons of Negro blood and African ancestry were regarded as ordinary members and entitled to consideration of the UNIA. Active members were those individuals who paid dues and ultimately had first claim to considerations of the UNIA. Consideration included assistance in illness and financial distress.

Each active member was assessed 25¢ per month, $1 each January, a 10¢ death tax per month, and a 5¢ tax to help pay a $75 death benefit to a deceased member's family. In addition, each active member was required to pay $5 annually into the African Redemption Fund. All high officials, members of the parent body, and local officials were required to subscribe to the Black Star Line stock. No specific number of stocks was required to be purchased by the individual. In addition to these dues and taxes, members of the various organizations within the UNIA were required to pay minimal dues.

Draper (1969) contends that the UNIA appealed mainly to recently uprooted African American migrants from southern states and those recently arrived from the West Indies who were emotionally stirred by nationalism and emigration incantations. Pickens (1921/1971), one of Garvey's contemporaries, felt that Garvey's influence was much more widespread and noted that "Garvey aroused the Negroes of Georgia as much as those of New York, except where the black preacher discouraged anything that threatened his income, or where white domination smothered every earthy hope" (p. 332). Closer analysis suggests that many African Americans from varied backgrounds supported the UNIA through membership or financial contributions.

J. A. Rogers, noted African American historian, and Claude McKay, Harlem Renaissance poet, wrote for the *Negro World*. T. Thomas Fortune, veteran civil rights fighter and dean of African American journalism, edited *Negro World* in his last years of life. C. J. Walker, hair care product mogul and millionaire, was a supporter of the UNIA, along with A. Phillip Randolph, founder of the Brotherhood of Sleeping Car Porters. Chandler Owen, who was a trained social worker via the National Urban League Fellowship Program, presided over one of Garvey's mass meetings in 1919 (DuBois, 1920/1971). Randolph, spoke at that meeting, but later became one of the UNIA's critics (Martin, 1976).

Ida B. Wells-Barnett, antilynching crusader, womanist, and activist, was a supporter of the UNIA and Garvey. Wells-Barnett first met Garvey when her husband, Ferdinand Barnett, invited him to their home for dinner in 1916. She found Garvey's ideas intriguing and invited him to speak at her Negro Fellowship League and Reading Room to raise money for his proposed school. Later, she was elected to serve as a UNIA delegate to the peace conference at Versailles (McMurry, 1998).

Organizations within the UNIA

There were at least three organizations within the UNIA, including the Universal African Legions, the Universal African Motor Corps, and the Universal African Black Cross Nurses. Membership in the Universal African Legions was open to active members between the ages of 18 and 55 who were in good health. The purpose was to teach these men military skills and discipline. The Legion was under the direct supervision of the Minister of the Legions. Its symbol was the sphinx. The Legion was a uniformed army with a military chain of command and stratification, and its members provided protection for the UNIA and the African American community against racist and unjust physical aggression. The Universal African Motor Corps was open to active members ages 15 to 45 and was to assist the Legion in the performance of its duties.

The Universal African Black Cross Nurses were to carry on a system of relief and to assist in mitigating the suffering caused by pestilence, famine, fire, floods, and other great calamities. They were to care for the sick and engage in preventive medicine. The Universal African Black Cross Nurses issued pamphlets on safety and accident prevention and instructed the public in sanitation and first aid. The organization was open to active female members ages 16 to 45. A central committee composed of the President General of the UNIA, the Surgeon General, and a Universal African Black Cross Nurse Directress directed the function of this corps of nurses. The Surgeon General was required to be a bacteriologist and the Directress was required to be a graduate nurse with three years of experience. A Black Latin Cross encircled by a red background in the center of a green field was the nurses' corps emblem. Girls were prepared at the age of 14 to join the nurses' corps.

Providing education and nurturing for children was a core component of the UNIA. The constitution outlined specific programs targeting children such as teaching prayer, discipline, African and African American history, and the UNIA & ACL's history and philosophy.

Funding

The UNIA was designed to establish economic solvency and independence in the African communities of the world. The major funding aim was to build an economic base—a key to the social and economic community practice model. Under the direction of the ACL, the business corporation of the organization, the Negro Factories Corporation managed the UNIA's laundries, restaurants, doll factory, tailoring and millinery establishments, and printing press (Martin, 1986). The Negro Factories Corporation was a key element in the UNIA's efforts toward resource development. One of the desired outcomes of the community social and economic development model, as Weil and Gamble (1995) note, is to prepare citizens to make use of social and economic investments. Garvey, for example, encouraged his followers to train and educate their children to have high self-esteem, unwavering race pride, and a positive self-concept. He was adamant that "Negro" children should play with "Negro dolls." To ensure that such dolls were available, the UNIA had to produce them, hence the establishment of the doll factory.

The Black Star Line Steamship Corporation was the ACL's greatest financial endeavor. It was incorporated in 1919 with a capital stock of $500,000. Shares had a par value of $5 each, and an individual could purchase a maximum of 200 shares. The multiple purposes of the line were to eliminate the racial discrimination suffered by African American passengers on White-owned lines and to provide jobs for African American seamen. The two most important needs that the UNIA leadership envisioned the Black Star Line fulfilling were (1) to provide transportation for African Americans to return to Africa and (2) to link together the African peoples of the world. African and West Indian merchants saw in it the hope of independence from racist White companies. Four ships were purchased as part of the line, but because of poor management, lack of fiscal planning, graft, and sabotage at the hands of White crewmembers, this venture fell into bankruptcy. Ironically, this venture was the largest and initially the most lucrative. It had the potential to be a key mechanism in a worldwide Black nation. It was, however, the key in the demise of the UNIA. Since Marcus Garvey decided to sell the line's stock through the mail, the U.S. government was able to convict him of mail fraud, incarcerate him, and then deport him back to Jamaica.

Leadership

Garvey was the avowed leader of the UNIA & ACL. He formulated its philosophy, directed its operations, and operationalized concepts of a world nation of Black people. Essentially, Garvey implemented a program for the self-determination of Black people throughout the world with Afrocentricity as the fundamental tenet. Crono (1955) describes Garvey as the "Black Moses," a short, chubby Black man who was charismatic in his leadership. With that charisma, Garvey galvanized 4 million active UNIA members by 1921 (Martin, 1986), providing leadership to the largest mass movement of Blacks in the world (Draper, 1969). Garvey's philosophy of leadership was simple. He felt that a leader must have superior ability; be ever vigilant in gathering useful, pertinent information; have personality; and be well groomed, well disciplined, self-possessed, self-reliant, and confident (Martin, 1986).

Decline of the UNIA & ACL

Many African American leaders rushed to critique the Garvey movement. DuBois (1920/1971) was critical of Garvey's ability to carry out his plan, noting that the goals were feasible, but "everyone of ability, knowledge, experience and devotion in the whole Negro race" (pp. 321–322) was needed for such a task. Pickens (1921/1971) lacked faith in the permanence of the Garvey movement, but was confident that the resulting "new racial consciousness of the Negro [would] endure" (p. 329).

Some years later, Martin (1976) discussed what he believes to be the key factors in the decline of the UNIA & ACL. The first is the economic depression of the 1930s, which diminished the financial support from the organization's membership. Second, Garvey's deportation left the organization without its charismatic leadership. Yet, even in Garvey's absence, economic support and membership participation were sufficient to hold the Eighth International Convention in Toronto, Canada, in August 1938.

Increasingly, financial troubles plagued the UNIA after the Black Star Line Steamship Corporation was forced to close its business doors. Membership eroded because of increasing fragmentation of the UNIA into splinter organizations, such as the Peace Movement of Ethiopia. Increased membership roles in other movements, including Father Divine, the Black Muslims, and the Moorish Americans, also contributed to the decline in UNIA membership and the organization's influence in the African American community.

Yet, the U.S. government might have been the single most significant factor in the decline of the UNIA & ACL. Martin (1976) links J. Edgar Hoover with the conspiracy to spy on the UNIA and to jail Marcus Garvey for mail fraud. Martin also connects George Tyler, who attempted to assassinate Garvey, with the U.S. government and with James E.

Amos. An ex-bodyguard of former President Theodore Roosevelt, Amos was at the time an African American agent of the Federal Bureau of Investigation. Martin contends that they were spying on the UNIA. It is without question that Marcus Garvey was considered a threat and that his personal and political powers were immeasurable. Furthermore, the lengths to which the U.S. government went to control Garvey and to destroy his movement continue to become more clear.

Conclusion

From a social welfare perspective, the UNIA & ACL provided a social and economic milieu conducive to individual, familial, and community development in an era when the local and national systems neglected to provide these services for African American people. Ironically, even though the UNIA & ACL declined rapidly after Garvey's death, its legacy lived and provided a model both philosophically and pragmatically for community practice among Black people worldwide.

References

Ak'bar, N. (1984). Afrocentric social services for human liberation. *Journal of Black Studies, 14*, 395–413.

Committee for Economic Development, Research and Policy Committee. (1995). *Rebuilding inner-city communities: A new approach to the nation's urban crisis*. New York: Author.

Crono, E. (1955). *Black Moses: The story of Marcus Garvey and the Universal Negro Improvement Association*. Madison: University of Wisconsin Press.

Draper, T. (1969). *The rediscovery of Black nationalism*. New York: Viking Press.

DuBois, W. E. B. (1971). Marcus Garvey. In J. Sochen (Ed.), *The Black man and the American dream: Negro aspirations in America, 1900–1930* (pp. 315–324). Chicago: Quadrangle Books. (Original work published 1920)

Garvey, A. (1970). *Garvey and Garveyism*. New York: Collier Books.

Garvey, M. (1923). *Philosophy and opinions*. New York: Universal Publishing House.

Germain, C., & Gitterman, A. (1987). Ecological perspective. In A. Manahan et al. (Eds.), *Encyclopedia of Social Work*, (18th ed., pp. 488–499). Silver Spring, MD: NASW Press.

Harris, R. (1978). *Garveyism and Marxism*. Harlem, NY: United Brothers Communications Systems.

Martin, E. P., & Martin, J. M. (1995). *Social work and the Black experience*. Washington, DC: NASW Press.

Martin, T. (1976). *Race first: The ideological and organizational struggle of Marcus Garvey and the Universal Negro Improvement Association*. Westport, CT: Greenwood Press.

Martin, T. (Ed.). (1986). *Marcus Garvey message to the people the course of African philosophy*. The New Marcus Garvey Library, No. 7. Dover, MA: The Majority Press.

McMurry, L. (1998). *To keep the waters troubled: The life of Ida B. Wells*. New York: Oxford University Press.

Miller, K. (1971). After Marcus Garvey—What of the Negro? In J. Sochen (Ed.), *The Black man and the American dream: Negro aspirations in America, 1900–1930* (pp. 336–344). Chicago: Quadrangle Books. (Original work published 1927)

Nembhard, L. (1978). *Trails and triumphs of Marcus Garvey*. Millwood, NY: Kraus Reprint Co.

Nobles, W. (1980). African philosophy: Foundations for black psychology. In R. Jones (Ed.), *Black psychology* (3rd ed., pp. 23–35). New York: Harper & Row.

Pickens, W. (1971). Africa for the Africans—The Garvey movement. In J. Sochen (Ed.), *The Black man and the American dream: Negro aspirations in America, 1900–1930* (pp. 325–330). Chicago: Quadrangle Books. (Original work published 1921)

Simon. B. (1994). *The empowerment tradition in American social work: A history*. New York: Columbia University Press.

Universal Negro Improvement Association (UNIA). *Constitution and Books of Laws*. Made for the Government of the Universal Negro Improvement Association, Inc., and African Communities League, Inc. of the World in effect July 1918. Revised and amended August 1921. New York: Author.

Weil, M. (1996). Community building: Building community practice. *Social Work*, *41*, 481–499.

Weil, M., & Gamble, D. (1995). Community practice models. In R. Edwards (Ed.), *Encyclopedia of Social Work* (pp. 577–594). Washington, DC: NASW Press.

White, D. (1999). *Too heavy a load: Black women in defense of themselves, 1894–1994*. New York: W.W. Norton.

CHAPTER 6

Ida B. Wells-Barnett

An Uncompromising Style

Tricia Bent-Goodley

As a pioneer journalist, crusader, "race woman," community activist, and club organizer, Ida Bell Wells-Barnett was relentless in her efforts for the rights of African Americans and women. Wells-Barnett saw herself as a Christian woman; today, she can be described as one of the premier women of her time and beyond. Though not a trained social worker, Wells-Barnett was a social researcher, a social activist, and a community organizer (O'Donnell, 1995; Peebles-Wilkins & Francis, 1990). She was known for being tenacious, direct, and uncompromising in her quest for social justice and the racial uplift of African American people.

While much has been written about the life of Wells-Barnett, most of the literature is written from a theological or journalism perspective. The review of her life within a social welfare framework is limited. Yet, she changed the fate of lynch law in the United States almost single-handedly. Without a clear understanding of the social welfare contributions of African American women, such as Wells-Barnett, social workers are left without the critical knowledge of the dynamics and unique experiences of African American social welfare leaders (Brown, 1989; Carlton-LaNey, 1997). A discussion of the interplay between race and gender is critical in understanding the life and work experiences of African American female social welfare pioneers (Giddings, 1984; Smith, 1985).

Wells-Barnett was a womanist. Walker (1983) suggested that womanism includes issues of race, culture, gender, economics, and political considerations for all people. Hine (1986) argued that womanism describes the double legacy of oppression and resistance among African American women. Townes (1993) stated that womanism includes some of the following essential characteristics: "outrageous, audacious, courageous or willful behavior" (p. 173). Essentially, the term *womanist* reinforces the need to address the concerns of gender, race, and class from a holistic perspective (Cannon, 1988; Carlton-LaNey, 1997; Hill-Collins, 1991; Townes, 1993; Walker, 1983).

From the social welfare perspective, Wells-Barnett made enormous contributions within the empowerment tradition. Empowerment is defined as a "process whereby persons who belong to a stigmatized social category throughout their lives can be assisted to develop and increase skills in the exercise of interpersonal influence and the performance of valued social roles" (Bryant-Solomon, 1976, p. 6). An empowerment tradition involves the commitment to encourage self-acceptance, collective responsibility, and the belief that one possesses political power (Gutierrez, 1990). This commitment can translate into diverse activities with the singular focus of personal, interpersonal, and collective liberation and power. Wells-Barnett worked as a race leader, crusader against lynching, and club organizer. While some believe that her confrontational style and spontaneity limited her leadership abilities (McMurry, 1998; Van Steenwyk, 1992), it can be argued that these traits demonstrate her true leadership.

Womanist Race Leader

Some describe Wells-Barnett as living before her time. She was born in 1862 in Holly Springs, Mississippi, to parents who were both newly freed slaves. She described her mother as deeply religious and famous for her culinary skills. Her father is described as an independent spirit, a skilled carpenter, and a community leader who served as a member of the first Board of Trustees of Rust College (originally known as Shaw University). Ida Wells had fond memories of growing up reading the paper to her father, particularly the political section that he enjoyed. On Sundays, Wells was allowed to read only the Bible, reinforcing a strong Christian belief that reigned throughout her life. In 1878, when Wells was 16, her parents, two brothers, and a sister were struck with yellow fever. All five died, leaving the young Ida Wells with five younger brothers and sisters to raise on her own. She chose to raise her siblings herself, although the Masons had agreed to do so in the absence of her parents. With the assistance of an aunt, Wells raised her brothers and sisters while maintaining an active social life and teaching.

Wells married Ferdinand Barnett in June 1895, and her four children were born soon after. She is one of the only women of her time known to hyphenate her name after marriage. Her desire for justice and equality did not diminish her role as a mother. Wells-Barnett "firmly believed in the importance of the presence of a mother in the home during her children's early years" (Duster, 1970, p. XXIII). As a mother, she attended parent-teacher meetings, organized the young boys in the community to protect themselves, and helped to bring needed resources to the larger community. Her daughter described her home as always filled with young male probationers requiring Wells-Barnett's assistance (Duster, 1970). She attended numerous political functions with her children. Her first son, Charles Aked Barnett, was known as the "Baby of the Federation" after attending the first national conference of the National Colored Women's Association. Despite the perception by others that she would no longer be as active in the fight for liberty and justice after motherhood, Wells-Barnett continued to marshal her efforts toward the antilynching crusade and racial uplift movement.

It was the railroad incident of 1884 that sparked her career in race work. Wells was a teacher in Shelby County, Tennessee. On her way to work one day, she was told to ride in the smoking car because of her race. Wells refused and was forced off the train by a conductor and several White male passengers. Enraged, she sued the Chesapeake and Ohio Railroad and won the case. Although the Supreme Court reversed the decision in 1887, Wells was well on her way to highlighting the injustices of segregation.

She began her journalism career by writing about the lawsuit for a small church paper. Wells had "an instinctive feeling that the people who had little or no school training should have something coming into their homes weekly which dealt with their problems in a simple, helpful way" (Duster, 1970, p. 23). She began to use the Voice of Iola in 1885 as her pen name and was later hired by and became part owner of *The Free Speech and Headlight*. Interestingly, this would not be her only experience with owning and running a newspaper. Wells-Barnett did not just strive to write for, but to own the vehicles of her message. She owned at least three newspapers during the course of her life and was elected the first woman officer of the National Colored Press Association in 1888. Wells-Barnett purchased the *Conservator* from her husband and began to work on the paper immediately thereafter (Duster, 1970).

Wells began a full-time journalism career, after seven years of teaching, by drawing attention to the unequal education of children in the Memphis school system (Adams, 1994). It was not long before she was known as the Princess of the Press. In describing the African American press and its editors, Penn (1891) wrote that "Miss Ida B. Wells, 'Iola,' has been called the 'Princess of the Press,' and she has well earned the title. No writer, the male fraternity not excepted, has been more extensively quoted; nor struck harder blows at the wrongs and weaknesses of the race" (p. 380). Wells was also described as acting like a man. Her tenacity and forcefulness were perceived as both a strength and liability. Historian McMurry (1998) noted that within "the middle- and upper-class black community of the late nineteenth century, the enthronement of the cult of true womanhood sought to empower African Americans as a whole by imposing a patriarchal dominance over black women" (p. 55). Wells struggled with the implications of sexism, her own idea of appropriate ladylike behavior, and her commitment to the cause of racial uplift.

In her capacity as journalist, Wells-Barnett wrote many essays and articles advocating racial justice for African Americans. One such article, entitled "Functions of Leadership," clearly demonstrated this notion. It was written to encourage upper-class African Americans to use their resources for African American economic, social, and political development (DeCosta-Willis, 1995, p. 182). Wells-Barnett firmly believed that upper-class African Americans had a particular responsibility to the community. The ideas of putting the race first and working toward the inclusion of African Americans in mainstream society were at the center of her arguments and actions. Wells-Barnett questioned all aspects of African American leadership—its role, commitment, and obligations to the community.

In 1893, Wells-Barnett went to Chicago to address her concerns regarding the organization of the World's Columbian Exposition. The exposition was coordinated to celebrate the 400th anniversary of the discovery of America. Wells edited a volume, with Frederick Douglass, Ferdinand L. Barnett, and I. Garland Penn as contributors, that protested the lack of African American participation in the Chicago World's Fair. The 81-page booklet articulated the concerns and experiences of African Americans and explored the role of lynching in American society.

Wells-Barnett wrote for numerous presses and race journals. She saw exposing race problems and pushing the discussion of race issues as her responsibility and lamented the lack of responsiveness from people whom she believed should be most vocal—ministers and journalists. She stated that "the pulpit and press of our own country remain silent on these continued outrages and the voice of my race thus tortured and outraged is stifled or ignored wherever it is lifted in America in a demand for justice" (Duster, 1970, p. 100). Wells-Barnett continued in the empowerment tradition. The Voice of Iola served as an uncompromising voice against the unequal treatment of African Americans. Through her journalism, Wells-Barnett provided African Americans with needed information and motivated them to acknowledge their personal, political, institutional, and economic power. She also encouraged them to acknowledge the contributions that African American women made to the preservation and sustenance of the community. Wells-Barnett recognized that community empowerment translated into political activism that served the best interest of the collective.

Crusade against Lynching

Wells-Barnett sought to expose the horrors and dispel the myths surrounding lynching. At that time, lynchings were thought to be a just response from angry White males attempting to defend the honor of White women who had allegedly been raped by African American men. Wells-Barnett was convinced that this perception was inaccurate. In order to obtain accurate information about this widespread and inhumane phenomenon, she researched incidents of lynching across the country, conducting thorough investigations, interviews, and reviews of secondary data.

In March 1892, her focus on lynching was intensified by an especially brutal and personal case in Memphis. Three African American businessmen were taken from the Shelby County jail, where they had been unjustly incarcerated, and lynched for having defended their store against an angry White mob. These three men—Thomas Moss, Calvin McDowell, and Henry Stewart—were co-owners of the popular and profitable People's Grocery Company. Moss was the president of this corporation and a close friend of Wells-Barnett. The lynching went unavenged by local authorities, who were believed to have been a part of the mob. Wells-Barnett was out of town at the time of the murders, but she received numerous accounts of the lynching. Saddened and enraged, Wells-Barnett encouraged African Americans to leave Memphis because they would not be treated with dignity and respect in such a place (Boyd, 1986; McMurry, 1998). She wrote about the incident in *The Free Speech* stating that "nobody in this section of the country believes the old threadbare lie that Negro men rape White women. If Southern

White men are not careful, they will over-reach themselves and public sentiment will have a reaction; a conclusion will then be reached which will be very damaging to the moral reputation of their women" (Harris, 1991, p. 16–17). This enraged Whites in the city; Wells-Barnett became the target of that rage. *The Free Speech* was destroyed three months after the printing of her commentary, and Wells-Barnett was told never to return to Memphis or she would also be lynched.

Wells-Barnett described lynching as a form of racial terrorism. She saw rape as an excuse for lynching. Wells-Barnett knew that White women were often willing participants until their liaisons were discovered, then the cry of "rape" became their cover. Moreover, she challenged Whites to look at the history of White men who had raped African American women during and after slavery without legal or social retribution. Wells-Barnett stated that once rape was eliminated as the reason for lynching African Americans, the truth would become clear. Essentially, she believed that lynching resulted from Whites' fear of African American political, economic, and social progress (McMurry, 1998).

Wells-Barnett then challenged the perception that the lynch mobs were composed of poor, ignorant Whites. She instead demonstrated in *Southern Horrors: Lynch Law in All Its Phases* that these actions were imposed by "leading business men" (Harris, 1991, p. 18). She firmly believed that the majority of White Americans did not realize the brutality and barbarism of lynching. It was her belief that if she were able to help Whites understand the barbarism involved in a lynch mob and its total lack of respect for law and order, then lynching would be outlawed. She enlisted the assistance of Europeans in this effort, believing that the Europeans would have the ability to affect the minds and thoughts of Americans. Thus, in 1893, Wells-Barnett traveled for two months throughout England, Scotland, and Wales publicly declaring the barbarism and lawlessness of lynching. She provided the Europeans with facts that could not be disputed by White America. In 1898, she returned to England for a six-month tour. Europeans, more than willing to speak out against lynching, formed an antilynching committee as a result of this trip.

Upon her return to the United States, Wells-Barnett continued her antilynching crusade throughout the North. In 1895, she published "A Red Record: Tabulated Statistics and Alleged Causes of Lynchings in the United States, 1892-1893-1894." She stated that "it becomes the painful duty of the Negro to reproduce a record which shows that a large portion of the American people avow anarchy, condone murder and defy the contempt of civilization" (Duster, 1970, p. 7). She provided a listing and categorization of all known lynchings between 1892 and 1894. It was found that African Americans charged with raping White women were often accused as a result of walking into the room of a White woman or brushing up against her (Harris, 1991; Townes, 1993). Furthermore, African Americans were the only group represented in the category identified as "no crimes charged." "No crimes charged" signified a lynching in which the person lynched was charged with no crime, but was lynched anyway. Wells-Barnett highlighted five specific interventions to eliminate lynching:

(1) bring the facts in the book to the attention of all acquaintances;
(2) get churches and civic groups to pass anti-lynching resolutions and send copies wherever outrages occur;
(3) call the South's attention to "the refusal of capital to invest where lawlessness and mob violence hold sway";
(4) think and act on independent lines in this behalf; and
(5) send resolutions to Congress supporting the Blair Bill to create an investigatory commission. (McMurry, 1998, p. 230)

Her effort resulted in the expansion of the Blair Bill, which called for an investigation of all rapes and lynchings from the previous 10 years.

Wells-Barnett continued to investigate lynching for the duration of her life. She published *Lynch Law in Georgia, Lynch Law in America*, and *Mob Rule in New Orleans,* and many other publications on the subject. Although her life was in constant danger, she remained committed to the antilynching movement.

Club Organizer

Wells-Barnett helped to establish the agenda for many African American women's clubs and national organizations. Her journalism experience and activism within the anti-lynching movement provided both entrance to and resistance from within these organizations. In addition to attempting to influence White women's civic clubs, she urged African American women to organize their own civic clubs (Ochiai, 1992). African American women, of course, already had a long history of organized women's groups extending as far back as the Female Benevolent Society in Philadelphia launched in 1793 (Townes, 1993). Non-secular African American women's groups flourished from 1885 to 1892. Some of the clubs even took the name of Ida B. Wells as a result of her notoriety and inspirational message. She organized the first civic club in Chicago for African American women. It was first named the Chicago Women's Club and then later renamed the Ida B. Wells Club.

The 1895 women's club convention in Boston brought together many of the African American women's clubs from across the nation. The convention leaders saw this meeting as an opportunity to support Wells-Barnett's work despite the criticism that had been levied against her by both African Americans and Whites (McMurry, 1998). The 1895 convention was of particular importance; it resulted in the creation of the National Association of Colored Women (NACW) a year later. Attending the meeting as the President of the Ida B. Wells Club and delegate of the Anti-Lynching Society in London, Wells-Barnett chaired the committee on resolutions and offered many suggestions as to the perpetuity of the organization. She left the meeting with several key responsibilities and roles: member of the *Woman's Era* editorial staff, secretary of the committee to publish the minutes, and representative of the Prison Congress of the United States. Yet, this would mark a shift in Wells-Barnett's participation in the NACW. Wells-Barnett later grew to disagree with the leadership of the NACW and the focus of the organization (Duster, 1970; McMurry, 1998).

The organization shifted its focus in 1900 from issues of social justice to issues of domesticity, focusing on the need for the African American woman to turn her attention to the improvement of her home. Wells-Barnett did not support this change and kept her attention on other national and local organizations.

Wells-Barnett was also busy as the secretary of the National Afro-American Council whose focus was to confront degenerating race relations and to help unite the African American race. In addition to her secretarial responsibilities, she was the national organizer of the antilynching bureau of the organization. Her participation in the Afro-American Council came to an end in 1903 when Booker T. Washington was elected president of the organization. Those individuals who had been labeled "radicals" no longer had a role to play in Washington's organization. Wells-Barnett was certainly labeled a radical and had spoken vehemently against Washington's ideologies. She felt that Washington's emphasis on industrial education was inappropriate and disrespectful, a throwback to African Americans' enslavement. She wrote, "This gospel of work is no new one for the Negro. It is the South's old slavery practice in a new dress. It was the only education the South gave the Negro for [the] two and a half centuries she had absolute control of his body and soul. The Negro knows that now, as then, the South is strongly opposed to his learning anything else but how to work" (Thompson, 1990, pp. 257–258). While she did not dispute the importance of industrial education, like W. E. B. DuBois, Wells-Barnett believed that higher education was instrumental to the progress of the race.

When DuBois developed the Niagara Movement with William Trotter in 1905, Wells-Barnett was a supporter of the movement, but was isolated from the planning of the endeavor because of many of her radical stances. In 1909, African American and White organizers came together to plan the National Negro Conference with over 300 people in attendance. Again, Wells-Barnett pushed for federal antilynching legislation and a bureau to track, investigate, and publicize lynchings. Instead of honoring her suggestion, delegates to the conference decided that a Committee of Forty would be established to address the need for a permanent organization. Wells-Barnett was not originally asked to participate on the committee. DuBois was the only African American member of the nominating committee. It was later explained that Wells-Barnett "was a great fighter, but we knew she had to play a lone hand. And if you have too many players of lone hands in your organization, you soon have no game" (McMurry, 1998, p. 282). However, she did eventually participate on the Committee of Forty and shared in shaping the plan for developing the National Association for the Advancement of Colored People (NAACP) when someone else stepped down to encourage her participation.

The NAACP was founded the following year. Wells-Barnett participated in the organization initially; however, she withdrew from her NAACP activities by 1915 as a result of Whites' control of the organization. She and her husband then joined the National Equal Rights League (NERL), which fought segregation and maintained a strong political focus (McMurry, 1998). Wells-Barnett was noted for working very closely with William Trotter, with whom she maintained a strong alliance for many years.

Wells-Barnett was an activist on the national and local levels. She made numerous contributions to her immediate community through women's clubs (Campbell, 1986; McMurry, 1998; Townes, 1993). She also participated in founding the League of Cook County Clubs of Chicago Women. She assisted in the development of the Frederick Douglass Center Women's Club in 1905, although she was denied the position of president. As Vice President, she actively participated in the club as a lecturer, teacher, and fundraiser, encouraging her husband to do the same.

Wells-Barnett began the Negro Fellowship League (NFL) in Chicago in 1910 as an alternative to settlement houses. The NFL began meeting at the Barnetts's home. The organization later provided a reading room, social/cultural activities, housing, and opportunities for social/political activism. In an effort to maintain the organization, Wells-Barnett became Chicago's first African American probation officer. Her salary allowed her to fund the center and provide social services to over 200 probationers (McMurry, 1998). The NFL kept its doors open for 10 years.

The Alpha Suffrage Club was established by Wells-Barnett in 1913 as the state's first African American female suffrage organization. She insisted that this group examine both the work of the race and the rights of African American women. This group engaged in massive voter registration drives for African American women—holding forums and going door-to-door. With over 100 members by 1914, the group's political clout increased.

Wells-Barnett continued her political activism along with her active commitment to various organizations. Her creation of the "Martyred Negro Soldiers" button during World War I led to a visit by U. S. Secret Service agents, who demanded that she give them the remaining buttons. She had developed the buttons to protest the lynching of 13 African American soldiers. Not only did Wells-Barnett not give the buttons to the agents, but she responded by upbraiding the African American leadership for their lack of retort on the issue. "I'd rather go down in history as one lone Negro who dared to tell the government that it had done a dastardly thing than to give my skin by taking back what I have said. I would consider it an honor to spend whatever years are necessary in prison as the one member of the race who protested" (Duster, 1970, p. 370).

Wells-Barnett was again elected president of the Ida B. Wells Club in 1924 while she continued to lead the Women's Forum in 1926 and the Third Ward Women's Political Club in 1927. She ran for the Illinois State Senate in 1929 at the age of 67 and lost bitterly (Van Steenwyk, 1992). While Wells-Barnett created and assisted in the development of local, state, and national organizations with individuals within and outside of the African American community, she forced organizations to stay focused on the liberation of African Americans and social justice for humanity. Wells-Barnett was often not popular for her rigid stances on African American race empowerment; nonetheless, she held steadfastly to her values and beliefs, willingly accepting the consequences of her actions.

Although Wells-Barnett never gave up her struggle for equity and justice, she was, nevertheless, dissatisfied with the fruits of her labor and was embittered and disappointed by the efforts that others made. She did not look to the future with optimism, but instead entered this essay in the concluding chapter of her autobiography.

> Eternal vigilance is the price of liberty, and it does seem to me that notwithstanding all these social agencies and activities there is not that vigilance which should be exercised in the preservation of our rights. This leads me to wonder if we are not well satisfied to be able to point to our wonderful institutions with complacence and draw the salaries connected therewith, instead of being alert as the watchman on the wall. (Duster, 1970, p. 415)

Ida B. Wells-Barnett died on March 25, 1931 from uremic poisoning.

Implications for Social Work Practice

Wells-Barnett spent her entire adult life engaged in service for race and gender uplift. She believed that as African Americans were uplifted, Whites, too, would grow and progress. Conscious of the impact of class and gender on African American relationships, Wells-Barnett acknowledged the importance of the interconnection between all African Americans, regardless of class or gender. She realized that the race could not truly become liberated until African American women and men worked together equally without the influence of sexism and classism.

Townes (1993) highlighted three factors that are common to a womanist Christian ethic: (1) creating a sense of self and learning to understand the power of spirituality lead to liberation; (2) restoring harmony and re-creating human relationships encompass reconciliation; and (3) assuming responsibility and accountability for the will of God is obedience. This womanist Christian ethic encompasses the core principles of an empowerment tradition and aptly describes the foundation upon which Wells-Barnett's work was based. It also provides options as to how to implement liberation principles individually, interpersonally, and within the larger sociopolitical context.

Liberation

Wells-Barnett worked for the liberation of African Americans and the larger society. She sought justice for all so that the United States might live up to its Constitution. Transformation of the individual and society were Wells-Barnett's desire. It was her belief that God guided everything and that He would support a cause that was just and right. Her leadership was focused on this goal.

Client empowerment and social justice are at the core of social work practice. Self-determination and self-knowledge provide the foundation for client empowerment. Both the client and social worker are challenged to have a strong sense of self. Social workers are further challenged to create an environment that speaks to social justice and equity for all people. It takes leadership that is tenacious and committed to achieve both goals.

Reconciliation

Wells-Barnett worked on several different fronts for the progression of African Americans and humanity. She attempted to help African Americans and Whites establish a new relationship based on harmony and justice. She provided individual and group counseling to young probationers. As a social advocate, she created vehicles to address social and political injustice. In her capacity as a community organizer, she established both local and national organizations. While serving as a social researcher, she investigated lynchings across the country, providing accurate documentation and assessments. The breadth of Wells-Barnett's work provides a model for contemporary social work practice. For her, the complexity of social problems demanded multiple problem-solving approaches. Like Wells-Barnett, today's social workers cannot afford to be narrowly focused, but must be able to employ multiple interventions and diverse techniques.

Obedience

Wells-Barnett was dedicated to the cause of African American and human liberation. Her allegiance was to the cause, not the individual or organization. While many see this trait as a lack of leadership (Holt, 1982; McMurry, 1998; Townes, 1993), I believe that her commitment to the cause was a true testament to her leadership. She believed that God had empowered her to do the work that she did and that God's will allowed her to continue because she was just in her pursuits. Her adage "God will fight my battles as long as I am right" (McMurry, 1998) empowered and sustained her when it seemed that all others were against her. Essentially, her religious faith inspired her uncompromising militancy. She never wavered from the task at hand, and she relied on her ability to organize and to rally support via the spoken and written word. Though her radical stance did not gain her popularity among many African American leaders of her time, her place in history is unchallenged.

Social workers are placed in compromising situations regularly. The test of true leadership is the ability to advocate in the best interests of the client despite institutional and societal mandates. Leadership does not guarantee popularity. Social workers must be willing to accept this challenge not only for the perpetuity of the profession, but also and most importantly for the progression of human rights and social justice.

Conclusion

Indeed Wells-Barnett provides a legacy of leadership for social workers as professionals and as people. She did not separate herself from her work. Her integrity was reflected throughout her personal and professional life. As a persistent force in the national and local community, she was respected for standing up for her convictions and fighting until her last breath for the liberation of all people. Her tenacious spirit, determination, and courage provide models for social workers, community leaders, and individuals. She is a role model for all who are interested in fighting for human liberation, equality, and social justice.

References

Adams, S. L. (1994). Ida B. Wells: A founder who never knew her place. *Crises, 101*, 43–46.

Boyd, M. J. (1986). Canon configuration for Ida B. Wells-Barnett. *The Black Scholar, 24*, 8–13.

Brown, E. B. (1989). Womanist consciousness: Maggie Lena Walker and the Independent Order of Saint Luke. *Signs, 14*, 610–631.

Bryant-Solomon, B. (1976). *Black empowerment: Social work in oppressed communities.* New York: Columbia University Press.

Campbell, K. K. (1986). Style and content in the rhetoric of early Afro-American feminists. *Quarterly Journal of Speech, 72*, 434–445.

Cannon, K. G. (1988). *Black womanist ethics.* Atlanta: Scholars Press.

Carlton-LaNey, I. B. (1997). Elizabeth Ross Haynes: An African American reformer of womanist consciousness, 1908–1940. *Social Work, 42*, 573–583.

DeCosta-Willis, M. (1995). *The Memphis diary of Ida B. Wells.* Boston: Beacon Press.

Duster, A. M. (Ed.). (1970). *Crusade for justice: The autobiography of Ida B. Wells.* Chicago: University of Chicago Press.

Giddings, P. (1984). *When and where I enter: The impact of Black women on race and sex in America.* New York: William Morrow.

Gutierrez, L. (1990). Working with women of color: An empowerment perspective. *Social Work, 35*, 149–153.

Harris, T., comp. (1991). *Selected works of Ida B. Wells-Barnett.* New York: Oxford University Press.

Hill-Collins, P. (1991). *Black feminist thought: Knowledge, consciousness and the politics of empowerment.* New York: Routledge.

Hine, D. C. (Ed.). (1986). *The state of Afro-American history: Past, present and future.* Baton Rouge: Louisiana State University Press.

Holt, T. (1982). The lonely warrior: Ida B. Wells-Barnett and the struggle for Black leadership. In J. H. Franklin & A. Meier (Eds.), *Black leaders of the twentieth century* (pp. 39–61). Chicago: University of Chicago Press.

McMurry, L. O. (1998). *To keep the waters troubled: The life of Ida B. Wells.* New York: Oxford University Press.

Ochiai, A. (1992). Ida B. Wells and her crusade for justice: An African American woman's testimonial autobiography. *Soundings, 75*, 365–381.

O'Donnell, S. M. (1995). Urban African American community development in the Progressive Era. *Journal of Community Practice, 2*, 7–26.

Peebles-Wilkins, W., & Francis, E. A. (1990). Two outstanding Black women in social welfare history: Mary Church Terrell and Ida B. Wells-Barnett. *Afffilia, 27*, 87–100.

Penn, I. G. (1891). *The Afro-American press and its editors.* Springfield, MA: Wiley and Company.

Smith, B. (1985). Some home truths on the contemporary black feminist movement. *Journal of Black Studies and Research, 16*, 4–13.

Thompson, M. I. (1990). *Ida B. Wells-Barnett: An exploratory study of an American Black woman, 1893–1930*. New York: Carlson Publishing.

Townes, E. M. (1993). *Womanist justice, womanist hope*. Atlanta: Scholars Press.

Van Steenwyk, E. (1992). *Ida B. Wells-Barnett: Woman of courage*. New York: Franklin Watts.

Walker, A. (1983). *In search of our mother's gardens: Womanist prose*. New York: Harcourt Brace Jovanovich.

CHAPTER 7

Lawrence A. Oxley
Defining State Public Welfare among African Americans

N. Yolanda Burwell

Modern social work education, practice, and research have evolved from numerous foundations. National leaders and events are routinely documented in social work texts and articles (Axinn & Levin, 1982; Barker, 1999; Day, 2000; Lundblad, 1995; Popple & Leighninger, 1993; Pumphrey & Pumphrey, 1961). Unfortunately, little scholarship has focused on *state* social work and social welfare histories. To compound this scarcity, knowledge of state or local social work pioneers of color is scant. A full understanding of social work's history and development cannot occur until these aspects are included. Every state has produced leaders and made historical milestones in social work.[1] People of color have been central to the development of the social work profession. Between 1925 and 1934, for example, the unsung African American social worker, Lt. Lawrence Augustus Oxley, directed a division of the State Board of Charities and Public Welfare in North Carolina.

Oxley is an important figure for two reasons. First, he contributed to the maturation of professional social work practice in North Carolina in three ways. He directed a successful state social welfare agency concerned with the specific needs of African American citizens in a southern state, organized these citizens to employ the first corps of social workers of color in various public agencies in more than 30 counties, and promoted social work education and training of African Americans through public welfare institutes and support of the Bishop Tuttle Memorial Training School of Social Work at St. Augustine's College in Raleigh.

Second, Oxley's work epitomized the self-help and empowerment tradition among African Americans. He tapped into existing resources and values of African American organizations and institutions, focusing on the collective strengths that people brought to the table, rather than their deficits. His work details resource development strategies, philanthropy, and institution building *before* New Deal initiatives and the governmental welfare state were created.

What is amazing is that he achieved all of this during the period of strict legal racial segregation in an agrarian state. Charged with upgrading social and health conditions for the 763,400 African Americans who faced staggering problems of poverty, disease, juvenile delinquency, and inadequate housing, Oxley operated in a climate of sanctioned bigotry and discrimination (Crow, Escott, & Hatley, 1992). His accomplishments demonstrate how one man garnered resources and power both within and outside of the African American community.

Following his achievements in North Carolina, he went on to work with the Department of Labor until 1957. During retirement, he became an advocate for the elderly. He died in 1973 having experienced three productive careers.

The Personal Side of Oxley

Today few people have heard of Lawrence Augustus Oxley and his pioneering social work in North Carolina or his work with the U.S. Department of Labor during the Great Depression. A published biography on this trailblazer does not exist. Though sometimes mentioned as a member of the Black Cabinet during Franklin D. Roosevelt's Administration, a full treatment of his life and work in North Carolina or the federal government has not been written. Yet, in the 1930s, he was considered one of the most influential state welfare leaders in the country (Washington, 1930).

Various photographs display Oxley, with his prominent forehead and piercing eyes, in front of a group of social workers or shoulder to shoulder with the Black Cabinet of President Roosevelt. He looks distinctive and self-assured. A study of Oxley's life shows that he carried this posture and presence of self throughout his various careers. He was a man who was out in front, leading the race and the way for others.

Born in Boston on May 17, 1887, to William J. B. and Alice Agatha, Oxley was a fair-skinned, middle-class, and privileged man. He was privately educated at Prospect Union Preparatory School in Cambridge and received special instruction from professors at Harvard University. He did not receive a degree from Harvard. A devout Episcopalian and active in the church throughout his life, Oxley prepared for the priesthood during his youth. "Had he been willing to enter the seminary, he would have won a scholarship" (Pitt, 1934, p. 6).

Known for his beautiful voice, he traveled for nine months in the British Isles with a company singing as "The Colored Serenader" in 1914. With the dangers of a world war imminent, Oxley returned to the United States and joined the Army. He rose from private to first lieutenant of the infantry. He became a Morale Specialist with the Morale Branch; few of his race held this position. He married Mamie Elizabeth Hill, a public health nurse. There were two daughters from this union.

Oxley became Commissioner of Conciliation in the Department of Labor under Secretary Frances Perkins in 1934. Within weeks, he was given the additional responsibility of Chief of Division of Negro Labor with the Bureau of Labor Statistics. Newspaper accounts and various conference reports show that Oxley traveled the country mediating labor disputes, assisting in the placement of Black workers where jobs were available, speaking on labor matters, and representing the Labor Department at various national events during the Depression years. He produced several research articles and updates on Black workers and directed two nationwide studies on organized labor and the Black worker. After 1937, Oxley worked with the U. S. Employment Service within the Department of Labor in various capacities. Newman (1973) credits him with contributing to equal employment opportunity efforts.

Following his forced retirement from the federal government in 1957 at the age of 70, Oxley became a staunch advocate for the elderly, fighting for their recognition and receipt of better services. He traveled over 7,500 miles as the national field coordinator of the senior citizens for presidential hopeful John F. Kennedy in 1960. Speaking all over the country, he was called the "unknown quantity" for securing victories in close elections in several states. Health care and hospitalization for the elderly were important topics that he promoted. His work laid a foundation for future Medicare legislation.

Oxley remained active until his death in 1973 at the age of 86 in Washington, DC A community organizer, mediator, and architect of social change all of his life, Oxley began his social work career in Raleigh, North Carolina.

Oxley and the Division of Work Among Negroes

Oxley made history at the age of 37. In 1925, he was named the director of the new Division of Work Among Negroes with the North Carolina State Board of Charities and Public Welfare[2]. Funded by the Laura Spelman Rockefeller Memorial Fund for six years, the Division of Work Among Negroes (the Division) was established to implement a statewide public welfare program for African Americans. This unit was a "venture in faith in the possibilities of a race to develop its own leaders and organize its social forces for community betterment" (Oxley, 1927, p. 16). Under Oxley's direction, the Division sought to accomplish two goals: to stimulate self-help among African American communities to work on their own pressing issues and to engage in intelligent studies of African American life and social conditions. The first of its kind in the nation, this experimental unit would become a major vehicle for identifying leadership and promoting community self-help among African American citizens in the state.

As one of the few Black Army Morale officers during World War I, Oxley came to this position with extensive military community service experiences. He conducted social surveys on conditions among Blacks in major cities like Cincinnati, Washington, Chicago, and Louisville. Prior to his appointment with the Division, he taught social science classes at St. Augustine's College in Raleigh. These experiences qualified Oxley as a "trained social worker" when he came to the Division.

North Carolina's program was the first of its kind in the country, and Oxley *defined* the scope and direction of state welfare work among African Americans. He dealt with everything from child abuse and neglect to problems at state institutions. He was a liaison with county officials as well as a mediator when racial conflicts arose. He worked with top African American and Caucasian leaders in the state. Oxley's work was multi-faceted. By all accounts, he was a "field" man, speaking in churches, organizations, and schools. He participated in professional social work and race relations conferences. He wrote numerous articles for mainstream and race-oriented publications about his work.

The following lengthy passage offers a glimpse of the special and extensive nature of Oxley's activities as a "trained social worker" with a state agency during his first four months. Over time, his responsibilities and engagements expanded. Success also increased his workload.

> During the first four months of the existence of the Bureau of Work Among Negroes the director, who is paid from the Rockefeller fund, has devoted his time first to the demonstration counties, and largely to Wake County. Here he has organized a county welfare committee of negroes, and a township committee in every township. He has laid plans for raising $1,500 among the negroes to employ a county negro worker, has secured subscriptions for this purpose to the amount of $1,400, about $1,000 of which has been paid into the hands of Mrs. T. W. Bickett, county superintendent of public welfare. Some work in the organization of the negroes has been done in Chatham [county]. The director has aided in a survey of the social agencies in a city of the State, has made a brief survey of conditions among negroes in several counties, has spoken before the Tri-State Inter-Racial Committee at Greensboro; the Older Boys Conference of the Y.M.C.A., Greensboro; Spring Conference of the Association for the Study of Negro Life and History, Durham; the meeting of the Inter-Racial Committee at Atlanta; at several school commencements. He has acted as assistant to the county superintendent of public welfare of Wake County in school attendance, probation, and general welfare work among the negroes. He has made various investigations for the State Board of Charities and Public Welfare. The bureau is abundantly justifying the faith of the Commissioner of Public Welfare in securing its establishment. (The Bureau of Work Among Negroes, 1925, p. 2)

Self-Help

When Oxley joined the Division of Work Among Negroes, Hattie Russell, a juvenile probation officer in Charlotte, was the only African American social worker identified in the state. Welfare work was segregated. African Americans were expected to work with their own people; Caucasians would work with theirs. Oxley faced the daunting task of building opportunities and resources for African Americans to work on their pressing issues in a racially divided and bigoted climate. Self-help was a viable solution for Oxley to promote.

Burwell (1996) notes that the self-help strategy offered several advantages. It was a helping ethos among African Americans (Martin & Martin, 1985; Pollard, 1978). It empowered African Americans to act as their own agents of positive change when governmental bodies and standard social work institutions cared little about their welfare. It was an expedient step. Scarce funds, limited staff, and rudimentary systems of services restricted broad public assistance to African Americans. Self-help among African Americans did not disturb the legal and customary segregation practices. Self-help advanced race improvement, but not race equality.

Fortunately, Oxley was a can-do administrator and a strong believer in self-help among African Americans. He insisted that "welfare work of a constructive nature" could not be put over on African Americans, but that, if it was to be worthwhile and permanent in character, they had to fully understand and assume a large degree of responsibility for solving their own problems (Oxley, 1927, p. 17).

With this as his charge, Oxley had organized African Americans in over 30 counties by the time he left the Division in 1934. Using locality development methods, Oxley helped Black residents to raise funds and to participate on advisory committees of local and state agencies (Burwell, 1995). Many of these communities secured their first African American county welfare worker or expanded parent-teacher associations or addressed recreational needs because of his efforts. A 1927 report of the Bureau of Social Service in Goldsboro, North Carolina, speaks to Oxley's impact.

> A new impetus was given the work by the coming of the colored family case worker. In January, the colored people, after much thought, under the direction of Lt. Lawrence Oxley of the State Board of Charities and Public Welfare and Professor Hugh Brown of the Goldsboro Colored Public Schools, put on a campaign and raised $1,200 for a worker. A report of the year's work among the Negroes will show what the worker has already meant to her group and the great help she has been to the office. (Bureau of Social Service, 1927, p. 1)

This kind of community organization and philanthropy was duplicated in county after county in North Carolina. By 1928, there were 26 African American social workers employed in county welfare offices. Fifteen held full-time positions, with an average monthly salary of $100. Black tenant farmers, domestics, mill workers, club women, entrepreneurs, and school children in 26 counties contributed about $15,000 toward salaries for several of the workers. They supplemented public funds with about $10,000 toward promotional expenses for this early corps of professional social workers (Oxley, 1929).

Oxley professionalized social work in the state. When E. E. Smith, President of the State Colored Normal School in Fayetteville, North Carolina, wrote Oxley asking about the duties and need for social workers among African Americans in 1928, Oxley responded in this way:

> The purpose of a social worker in a Negro community is for the awakening of a social consciousness of the community to its needs and desire of self-help. The Negro social worker in North Carolina, particularly in these pioneer days is expected to serve as probation officer, big sister and big brother to the underprivileged Negro

> child and be able to intelligently understand the social needs of the community and initiate programs of community service with which to satisfy, at least in part, these needs. (Oxley to E. E. Smith, January 11, 1928)

He advanced community organization as a social work method when professional practice methods were just evolving. He promoted the Division and community organization at social work conferences, at public welfare institutes, and through courses at Bishop Tuttle Memorial Training School of Social Work, a professional school for Black women at St. Augustine's College. Oxley advanced the Division of Work Among Negroes, social work, and his own methodologies so well that he was often consulted by other states wanting to set up similar units. Atlanta University's Dean of the School of Social Work, Forrester B. Washington (1930), notes that, of the five African Americans employed in state public welfare, Oxley held the most important position. Oxley's work was so significant that the state legislature made the Division of Work Among Negroes a permanent unit within the State Board of Charities and Public Welfare in 1931.

Social Research

Tremendous strides were made in social welfare initiatives under Oxley's stewardship. He oversaw state institutions that served African Americans and worked diligently with state and county agencies to improve the pressing social conditions facing Black citizens. The paucity of accurate information on African Americans troubled Oxley. Recognizing the importance of research and "intelligent study of Negro life" (Larkin, n.d., p. 2), Oxley produced comprehensive studies on child welfare, crime, and unemployment for the state and assisted counties in documenting local needs. The survey method of data collection was crucial to Oxley's work. His thorough reports often made the difference between acceptance and rejection of his recommendations. His work in Gaston County is illustrative.

In 1926, Gaston County commissioners and the county welfare superintendent, Ms. Gertrude Keller, invited Oxley to study the needs of African Americans in their county. After spending a week in Gastonia and the county, Oxley submitted a comprehensive report in which he recommended a full program of welfare work that included health work in the school, the erection of a tuberculosis annex at the local hospital for African Americans, and other health measures. Oxley recommended a $4,000 budget with his report. Commissioners and city officials accepted his recommendations. The City of Gastonia agreed to appropriate $600 and the county put up $1,000.

> The remainder will be derived from various sources such as the sale of tuberculosis seals, fees from the patients at the hospital, private subscriptions from Negroes and special gifts. The county will repair the hospital, which will cost about $500 and it is expected that the annex for tubercular patients will cost about $2,500. ("News from the Bureau of Work Among Negroes," 1926, p. 2)

Kate Burr Johnson, the Commissioner of the State Board of Charities and Public Welfare, commented on this specific effort.

> This is a specific and a very interesting instance of the kind of service which the various bureaus of the State Board of Charities and Public Welfare are prepared to give to the counties of the State. A careful survey of the field by an experienced social worker often results in a deeper interest and stronger support. The plan which has been accepted by Gaston County and the city of Gastonia is a sound one and will be of increasing benefit to the Negro people of the community since it was carefully planned to suit their needs. ("News from the Bureau of Work Among Negroes," 1926, p. 2)

Social Work Education

Oxley was vexed by the dearth of trained African American social workers. To respond to this need, Oxley began annual public welfare institutes to supplement the training and staff development needs of African American workers. He organized nine North Carolina Public Welfare Institutes for Negroes where some of the most prominent social workers of both races made presentations. Participants from North Carolina, South Carolina, and Virginia were introduced to social work methods, knowledge and skills, and the latest developments occurring on the state and national levels. Since African Americans could not attend the University of North Carolina's social work program, these popular and well attended institutes filled an important educational void for early African American social workers in the state. The institutes continued until 1945.

A firm believer in education and training, Oxley was instrumental in steering many young women to Bishop Tuttle Memorial Training School of Social Work on St. Augustine's College campus in Raleigh, North Carolina, and others to the Atlanta University School of Social Work.

Oxley vigorously directed the Division of Work Among Negroes for nine years. The fact that Oxley accomplished all that he did in a racially segregated state during the Depression years is amazing, because he operated in a hostile climate that squashed race equality. He had to walk a curious tightrope of race relations. He could not afford to upset the racial etiquette systems; agitation and protest were not in his repertoire. But he used other tactics. For example, he retained the title "Lieutenant" throughout his tenure with the Division. This was so Whites would address him with a proper title. Two references give clues to his deportment:

> Oxley has rendered an important service as a mediator between the races. He is called upon frequently by state officials to interpret the attitude of the state to his people. For instance the night of the mob violence in connection with the Mansel case in Asheville in 1925, Oxley was sent to that city to prevent race rioting. A huge mass meeting was called on Sunday afternoon and Oxley spoke before an

> audience that jammed the building, an audience of incensed Negroes who were verging on rebellion. The crowd went away placated. He was frequently called upon to investigate cases for parole. Every one of his recommendations for clemency in cases of capital sentence has received favorable action. ("Negro Welfare Program Falls Back Upon State," 1931, p. 7)

In a special report on his progress, Oxley (1925) detailed activities of his unit in various cities during his first year as director. He indicated that a Miss M. E. Gilkerson was the Negro Assistant to the Guilford County Welfare Superintendent. She was from Ohio and found difficulty in adjusting to the ways of the South and race matters. Though he acknowledged the superintendent possessed "groundless" racial fears, Oxley went on to say, "This is not the time to muddy the clear stream of Public Welfare in North Carolina by injecting the race question or the matter of race relationships. Wise selection of personnel, proper organization and a common sense attitude will solve this problem" (p. 2).

Tensions increased with the start of the Great Depression. The Depression years were difficult for everyone in North Carolina. Oxley had the added responsibility of overseeing unemployment relief efforts among African Americans after 1932. He also experienced serious salary cuts during this time (Shepard to E. Pou, November 4, 1933). Through assistance from influential people like educator and advisor to President Franklin Roosevelt, Mary McLeod Bethune, and the founder of North Carolina Mutual Insurance Company, C. C. Spaulding, Oxley secured a position in the Department of Labor in 1934 and left North Carolina. James E. Shepard, the President of North Carolina Central College and one of the state's leading African Americans, wrote to U.S. Representative Edward Pou of Oxley,

> Lieutenant Oxley has served the colored people in North Carolina in a way which is hardly appreciated by those of us who come in contact with his work from day to day. He has alleviated difficulties between the races, has sought to instill lessons of peace and harmony and in every way been a valuable citizen. (Shepard to E. Pou, November 4, 1933)

William R. Johnson directed the Division of Work Among Negroes from 1934 to 1943. John Larkin assumed the leadership of this unit for the next 20 years until segregated services were dismantled.

Conclusion

Oxley accomplished a great deal during his lifetime. For historical purposes, his work is important on many fronts. He *defined* state public welfare work among African Americans as a viable and responsible field of practice. His was the model that other states copied. Washington (1930) noted, "Scattered about the country there are other Negroes directing bureaus of colored work for state departments of welfare, notable among them are William Jennifer of Michigan, Maude B. Coleman of Pennsylvania, J. G. Robinson of West Virginia and J. A Robinson of Tennessee" (p. 6). The benefits and leadership these men and women gave deserves historical attention.

New or revised evidence about social work by African Americans with African Americans arises from historical studies like these. They encourage new paradigms of engagement with communities of color—as producers, philanthropists, and institution builders (Burwell, 1995). Historically and today, communities of color are more than recipients and objects of service.

The Division of Work Among Negroes acquaints social workers with a fascinating network of Black and White social welfare and social work practitioners in a southern state between 1920 and 1960. Some are known, but *many* are unknown to the social work record. Oxley was responsible for investigating and reporting on private and state institutions that served African American citizens. He actively worked with the leaders of Efland Home for Colored Girls. Founded by the North Carolina Federation of Colored Women in 1925, Efland Home was a residential center for troubled girls. Burwell (1994b) notes that this federation of 100 women's clubs funded and operated Efland Home for 14 years. Prominent race women like Charlotte Hawkins Brown of Sedalia, North Carolina, and Marie Louise Clinton of Charlotte, North Carolina, were involved with the operation and upkeep of the home and numerous social welfare efforts in the state.

Less known, yet very important to the state's social work history, is Bertha Richards. She headed Bishop Tuttle School of Social Work at St. Augustine's College. A Caucasian who was trained as a librarian, Richards was very instrumental in producing some of the first professionally trained African American social workers in the state. Oxley worked closely with Richards and the school throughout his directorship. She was present at the first social work institute sponsored by Oxley and the Division of Work Among Negroes in 1926. In fact, many of the social work institutes were held at the St. Augustine College campus after 1928 because it could accommodate the large number of attendees.

More than 30 social workers who were the first African Americans employed in county welfare agencies in the 1920s and 1930s were the direct result of Oxley's work. These workers often were the first of their race and the only person of color working in county welfare agencies. They faced hostile attitudes and negative practices. Some advanced the profession through publications and presentations at professional conferences (Burwell, 1994a). These local pioneers merit further research.

Oxley served under two commissioners of the State Board of Charities and Public Welfare, Kate Burr Johnson and Mrs. W. Thomas Bost. He interacted with over 40 county welfare superintendents. Wake County's welfare superintendent, Fannie Yarborough Bickett, was one of the first to employ Oxley's skills. An attorney by trade and a former first lady of the state, Bickett was an active club woman. She was the sole Caucasian and chair of the board of Efland Home for Negro Girls (Moore & Hamrick, 1989). These top social welfare administrators sanctioned Oxley's efforts. Their progressive stances supported his work among African Americans. Despite their groundbreaking contributions around public assistance and social work and social welfare in the state, the record is now silent on them.

Oxley's work with the Division informs social workers about proactive African American participation at state and local levels. The Division had a Negro Advisory Committee that met regularly. The Committee consisted of influential members like Mary Jackson McCrory, wife of the president of Johnson C. Smith College and a leader in the YWCA movement, and educator Charlotte Hawkins Brown. These power brokers brought clout, information, and meaning to the Division. They lobbied, counseled, and questioned Oxley and the State Commissioners on matters affecting African Americans in the state. Though this group had no enforcement or regulatory powers, they did facilitate and influence social welfare initiatives behind a veil of segregation in a southern state.

Every state has a Lawrence Oxley. It is simply a matter of unearthing this "lost" history and giving voice to such achievements. As modern social work practitioners, we stand on the shoulders of pioneers like Lawrence Oxley. They have given us fascinating lessons of empowerment, self-determination, and institution building.

Notes

1. There are three threads of professional social work and welfare development in North Carolina. Accounts of social work history in the state begin and end with the establishment of the School of Public Welfare at the University of Chapel Hill in 1920 and the contributions of sociologist Howard Odum. Aydlett's (1947) history of the North Carolina State Board of Public Welfare introduces early governmental changes and personalities that shaped services and welfare in the state. Second, the numerous women's clubs and church and professional groups spawned many social welfare initiatives and agencies. Third, the parallel development of services and institutions that African Americans created to attend to their educational, health, and child welfare needs contributed to the foundation for social work and social welfare.

2. The North Carolina State Board of Charities and Public Welfare received expanded powers in 1917 from the state legislature and organized the provision of welfare through county auspices. Seven divisions oversaw the needs of the most vulnerable citizens in the state: the county organization, child welfare, institutions, mental health and hygiene, education and publicity, school attendance, and work among Blacks.

References

Axinn, J., & Levin, H. (1982). *Social welfare—A history of the American response to need* (2nd ed.). New York: Longman.

Aydlett, A. L. (1947) The North Carolina State Board of Public Welfare, *The North Carolina Historical Review, 47*, 1–33.

Barker, R. L. (1999) *Milestones in the development of social work and social welfare*. Washington, DC: NASW Press.

Bureau of Social Services. (1927). Weil Papers. Goldsboro Bureau of Social Services. North Carolina Division of Archives and History. Box 1488.71.

The Bureau of Work Among Negroes. (1925, May). *Public Welfare Progress, 6*, 2.

Burwell, N. Y. (1994a). North Carolina Public Welfare Insitutes for Negroes, 1926–1946. *Journal of Sociology and Social Welfare, 21*, 55–66.

Burwell, N. Y. (1994b). *The North Carolina Federation of Negro Women and the Efland Industrial Home for Negro Girls*. Paper presented at the National Conference of the Association for the Study of African American Life and History, Atlanta, GA.

Burwell, N. Y. (1995). Shifting the historical lens: Early economic empowerment among African Americans. *Journal of Baccalaureate Social Work, 1*, 25–37.

Burwell, N. Y. (1996). Lawrence Oxley and locality development: Black self-help in North Carolina, 1925–1934. In I. B. Carlton-LaNey & N. Y. Burwell (Eds.), *African American community practice model* (pp. 49–69). Binghamton, NY: Haworth Press.

Crow, J. J., Escott, P. D., & Hatley, F. J. (1992). *A history of African Americans in North Carolina*. Raleigh, NC: North Carolina Division of Archives and History.

Day, P. (2000) *A new history of social welfare* (3rd ed.). Boston: Allyn & Bacon.

Larkin, J. (n.d.). A history of the unit of Work Among Negroes. Raleigh, NC: North Carolina State Board of Charities and Public Welfare.

Lundblad, K. S. (1995). Jane Addams and social reform: A role model for the 1990s. *Social Work, 40*, 661–669.

Martin, E. P., & Martin, J. M. (1985). *The helping tradition in the Black family and the community*. Silver Spring, MD: NASW.

Moore, J. C., & Hamrick, G. (1989). *The first ladies of North Carolina*. Charlotte, NC: Heritage Printers.

Negro welfare program falls back upon the state. (1931, January). *News and Observer*, p. 7.

Newman, D. (1973). *Urban policy of Lawrence A. Oxley Chief, Division of Negro Labor of the Department of Labor with a case study of Chicago, 1934–1939*. Unpublished manuscript. Department of Labor files. National Archives.

News from the Bureau of Work Among Negroes. (1926, October). *Public Welfare Progress, 7*, 2.

Oxley, L. (1925). Special Report—Bureau of Work Among Negroes January 1 to March 31, 1925. Unit of Work Among Negroes Papers. North Carolina Division of Archives and History. Box 234.

Oxley, L. (1927). North Carolina's Welfare Program for Negroes. *The Southern Workman, 56*, 16–25.

Oxley, L. (1928, January 11). Letter to E. E. Smith. Unit of Negro Work Papers. North Carolina Division of Archives and History, Box 234.

Oxley, L. (1929). Organizing the North Carolina Negro community. *The Southern Workman*, 3–11.

Pitt, L. (1934, May). New Deal personalities. *Journal and Guide*, p. 6.

Pollard, W. (1978). *A study of Black self-help*. San Francisco: R & E Associates.

Popple, P., & Leighninger, L. (1993). *Social work, social welfare and American society* (2nd ed.). Boston: Allyn & Bacon.

Pumphrey, R. E., & Pumphrey, M. W. (1961). *The heritage of American social work*. New York: Columbia University Press.

Shepard, J. (1933, November 4). Letter.to Edward Pou. Unit of Negro Work Papers. North Carolina Division of Archives and History. Box 233.

Washington, F. (1930, January). Headway in social work. *The Southern Workman, 59*, 3–9.

CHAPTER 8

George Edmund Haynes and Elizabeth Ross Haynes

Empowerment Practice among African American Social Welfare Pioneers

Iris B. Carlton-LaNey

The first two decades of the 20th century marked the movement of social work toward professionalization. The roles played by volunteers were becoming increasingly subordinate as paid workers replaced them in many social agencies and organizations. African American social workers placed themselves squarely within the movement toward professionalization, even though their White counterparts did not always embrace them warmly. The African American social work and social welfare movement provided a new avenue of opportunity for many young, well educated African American men and women.

While African Americans and Whites engaged in numerous charitable activities during the period of the Progressive Era, the dominant trend of that period was a conservative triumph (Kolko, 1963). Conservative solutions to the emerging problems of an industrial society were applied under nearly all circumstances. Business and political leaders shared the same basic belief in defining the public good. Essentially, their primary goal was to preserve the basic social and economic relations critical to a capitalist society. The goals of business and the rest of the public became synonymous. Business leaders defined the limits of political intervention and specified its major form and thrust (Kolko, 1963). Furthermore, the economic booms and busts of this era created a volatile economy and heightened inequality (Abramovitz, 1998). Consequently, the glaring paradox of progress and poverty became quite apparent in American society between the years of 1890 and 1920.

African American migrants, along with their European immigrant counterparts, flocked to urban centers to experience the prosperity that was available to so many others who benefited from the industrial wave of success at the turn of the 20th century. For African Americans, however, *escaping* was critical to their decisions to move cityward. They moved to escape the tremendous poverty created by the southern plantation sharecropping system, the ravages of the cotton boll weevil, the destruction of the earth by the quest for bauxite, unusual floods, and the intense racial discrimination, lynchings, and overall dehumanizing treatment levied at the hands of southern Whites. Exaggerated stories of success in the northern cities, along with the promises from labor agents of jobs and the lure of free railroad tickets to the North, provided further impetus for African American migration (DuBois, 1912; Fulks, 1969; Haynes, 1924/1978).

These urban arrivals were ill prepared to live in the cities of the North. Their efforts to escape the oppression of the rural South were thwarted by similar discrimination in the cities of the North. In addition to the myriad social problems that African American migrants faced in the cities, they also encountered a social service delivery system that was unwilling to acknowledge them as "worthy" recipients of services. White immigrants were also judged "worthy" or "unworthy" by virtue of their willingness to work, moral fitness, extravagance, or moral defects. However, African Americans were labeled "unworthy" by virtue of skin color and generally relegated to the periphery of the social welfare system.

An organized system of African American self-help emerged, in part, because of the group's overwhelming exclusion from full participation in the American social welfare system. Another reason, and one that had its roots in their African heritage, was the desire and propensity to take care of their own. The African American social welfare system developed parallel to the one that Whites established for themselves. Their self-help welfare system included building private institutions, like churches, hospitals, old folks homes, orphanages, and schools, as well as establishing organizations like the National Association of Colored Women (NACW), the National Association for the Advancement of Colored People (NAACP), and the National Urban League (NUL). These individuals and organizations even raised private monies to hire African American workers for public agencies when White officials refused either to hire African Americans or to designate White workers to serve African American clients.

Self-help and mutual aid became an institutionalized part of the African American community; these services developed on the heels of and encompassed the West African tradition of social obligation that emphasized the collective good, as opposed to the Western focus on the individual. Mutual aid was perfected in the United States during the African American enslavement. Through mutual aid, the slave community and later the emancipated freedmen and women engaged in their greatest form of resistance—group and individual survival. Peebles-Wilkins and Koerin (1992) note that "community action" superseded the ideal of mutual aid and provided a foundation for the development of African American empowerment–based social welfare and social work.

Race pride, race consciousness, and racial uplift were also essential elements of African American social work and reform. According to Locke (1925/1965), the race-proud intelligentsia of the early 1900s showed a "belief in the efficacy of collective effort" and "in race cooperation" (p. 91). Essentially, race pride served as a mechanism for group solidarity and helped to undercut class differences between the social workers and the people that they served (Chandler, 1995). Race pride emphasized a collective conceptualization of human beings and their group survival.

Social debt, another element of African American social welfare, was closely connected to race pride and refers to the obligation or indebtedness that African Americans felt toward each other as a result of achievement and some modicum of success (Carlton-LaNey, 1999). These elements—self-help, race pride, and social debt—were fundamental to African American social work and social welfare at the turn of the century and were an essential part of the services and programs that professional and lay practitioners developed and delivered to those in need.

Martin and Martin (1995) contend that gender was critical to the way that social work developed in the African American community. They assert that African American male social workers did not build on the African American helping tradition of which the elements of self-help, race pride, and social debt were a part. Instead, they pursued an assimilationist course and sought interracial alliances as a mechanism for successful social work practice. African American female social workers, on the other hand, used extended family concepts to work with African American people of all ages to fulfill social service needs. Essentially, African American female social workers "brought extended family values into a larger context of social obligation" or social debt (Martin & Martin, 1995, p. 176). These two approaches to African American social work reflected the two emerging philosophies of racial development that existed at the time. According to E. Franklin Frazier (1927/1965), African American people either "undertook to conform in every respect to the culture about them" or held to the belief that "they should develop their own unique culture" (p. 97).

Martin and Martin's extended family paradigm reflects an Afrocentric perspective. Essentially, their notion of the helping tradition among African Americans emphasizes sharing, cooperation, and social responsibility (Ak'bar, 1984; Daly, Jennings, Beckett, & Leashore, 1995). Afrocentric practice also embraces the empowerment tradition and focuses on the interconnectedness of all things and the oneness of body, mind, and spirit. The emphasis is on the development of the collective, rather than the individual, along with pervasive, experiential, and participatory spirituality (Turner, 1991).

The African American social workers of the Progressive Era, whether operating from an African helping tradition or from an assimilationist perspective, were sincerely committed to mobilizing resources for community members in need. The "worthy versus unworthy" argument was a consideration in their service provision; however, the importance of racial uplift often overshadowed this spurious argument, since they were aware that the White professional community generally considered both the service provider and the recipient to be unworthy. Social workers and social welfare leaders provided a myriad of services and programs that included direct social provisions as well as intangible services, all designed to meet basic human needs and to alleviate human suffering. Through their web of affiliation, personal and political power, hard work, and determination, these leaders were active in a wide range of organizations that gave them community access and influence. The careers of the Haynes family illustrate the empowerment-based concept that characterized social work practice for some African American social workers at the beginning of the 20th century.

Introducing the Haynes Family

The Hayneses included Dr. George Edmund Haynes (1880–1960), sociologist, social worker, and cofounder of the NUL; his wife, Elizabeth Ross Haynes (1883–1953), womanist, politician, and labor expert; and his younger sister Birdye H. Haynes (1886–1922), a settlement house matron in prominent social settlements in both Chicago and New York. (The career of Birdye Haynes is discussed in detail in chapter 3.) The Haynes family legacy is one of commitment to service and education for service. For them, social work was a calling and an obligation, one that required them to give to those African Americans who did not have the same access to opportunity that they enjoyed. It required them to model expected and accepted behavior and to demand as much from others as they were willing to give of themselves.

The Hayneses were very well educated, among the "talented tenth" of the race, and politically influential in the African American community. Both George and Elizabeth graduated from Fisk University in Nashville in 1903. George Haynes was a professionally trained social worker and, in 1910, became the first African American to graduate from the New York School of Philanthropy; in 1912, he became the first to earn a doctorate in sociology and economics from Columbia University. Elizabeth Ross Haynes earned a master's degree in sociology from Columbia University in 1923. Both also studied at the University of Chicago during their summer terms, Elizabeth in 1905 and 1907 and George in 1906 and 1907. These educational achievements were exceptional, since only 1 percent of African Americans, both male and female, had four or more years of college as indicated by data in 1940—the earliest year for which such figures are available (Gordon, 1991).

The Hayneses were members of the African American intelligentsia. They recognized that their roles were pivotal in tackling the problems that confronted African American people. George Haynes was not born of privilege, although Elizabeth Ross was born to parents who amassed some land and wealth in segregated and impoverished Lowndes County, Alabama, after emancipation. George and Elizabeth wed at the Fisk University Chapel and had one son, two years after their marriage in 1912. Gordon (1991) speculates that many African American women reformers, like Elizabeth Ross Haynes, had low fertility rates either because they used some form of birth control or because they led lives very independent from their husbands, causing long physical separations. While Ross Haynes was a womanist who led a very independent life, she, nonetheless, was quite traditional in many ways, embracing the cult of true womanhood and giving up paid employment upon her marriage to George Haynes. Furthermore, she relocated with him whenever his work required that he move, and she accepted the life of a professional volunteer and unpaid consultant throughout much of her career. Her relationship with her husband was very close. She also maintained a close relationship with her sister-in-law and affectionately referred to her as "Bert." Birdye Haynes, in turn, called Elizabeth "Rossie" and often communicated with her about the health and the well-being of her young nephew (Carlton-LaNey, 1997).

George Haynes and Elizabeth Ross Haynes were prominent pioneer advocates and crusaders of social justice. Only within recent years, however, has the social work profession acknowledged George Haynes as a pioneer. His involvement with NUL is usually the only acknowledgment that he is accorded. The importance of the NUL to the development of the emerging social work profession and to social work education is seldom discussed. Ross Haynes, whose work, according to Guichard Parris (personal communication, September 1980), was probably more contributory in breadth than her husband's, has yet to be acknowledged as a pioneer in the social work and social welfare profession. Her contributions may yet be recognized, as the journal *Social Work* published an article on her life and career in 1997 and African American women's history has identified Ross Haynes as playing an important role in the advocacy of women's rights and in women's labor issues. The Haynes's work, albeit generally ignored by the social work profession, was in response to the many social problems and individual hardships that confronted the African American community. Moreover, their work contributed to social work and social welfare on both the macro and micro levels and empowered those that they served.

The terms "race man" and "race woman" aptly describe these two pioneers. According to Drake and Cayton's 1945 discussion, a "race man" is an individual who is reputed to be uncompromising in his fight to ensure African Americans equal access to opportunity. He is proud of his race and culture, and he engages in activities to benefit his people. With many of the same attributes, the "race woman" has less power than the "race man," but she is regarded with less suspicion by the African American community. The race woman understands the circumstances of her people and is likely to engage in studies of their social, economic, and political conditions. Her work is always to uplift the race and to teach appropriate, suitable, and necessary life skills. George and Elizabeth Haynes's careers reflect the dimensions of empowerment practice to which Simon (1994) refers in her discussion of the empowerment tradition of American social work.

Simon (1994) has identified four dimensions of empowerment practice that emerged in the period from 1893 through 1917. This empowerment practice was designed "to increase poor and stigmatized persons' capacities to act on their own behalf and to obtain a fairer share of social justice and resources (p. 73)." The dimensions include (1) mobilization of immediate material aid in conjunction with the provision of psychological reassurance and support, (2) the teaching of specific skills needed in survival, (3) the active enlistment of clients' or neighbors' participation and preferences in problem solving, and (4) the public, educative, and advocative uses of the findings of social investigations.

Offering Concrete and Social Support

George Edmund Haynes was cofounder and first executive director of the National League on Urban Conditions Among Negroes (NLUCAN), later renamed the NUL. Through this organization, he established the earliest social work training program for African Americans at Fisk University, predating both the Atlanta School of Social Work (1920) and the Bishop Tuttle Memorial Training School of Social Work (1925) at St. Augustine College in Raleigh, North Carolina. The NUL, founded in 1911, became the major social work organization in the African American community. George Haynes worked to provide skilled social work services to the population of African Americans migrating from the South to urban centers in the North. The NUL was one of the major social welfare movements of the Progressive Era. It was comparable in influence and impact to the Charity Organization Society and the social settlement house movement.

Through the NUL, George Haynes and others offered an array of concrete social and support services, such as employment, education, daycare, wholesome leisure activities, and housing services. Like other social workers of the day, George Haynes saw social change as simply another layer of social work practice. He never saw social change as more important than responding to the immediate needs of the African American community, families, or individuals who were suffering. He was as easily immersed in negotiating with wealthy philanthropists or planning with university administrators as he was in conducting social work and social welfare research or providing direct services to victims of disasters. He was also adept at interdisciplinary team work, as was evident when he established residency policies for social work students' field practicums at Nashville's Bethlehem House Settlement or coordinated disaster relief for the victims of the East Nashville fire of 1916 (Carlton-LaNey, 1985).

The East Nashville fire destroyed the homes of 324 African Americans and 301 Caucasian families on March 22, 1916. Haynes was then Director of the Department of Social Science and Social Service at Fisk University. He, his assistant Paul Mowbray, and the Fisk social work students played a significant role in providing relief to the fire victims in the community surrounding the university. Divided into two teams of field staff and office staff, the students developed and maintained an orderly means of relief distribution for each recipient of service, made personal visits to the temporary addresses of all applicants to inspect their circumstances, and provided emergency food and clothing to each applicant. To service the emergency needs of the fire victims, Haynes worked with several groups and organizations, including the Nashville Negro Board of Trade, a group that worked for community progress and self-help, and the Commercial Club, an all White local business organization. Through the mutual cooperation of these diverse groups, interest was stimulated for the founding of the Public Welfare League, which later became an affiliate of the NUL (Carlton-LaNey, 1987).

Like her husband, Elizabeth Ross Haynes was comfortable with and capable of various aspects of social service delivery. Ross Haynes was a philanthropist who articulated a womanist consciousness. Her life's work incorporated the numerous issues of race, gender, culture, economics, and politics. She began her social service work with "colored students" for the Student Department of the National Board of the Young Women's Christian Association (YWCA), traveling to college campuses where branches of the "Y" were established for African Americans. George Haynes held a similar position with the Young Men's Christian Association (YMCA) before entering the New York School of Philanthropy. The direct social services that they provided to African American college students included program advising about the association, assistance in planning and implementing the annual conferences, individual student interviews, and new associations organization.

Ross Haynes offered concrete social and support services to many throughout her career. The work that she did for the young women of the YWCA involved providing support and encouragement. She noted that often she found many of the young women burdened with heavy work requirements as domestics to support their education by day and occupied by the demands of schoolwork at night. Nonetheless, she remarked that the students were generally "cheerful and determined to push ahead, [but] occasionally an almost discouraged girl has made her way to my room seeking advice, information, and more than all a word of encouragement" (Ross, special report to the YWCA Board, 1909). On her many visits to the college campuses, Ross Haynes was always observant, keeping a particular eye out for the student who showed unusual promise. On visiting Paine College, which she described as "one of the strongest Associations on the field," she noted that the president of the local Association was impressive and someone "worthy of being kept in mind as a possible Association worker somewhere" in the future (Ross, 1909).

Haynes was also a club woman, an elected officer, a social scientist, and part of a network of African American college-educated women who saw as their mission racial uplift and protection and advancement of women. As Gordon (1991) indicates, Haynes and women like her taught, mentored, and even self-consciously trained each other. This occurred in colleges, sororities, women's clubs, and through the YWCA and the NACW. A selfless person, Ross Haynes took every opportunity to mentor and support younger women and colleagues alike. For example, when she resigned her position with the YWCA, she recommended a fellow Fiskite, Cecelia Holloway, for the position and participated in the young woman's training and acclimation to the YWCA. Ross Haynes rejoined the YWCA in 1922, when she was named to the newly created Council on Colored Work. In 1924, she became the first African American member of the Association's national board, a position that she held for the next 10 years (Carlton-LaNey, 1997).

Ross Haynes was also a philanthropist. As Ida B. Wells-Barnett's antilynching campaign was sometimes considered "philanthropy," Ross Haynes's master's thesis, entitled *Negroes in Domestic Service in the United States*, was a form of philanthropy that pole vaulted the issues of African American women's labor onto a national agenda. Before completing her master's thesis, Ross Haynes had served as a special aide to Mary Van Kleeck who was Director of the Department of Labor's Women in Industry Service, later named the Women's Bureau (Carlton-LaNey, 1997). Ross Haynes was a philanthropist in the traditional monetary sense as well. She contributed monies to various worthy causes that supported "the race," such as Alabama's unique and successful Calhoun Colored School and Social Settlement, a combination of serious elementary education and secondary education and a version of industrial training and social settlement work.

Teaching Skills Needed in Daily Urban Life

Both George Haynes and Elizabeth Ross Haynes identified teaching, education, and skill development as critical to the survival and empowerment of the African American community, family, and individual. For George Haynes, the NUL Fellowship Program was one way to empower both African American social workers and their clients. He believed that securing and training African American social workers was the most pressing need of the NUL. In his mind, these students should be intimately familiar with the communities and clients whom they served. To that end, he developed a social work training program that included two African American history courses and that required the students to live as "settlers" within the communities' African American settlement houses. He negotiated with Bethlehem Center, a social settlement opened in 1913, to provide the "laboratory" experience that he believed was imperative for social work training. The Fisk students renovated and staffed the Center, which provided an array of services and programs, including Camp Fire Girls, three courses in domestic science, kindergarten, a sewing school for children, a junior and intermediate boys' club, and a men's cooperative club. George Haynes was uncompromising with the worried mother who inquired about the necessity of her fragile daughter living in a community settlement house. He diplomatically informed the parents that this was a needed part of the training program and that every effort had been made to ensure the health and safety of the student "settlers." George Haynes believed that the most direct way of influencing the customs and habits of a people was to give them "teachers and exemplars of their own kind" (Haynes, 1910) as role models. He strongly believed that it was the students' intimate involvement with the community that surrounded Fisk University that helped to prepare them for the crisis that was associated with the East Nashville Fire of 1916.

The NUL, under George Haynes's direction, also provided direct social services to the new arrivals from the rural South. The organization, for example, sent potential migrants information about life in northern cities, warned them of the dangers that lurked there, and tried to help those who resolved to come despite the warnings. It also stationed travelers' aid workers at critical points along the journey to help to protect vulnerable, unsuspecting travelers as they journeyed northward (Weiss, 1974), a practice that resembled Victoria Earle Matthews's earlier efforts to protect young women traveling alone to the cities.

Elizabeth Ross Haynes was also committed to teaching life skills as a way to empower African Americans. She was a member of several speakers' bureaus, tutored young children, and participated in clubs and organizations that had as part of their mission nurturing girls, young women, and elders alike. For example, through the Alpha Kappa Alpha Sorority, Ross Haynes conducted annual literary contests for high school girls in New York and New Jersey. The contests not only gave these girls an opportunity to develop their literary skills, but also provided an opportunity for the girls to interact with well educated high-achieving African American women. The sorority women, who were themselves excellent role models for the young contestants, also brought in prominent literary giants, including Langston Hughes and Countee Cullen, to judge the contest (Carlton-LaNey, 1997). Ross Haynes also spent some of her vacation time in Alabama, tutoring children in her community for several hours each afternoon. Later, commenting on the desperate conditions of her neighbors in Lowndes County, Alabama, she expressed fear that the children's very early marriages were certain to ensure a life of poverty and want. Furthermore, problems such as very poor schoolteachers, incompetent ministers, and unworthy lawmakers exacerbated the problems confronting her neighbors. While Ross Haynes's access to this population was limited, she nonetheless could continue to have an impact on the life of her community and on the skills that residents developed by supporting the Calhoun Colored School and Social Settlement through her annual monetary giving.

Involving Clients as Participants

Simon's (1994) third dimension of empowerment practice involves the clients as participants in meeting their own needs. A good example of the involvement of clients actively shaping their problem-solving strategies can be seen in the NUL's newcomers' dance. This dance was an opportunity for new arrivals to cities and those who had been integrated into the life of the city to meet informally and socially, and to offer advice, information, and support to each other. In another example, George Haynes understood the important role that established community institutions such as the church had. "The Negro church organizations," he asserted, "have a willingness and zeal for service which has brought results." The migrants, Haynes indicated, were coming to the North "seeking opportunity for self-development and self-determination," and the social worker needed to help them to realize their dreams and to integrate their lives in the community as they saw fit (Haynes, 1924/1978, p. 297).

Elizabeth Ross Haynes's focus on involving people in their own problem solving is most apparent in her admonition to women to move forward and seek opportunities for personal growth and development instead of pushing their men forward. She felt that women needed to mobilize and have a voice in the politics that affected their lives. She believed that the time was right "for women … to step forward as aspirants, bargainers, and if necessary, contenders for the choicest official plum" (Haynes, n.d.). Haynes similarly encouraged all African American women to struggle constantly against restricted job opportunities and to search for economic independence.

Making Agency Data Publicly Useful

Finally, a fourth building block of empowerment practice involves making agency data publicly useful. Both George Haynes and Elizabeth Ross Haynes were social scientists who conducted scholarly research and presented their findings via public speeches, published articles, and books. Elizabeth published scholarly research on African American women's labor issues entitled *Two Million Negro Women at Work* and *Negroes in Domestic Service in the United States*. She also disseminated knowledge through consultation with various organizations and institutions, including the U.S. Department of Labor's Women in Industry Service. In 1921, Ross Haynes published *Unsung Heroes*, a children's book, and in 1952, she completed *The Black Boy of Atlanta*, a biography of Major Richard Robert Wright, a college president and banker. Her works aimed to impart information and to engender race pride and understanding. Ross Haynes became a writer of some prominence. A Los Angeles YWCA girls' group voted to name its club the "Elizabeth Ross Haynes Club" in honor of her work with the YWCA and her literacy contributions. Her literary prowess was further recognized with her acceptance of an invitation to become an honorary member of the International Mark Twain Society, a public acclaim for her contributions to literature.

George Haynes was a prolific writer, completing more than 60 articles and five books during his lifetime. Like his wife, his research was disseminated via books, articles, speeches, and reports. The Columbia University Press published his doctoral dissertation, *The Negro at Work in New York City*, in 1912. He also published several other books including *The Trend of the Races* (1922) and *Africa—Continent of the Future* (1950).

Haynes was also a meticulous record keeper and wrote elaborate and copious reports that became part of the public record of the Fisk University Department of Social Sciences or the NUL. For example, his account of the events surrounding the East Nashville Fire of 1916 provided a clear and detailed description of each step that Haynes, his associate, the students, and others who joined the relief work took throughout the process. Haynes disseminated this report to various individuals and organizations across the country, including B. G. Brawley, Dean at Morehouse College in Atlanta; Roswell McCrea, Dean of the Wharton School of Finance and Commerce in Philadelphia; and the NUL's Executive Board (Carlton-LaNey, 1987).

In sum, George Haynes and Elizabeth Ross Haynes's careers, based on the elements and dimensions that identify African American social work and social welfare practice (Carlton-LaNey, 1999) exemplified the aspects of empowerment practice that emerged between 1883 and 1917. The way that they approached their work may not appear surprising to today's reader, but an understanding of the obstacles and barriers that stood before them during the early part of the 20th century makes their career successes quite extraordinary. The fact that their stories are largely untold and their contributions generally ignored is also extraordinary and unacceptable in a profession that embraces diversity and stands as a model for other disciplines and fields of human services.

References

Abramovitz, M. (1998). Social work and social reform: An arena of struggle. *Social Work, 43*, 512–526.

Ak'bar, N. (1984). Afrocentric social services for human liberation. *Journal of Black Studies, 14*, 395–413.

Carlton-LaNey, I. B. (1985). Fisk social work students' emergency relief work following the East Nashville fire of 1916. *Tennessee Historical Quarterly*, *44*, 371–379.

Carlton-LaNey, I. B. (1997). Elizabeth Ross Haynes: An African American reformer of womanist consciousness, 1908–1940. *Social Work*, *42*, 573–583.

Carlton-LaNey, I. B. (1999). African American social worker pioneers' response to need. *Social Work*, *44*, 311–321.

Chandler, S. (1995). That biting, stinging thing which ever shadows us: African-American social workers in France during World War I. *Social Service Review*, *20*, 408–514.

Daly, A., Jennings, J., Beckett, J., & Leashore, B. (1995). Effective coping strategies of African Americans. *Social Work*, *40*, 240–248.

Drake, S., & Cayton, H. (1945). *Black metropolis*. New York: Harper & Row.

DuBois, W. E. B. (1912). Play for Negroes. *Survey*, *28*, 614–642.

Frazier, E. (1965). E. Franklin Frazier on the ambivalence of Negro intellectuals. In F. Broderick & A. Meier (Eds.), *Negro protest thought in the 20th century* (pp. 97–102). New York: The Bobbs-Merrill Company, Inc. (Original work published in 1927).

Fulks, B. (1969). *Black struggle*. New York: Dell Publishing Company.

Gordon, L. (1991). Black and white visions of welfare: Women's welfare activism, 1890–1945. *Journal of American History*, *78*, 559–590.

Haynes, April 12, 1910, George Edmund Haynes Papers, Fisk University.

Haynes, E. (1923). Negroes in domestic service in the United States. *Journal of Negro History*, 8, 507–565.

Haynes, G. (1978). Negro migration: Its effects on family and community life in the north. In E. Ross (Ed.), *Black heritage in social welfare 1860–1930* (pp. 293–297). Metuchen, NJ: Scarecrow Press. (Original work published 1924)

Kolko, G. (1963). *The triumph of conservatism: A reinterpretation of American history, 1900–1916*. Chicago: Quadrangle Books.

Locke, A. (Ed.). (1965). *The new Negro*. In F. Broderick & A. Meier (Eds.), *Negro protest thought in the 20th century* (pp. 91–92). New York: Bobbs-Merrill Company. (Original work published 1925)

Martin, E. P., & Martin, J. M. (1995). *Social work in the Black experience*. Washington, DC: NASW Press.

Peebles-Wilkins, W., & Koerin, B. (1992). Moral goodness and Black women: Late nineteenth century community caregivers. In N. Reid & P. Popple (Eds.), *The moral purposes of social work* (pp. 155–172). Chicago: Nelson-Hall Publishers.

Ross, E. (1909). Report to the YWCA Board; YWCA Archives, New York.

Simon, B. (1994). *The empowerment tradition in American social work: A history.* New York: Columbia University Press.

Turner, R. (1991). Affirming consciousness: The Africentric perspective. In J. E. Everett, S. S. Chipungu, & B. Leashore (Eds.), *Child welfare: An Africentric perspective* (pp. 36–57). New Brunswick, NJ: Rutgers University Press.

Weiss, N. (1974). *The National Urban league, 1910–1940.* New York: Oxford University Press.

CHAPTER 9

Janie Porter Barrett and the Virginia Industrial School for Colored Girls

Community Response to the Needs of African American Children

Wilma Peebles-Wilkins

Virginia will not forget that she is indebted to the colored women of the Commonwealth for the Industrial Home School.

—J. E. Davis, 1920

Historically, African American child welfare services have evolved as a response to exclusion, differential treatment, segregation, and other forms of racial oppression (Billingsley & Giovannoni, 1972; Smith, 1991; Stehno, 1988). Internal social reform and selective services for African American children have resulted from mutual aid–oriented responses on the part of African American churches and voluntary associations and benevolence originating from interracial cooperation, the work of Caucasian philanthropists, and governmental sponsorship. The Virginia Industrial School for Colored Girls, founded in 1915, was initially maintained by the Virginia Federation of Colored Women's Clubs through organized interracial cooperation. Existing today as the Barrett Learning Center, this institution responded to dependent and delinquent African American girls and exemplifies the fulfillment of one of the national directives of the National Association of Colored Women. Using guiding principles from educational theory and from the Child Welfare Department of the Russell Sage Foundation (forerunner of the Child Welfare League of America), the Virginia Industrial School, under the leadership of Janie Porter Barrett, provided "convincing reform efforts" by means of a humanistic living and learning environment and preparation for transition to the community (Davis, 1920, p. 358).

Child Welfare Work and the African American Community

Between 1877 and 1900, the status of African Americans was being socially redefined (Ogbu, 1978). In general, conditions for impoverished African American children in the South were deplorable. Emancipation resulted in the problem of who would care for dependent African American children. African American children were excluded from any meaningful and structured governmental care aside from the in-home services offered to former slave families by a few pre–Civil War private orphanages (Billingsley & Giovannoni, 1972, pp. 27–33), the orphanages established by the short-lived Freedman's Bureau and almshouses. Mutual aid organizations and voluntary associations or self-help efforts became the dominant mode of care for dependent African American children immediately after emancipation and beyond (Billingsley & Giovannoni, 1972). African American status was based on separation laws and customs between 1900 and 1930 (Ogbu, 1978), and the existing governmental child welfare system was not adequately responding to the needs of African American children.

The child-saving activities of the mid-nineteenth through the early twentieth centuries led to the establishment of industrial schools and other institutions primarily for the care of poor Caucasian immigrant children who were dependent, abused, neglected, or delinquent. For the most part, African American children were not the focus of the early crusade for children. Although the juvenile court system was established as early as 1899, the practice of putting African American children in jail persisted in many communities well into the twentieth century. In 1976 in Virginia, for example, 75 years after the practice was prohibited by state law, a large number of children under age 15 were still being jailed, generating community concern ("Child Jailings," 1976). As segregation customs and laws persisted, young dependent African American children were either jailed or sent to reform schools even when not delinquent because communities were slow to respond to the need for home finding and family-based foster care services for African American children.

During the early decades of the twentieth century, voluntary associations founded by African American women began to confront the unmet needs of African American children and youth. Kindergartens, day nurseries, and schools for dependent and delinquent African American children were developed in response to the racial uplift mandates emanating from the philosophy of the National Association of Colored Women. Founded in 1896, this association represented African American club women from coast to coast in about 40 states. Its organizational philosophy was promulgated by the first president, Mary Church Terrell, whose words (1899) are typical of the club women's collective moral authority in the African American community:

> As an Association, let us devote ourselves enthusiastically, conscientiously, to the children. . . . Through the children of today, we must build the foundation of the next generation upon such a rock of integrity, morality, and strength, both of body and mind, that the floods of proscription, prejudice, and persecution may descend upon it in torrents, and yet it will not be moved. We hear a great deal about the

> race problem, and how to solve it . . . but the real solution of the race problem, both so far as we who are oppressed and those who oppress us are concerned, lies in the children. (p. 346)

The perceived internal social reform duties of African American club women to the race are best chronicled and understood through their autobiographical and other personal and biographical accounts. Community perceptions, as expressed in anecdotal accounts in the African American news media, are also useful. For the most part, child welfare services that developed through the club women's movement were residual in nature and were replaced by institutionalized social welfare arrangements after the Great Depression. After the Progressive Era, the broader crusade for children, as noted by Chambers (1963), expanded into other family welfare areas, and the new focus was on developing non-institutionally based services. These changes undoubtedly had some impact on services for African American children. Some private services for the children persisted until the 1940s, but these were discontinued because of inadequate funding and likely also because of increased governmental alternatives for the African American community after World War II (Axinn & Levin, 1982). Others persisted as privately supported institutions, and still others were subsumed under state auspices.

For example, in Kansas City, Missouri, the Colored Big Sister Home for Girls, founded by Fredericka Douglass Sprague Perry in 1934, existed as a state-contracted private institution through the 1940s. Perry, together with the Colored Big Sister Association, began the first home-finding services for African American children in Kansas City, Missouri, because standard home placement services by the local Community Charities Chest Committee were not available to African American children. Instead, dependent young girls released from the local orphanage at age 12 were sent to the state institution for delinquents until the age of 17. Home-finding efforts eventually culminated in the establishment of a residential care facility. The Big Sister Home helped these young girls move into the community by affording access to schools, training in homemaking skills, and employment placements in private homes (Peebles-Wilkins, 1989, p. 40). Another example of institution-building involved the founding by Carrie Steele of an orphanage in Georgia to care for infants and children she found abandoned in the Atlanta Terminal Railroad Station where she worked as a maid. The Carrie Steele Orphan Home was constructed and chartered as a nonprofit institution in 1888 after a successful community fund-raising effort by Steele. She had previously been caring for these children in her own home at night and watching them play in the terminal by day. In 1923, the Home became a United Way–supported agency and exists today as the Carrie Steele-Pitts Home, serving about one hundred neglected, abused, abandoned, or orphaned children of all races, from six to 18 years of age (*Carrie Steele-Pitts Home, Inc.*, 1988). The Virginia Federation of Club Women turned the Virginia Industrial School over to the state in 1920; today it continues to operate as the Barrett Learning Center in Hanover County, Virginia, a public agency for juvenile delinquents of all races (Table 1 presents a chronological development of the Virginia Industrial School).

Table 1. *Chronological Development of the Virginia Industrial School*

Date	*Historical Development*
1911	Fund-raising began
January 1913	147 acre farm site purchased for Virginia Industrial Home School for Colored Girls
May 1913	First board meeting
January 1915	First two girls admitted
November 1915	Barrett appointed superintendent
1916	First cottage built
1919	Second cottage and school building added
1920	Placed under state control, renamed Virginia Industrial School for Colored Girls
1927	Superintendent's residence built
1940	Barrett retires as superintendent
1950	Renamed Janie Porter Barrett School for Girls
1965	School is racially integrated
1970s	Renamed Barrett Learning Center

Source: Compiled from the cited primary source data in the Peabody Collection, *Leader* (1916); Hampton University and the *Virginia Welfare Bulletin* (1956).

Barrett's Home School

Internal child welfare reform and services by African American club women, like settlement house services provided by Lillian Wald and Jane Addams, reflected the personality traits of the founders (Kogut, 1972). Such was the case with the Virginia Industrial School for Colored Girls with its flowering, landscaped campus. Scott (1992, p. 90), noting that the Virginia Industrial School became a model school that other states tried to emulate, described a visible atmosphere of trust and hope attributable to Barrett's personality. In addition to her unique skills in facilitating a growth-promoting milieu at her home school, Barrett's skill in developing and maintaining interracial group support also contributed to the amount of financial and material resources available and the level of broad-based community endorsement for the school. Barrett's successful approach to delinquent African American girls was likely the result of a combination of her ability to effectively incorporate consultation from Hastings Hart of the Russell Sage Foundation and child welfare practices later promoted by C. C. Carstens, first director of the Child Welfare League of America.

Janie Porter Barrett was born in Athens, Georgia. She was reared as a family member in the Skinner home, where her mother was employed as a housekeeper and seamstress. Educated in mathematics and literature in a Caucasian family, she was exposed to persons of privilege and refinement and grew up with a lifestyle atypical of the African American community. Her mother later sent her to Hampton Institute in Virginia, where she was trained as an elementary school teacher. At Hampton, Barrett (1926) was inculcated with patriotic, altruistic values and a sense of duty to her race, learning lessons "in love of race, love of fellow-men, and love of country" (p. 361). Her worldview led to the development of an industrial home school based on a philosophy of social and human development lodged in educational programming.

The Industrial Home for (Wayward) Colored Girls opened its doors in Hanover County near Richmond in 1915 on a 147-acre site purchased by the Virginia Federation of Colored Women's Clubs, an organization also founded by Barrett, its first president, between 1907 and 1908 (Peebles-Wilkins, 1987). At the time the school was founded, it was estimated that about 500 young African American girls needed supervised care, training, and rehabilitation. The farmland with a farmhouse had been purchased in 1914, but the federation had been gradually raising money since 1911 and anticipated paying for the land in full after five years (Aery, 1915). Urged on, however, by the sentencing of an eight-year-old African American girl to six months in jail, "every woman gave until she could feel it" (Barrett, 1926, p. 356). Having raised $5,300, the federation paid for the land, chartered the school, and designated the farmhouse as Federation Cottage after the club women's organization. Barrett's encounter with the judge to get custody of the eight-year-old girl gives us a glimpse of differential perceptions and the handling of dependent African American girls by the Virginia juvenile justice system.

Prior to establishing the Industrial Home, Barrett had already established a Child Welfare Department at the Locust Street Settlement. In addition to providing guidance for young mothers and helping children through adolescence, a committee from the Child Welfare Department had been successfully removing under age African American children from jail to alternative placements (Daniel, 1931, pp. 57–58). A Negro reform school had been founded by the Virginia African American community as early as 1897 (Ludlow, 1904), but putting African American children in jail and the lack of differential planning for dependent African American children persisted. Barrett read about the sentencing of the eight-year-old child in the newspaper and immediately appealed to the judge in Newport News, Virginia, to send the child to the Weaver Orphan Home in Hampton, Virginia, where Barrett was living. The judge, viewing the child as a criminal who was in court because African American women needed to look after their children, only reluctantly released the child into Barrett's care. Thus, Barrett (1926) was able to "save Virginia the disgrace of making a baby like this serve a sentence" (pp. 355–356).

A juvenile court was established in Newport News shortly after Barrett's encounter, but this rather dramatic example of the need for a more specialized facility for dependent African American children served to raise the consciousness of both the African American and Caucasian middle class communities. The federation quickly recognized that the support of men and women of both races was necessary to fully realize its goals.

Some state support was necessary to supplement private fund-raising, but the Virginia state governmental system had a practice of not allowing any women—Caucasian or African American—to receive and manage funds. For the facility to be considered for a state financial appropriation, a board consisting of Caucasian women and businessmen was recommended. Barrett, however, recognized that continued and active participation by the African American community was essential to ensure the success of the girls and the home school. (For example, some of the private fund-raising was associated with donors who had been cultivated by Hampton Institute.) Although organizing an interracial board in segregated Virginia was discouraged, after much persistence and with a great deal of effort, Barrett was able to organize such a board of both men and women from the North and South to obtain a small state supplement (Aery, 1915). The school opened in spite of "vigorous protests" from the local Caucasian community, with Barrett stating, "Beg them to give us a chance—to try us. If the school proves objectionable, I promise to move it" (Daniel, 1931, p. 59). To ensure success of her home school, she took on the position of superintendent. Board members, along with federation club members, played key roles in supporting Barrett as superintendent, raising funds, visiting similar schools in the North, enlisting community endorsement, and helping to identify homes where girls could be placed when ready for the community.

Although sources do not afford a great many details on the child welfare consultation provided to the Industrial School, the operations of the school itself shed light on the influences of the Child Welfare Department of the Russell Sage Foundation and of the standards set by the Child Welfare League of America between 1921 and 1925. The delinquency institution was expected to have social responsibilities, which included ensuring that institutionalization was the last resort, providing adequate preparation for parole once children were admitted, and conducting investigation and follow-up in discharge planning (Harrison, 1985, pp. 590–594). Before officially opening the home school, advice about industrial training was sought from Dr. Hastings Hart at Russell Sage. The Russell Sage Foundation cottage plan was used to create a homelike environment for the girls. The operations of the cottage system and the overall operations and goals of the industrial home for girls modeled the social responsibilities of a delinquency institution. Barrett's pioneering leadership style in relation to the delinquent is best characterized as transformational. The home school was viewed as a "moral hospital," and the word *wayward*, although popular vernacular during the time, was never used by the school even though it does appear in the early media (Aery, 1915; Daniel, 1931; "An Industrial School," 1913; "Schools for Wayward Girls," 1916).

Admissions and Intake

All residents were admitted to the home school on referral from the State Board of Welfare. Ultimately, all girls admitted were considered incorrigible and without other placement options in the community. In addition to Harris Barrett's cottage, the superintendent's residence and three other cottages were on the campus of the industrial home school, including Federation Cottage, the farmhouse part of the initial purchase and the Hanover and Virginia Cottages, built with additional state appropriations

Table 2. *Barrett's Behavioral Marking System (Demerits)*

Escapes	All Credits	Quarreling	50
Insubordination	350–1500	Discourtesy	10
Stealing	150	Inattention	10
Lying	150	Laziness	50–200
Impudence	150	Disorder	10
Insolence	150	Uncleanliness	50
Disrespect	150	Fighting	150–200
Disobedience	25–100	Carelessness	10

Source: Barrett's Seventh Annual Report, cited by Daniel (1931, p. 69).

(Aery, 1919, pp. 473–474). Virginia Cottage was used for the intake and admissions process. Upon arrival, each girl was assigned to Virginia Cottage for social assessment; "I require them to tell me the whole truth about their past . . . when I know everything, I understand better how to help" (as quoted in Daniel, 1931, p. 61). Then, starting with a clean slate, a peer system with Big Sister assignments was used to help each resident learn the school's expectations. After a 10-day period of instruction about the rules and regulations, girls were given demerits for lapses in behavior, personal appearance, and work habits, and negative points were accumulated. Table 2 shows the marking system.

The school operated on an honor system, with each girl working toward becoming an "honor girl" wearing the "white dress," and being promoted to Federation Cottage, the highest of the cottages. Discipline at the home school was strict, with team groups consisting of ten residents assigned a team lieutenant and a captain to monitor behavior. School matrons followed up on any necessary disciplinary action. In addition to the demerit system, silences were also used as a form of discipline. A biographical account of Janie Porter Barrett by Daniel mentions, without giving descriptive details, a "Thinking Room" for the "development of moral strength" (Daniel, 1931, p. 68). One is left with the impression that the so-called "thinking room" was some form of isolation resembling "quiet rooms" used in psychodynamic forms of therapeutic treatment for children who lose control.

Preparation

The goal of the industrial home school was to help each girl gain self-control and develop home-life skills in preparation for independent community living. The home school, like other educational programs for African American girls, was focused on domestic sciences and household skills. Preparation for jobs accessible to African American women was a programmatic goal that concentrated on social role adaptation in the face of racial segregation and oppression; well into the 1950s, the majority of African American women were employed as domestics. Educational preparation paralleled the public school curriculum through grade 8, and the academic content was supplemented with other opportunities such as programs to promote English-proficiency skills. Religious training, crop harvesting, and household management were all part of the vocational education program. Applied agricultural training was instituted on the basis of two rotating teams, one of farm girls learning to work the farm and the other of house girls learning household management. A supply-demand approach was used because household domestics were more easily placed. Like contemporary chef school or contemporary culinary arts training programs, the residents actually prepared the dining table and meals. Neighbors in the community helped subsidize the school by giving the residents laundry and sewing work. Such community services no doubt strengthened Barrett's relationship with the neighbors.

The curriculum also included appreciation for nature and pleasurable use of leisure time, such as bird-watching, plant growing, and a range of sports, theater, and other organized recreational activities. "Clean, straight living" (Barrett, 1926, p. 357) could be considered the hallmark of the institution. Patriotism and responsible citizenship were stressed even though the residents often expressed skepticism in the face of differential treatment, segregation, and oppression. As in the segregated public schools, Negro History Week was observed and celebrated during the second week of February. The purpose of this observance was to instill racial pride and to teach residents about the accomplishments of successful African American men and women.

Several other prevailing themes that characterize a humanistic but structured, kind, and caring learning environment are identifiable in descriptions of the home school's pedagogy and day-to-day operations. Highly valuing and taking pride in her education at Hampton Institute, Barrett was committed to transmitting to others the lessons she learned there. The Golden Rule was applied at the school, and behavioral expectations were applied both to personnel and to residents. As one might anticipate, attendance and staff shortages were an administrative concern. Personnel were expected to be committed, efficient, and trained, with "sane judgment, kind hearts, and the ability to direct intelligently" (Daniel, 1931, p. 70; Davis, 1920, p. 364). Cooperation from residents was enlisted by not embarrassing or humiliating any of the girls. Each girl was accepted, given the chance to start over, and treated kindly ("Hampton Woman Honored," 1916). Open communication and free expression were supported by impromptu "open forums" for group discussion, as requested by the residents. "Character training exercises issued by the National Association of Child Welfare (Child Welfare League)" were also used, and there were group discussions and problem-solving sessions based on life course simulations (Daniel, 1931, p. 67).

Parole

Girls were honorably released from the institution after successful completion of parole, which was possible after two years of satisfactory performance. Home school residents could be paroled to employment situations under supervision in either African American or Caucasian homes or to their own families. The investigation process described by C. C. Carstens was carried out by an application and screening process that eventually included investigation and approval by the state welfare department. After approval and a thorough explanation of a resident's needs and supervision requirements, a contractual agreement was signed between the Industrial School and the employer family. Each resident was required to send two dollars of her earnings back to the home school. A bank account was established for each girl. Initially, one dollar went into her bank account and the other dollar was credited to the institution until costs associated with a clothing allowance purchase for parole were recovered. Afterwards, all the money went into the resident's account, and the resident left the institution with money when officially discharged. In addition to written communication between Barrett and the residents, reports were required from the individual responsible for the parolee. If the resident had difficulty adjusting, more contact between the home and the school was required. Early on, Barrett began to see the need for a parole officer to do close follow-up supervision.

Paroling residents to their own homes was less frequent. Socioeconomic and environmental circumstances caused concern about the residents' vulnerability to prostitution and other avenues to illegal income. Barrett expressed the need for child welfare advocacy for poor families as a deterrent to delinquency.

Discharge

After two years of successful parole, the residents were discharged with a graduation or a closing exercise. In a 14-year period, 33 percent of the residents were discharged because they were no longer minors, about 42 percent were discharged after successful parole, two percent of the residents had died, and less than a half a percent of the girls had successfully run away (see Table 3).

Table 3. *Admission Outcomes, 1915–1929 (N=823)*

Discharged after parole	343
Discharged due to majority age	272
In community school	100
Died	20
Transferred to:	
Hospitals for feebleminded	20
Piedmont Tuberculosis Sanatorium	2
State Board of Welfare	3
Ran away, still at large	4
Paroled under supervision	59

Source: Table is a modification of statistics reported in Daniel (1931, p. 77).

Anecdotal accounts do suggest parole recidivism and residents with poor health status. These factors, coupled with admission during the late teens and the inability to comply consistently with the rules of the system, likely account for the 33 percent of the residents who stayed in the institution and were released when they became adults.

Conclusion

This article examines one historical response by the African American community to the exclusion of African American children from turn-of-the-century child welfare services. As Barrett (1926) noted:

> Rendering service, climbing to a higher plane of citizenship, and uplifting those farthest down was what the women of the Virginia Federation had in mind when they started out to establish the Virginia Industrial School. At that time there was no place except the jail for a colored girl who fell into the hands of the law; so there was no question about the need for such an institution. (p. 355)

Today, one of the prevailing concerns in the child welfare system involves overinclusion of African American and other minority children in the existing forms of out-of-home care. Juvenile detention is sometimes the only available recourse for African Americans from low-income families, who should instead receive outpatient therapy, adequate child care, or sufficient family preservation services.

The considerations associated with the entrapment of minority children in out-of-home placements extend far beyond the juvenile justice system and expand to the entire child welfare system. Certainly, many of these considerations are manifestations of unemployment, poverty, the breakdown of the family structure, and other life circumstances associated with oppression and social and economic injustices. For these reasons, it is the philosophical response to oppression described in this historical account that has the greatest relevance for contemporary child welfare services.

Several prevailing themes of equal importance are noteworthy in this example of internal social reform within the African American community:

- Collective responsibility and self-development as well as external community involvement and interracial cooperation
- Description of life circumstances and advocacy for the needs of children
- Utilization of the existing knowledge base about the needs of children and quality child welfare services
- Collaborative efforts of the public and private sector to promote new service initiatives
- Employment of trained personnel for humane and skillful child welfare interventions
- Persistent and consistent concern for the quality of care

- Instilling children with values that promote responsible citizenship and social responsibility
- Development of personal and racial pride by means of programs that preserve racial heritage and promote social justice
- Dedication, commitment, and concern for others.

The contemporary crisis in youth services is complicated by the increasing prevalence of drugs, gang involvement, and violent juvenile crimes. As the child welfare system continues to seek innovations, current initiatives for African American children should be informed by the past. The present account suggests that, at a minimum, quality child welfare services for the African American community should involve the training, hiring, and continued professional development of all child welfare workers by means of such opportunities as those available in the Title IV-E training grants. Communities that still have a shortage of African American and other minority social workers should develop aggressive efforts to ensure the inclusion of these workers in hiring and training efforts. Diversity training and promotion of culturally sensitive assessment and intervention strategies should be included in supervision and staff development. Social support network analysis and the inclusion of these networks in child welfare service plans are also important goals (Thompson & Peebles-Wilkins, 1992; Tracy, 1990).

(Reprinted by special permission of the Child Welfare League of America from Child Welfare, *Vol. LXXIV, No. 1, 1995, pp. 143–161.)*

References

Aery, W. A. (1915, November). Helping wayward girls. *Southern Workman*, 598–604. Hampton, VA: Peabody Collection, Hampton University.

Aery, W. A. (1919, October). Industrial Home School for Colored Girls at Peake in Hanover County, VA. *Southern Workman*, 473–474. Hampton, VA: Peabody Collection, Hampton University.

An Industrial School for wayward girls. (1913, July 3). *New York Age*. Hampton, VA: Peabody Clipping Book 28, Huntington Memorial Library, Hampton University.

Axinn, J., & Levin, H. (1982). *Social welfare: A history of the American response to need* (2nd ed.). New York: Longman Press.

Barrett, J. P. (1926, August). The Virginia Industrial School. *Southern Workman, 55*, 352–361. Hampton, VA: Peabody Collection, Hampton University.

Billingsley, A., & Giovannoni, J. M. (1972). *Children of the storm: Black children and American child welfare*. New York: Harcourt, Brace, Jovanovich, Inc.

Carrie Steele-Pitts Home, Inc. 100 Years, 1888–1988: Share the Legacy. (1988). Atlanta, GA: Author.

Chambers, C. A. (1963). *Seedtimes of reform*. Minneapolis, MN: University of Minnesota Press.

Child jailings decline in Virginia. (1976). Richmond, VA: Education and Schools Industrial, Juvenile Delinquency Clipping Files, Richmond Public Library.

Daniel, S. (1931). *Women builders*. Washington, DC: Associated Publishers.

Davis, J. E. (1920, August). A Virginia asset: The Virginia Industrial School for Colored Girls. *Southern Workman, 49*, 357–364. Hampton, VA: Peabody Collection, Hampton University.

Hampton woman honored. (1916, February 23). *Amsterdam News*. Hampton, VA: Peabody Clipping Book 28, Huntington Memorial Library, Hampton University.

Harrison, D. (1985). C. C. Carstens: Permanency planning pioneer. *Child Welfare, 64*, 587–597.

Janie Porter Barrett School for Girls. (1956, February). *Virginia Welfare Bulletin, 34*(2), 9. Richmond, VA: Education and Schools Industrial, Juvenile Delinquency Clipping Files, Richmond Public Library.

Kogut, A. (1972). The settlements and ethnicity: 1890–1914. *Social Work, 17*, 22–31.

Ludlow, H. (1904). Virginia Negro Reform School. *Southern Workman, 33*, 606–616. Hampton, VA: Peabody Collection, Hampton University.

Negro Home School building to be dedicated. (1916, May 9). *Leader*. Hampton, VA: Peabody Clipping Book 28, Huntington Memorial Library, Hampton University.

Ogbu, J. (1978). *Minority education and caste*. New York: Academic Press.

Peebles-Wilkins, W. (1987). Janie Porter Barrett (1865–1948). In A. Minahan (Ed.), *Encyclopedia of social work*, 2, (pp. 914–915). Washington, DC: NASW.

Peebles-Wilkins, W. (1989). Black women and American social welfare: The life of Fredericka Douglass Sprague Perry. *Affilia, 4*(1), 33–44.

Schools for wayward girls. (1916, February 6). *Chicago Defender*. Hampton, VA: Peabody Clipping Book 28, Huntington Memorial Library, Hampton University.

Scott, A. F. (1992). Janie Porter Barrett. In D. C. Hine (Ed.), *Black women in America: An historical encyclopedia* (pp. 90–92). New York: Carlson Publishing Company.

Smith, E. P. (1991, March). *Promoting policy change through funding withdrawal: The Race Discrimination Amendment of 1942*. Presentation at Social Welfare History Group Symposium, Council on Social Work Education, Atlanta, GA.

Stehno, S. M. (1988). Public responsibility for dependent Black children: The advocacy of Edith Abbott and Sophonisba Breckinridge. *Social Service Review*, 485–489.

Terrell, M. C. (1899). The duty of the National Association of Colored Women to the race. *Church Review* (pp. 340–354). In Mary Church Terrell Papers. Washington, DC: Moorland-Spingarn Research Center, Howard University.

Thompson, M., & Peebles-Wilkins, W. (1992). The impact of formal, informal, and societal support networks on the psychological well-being of Black adolescent mothers. *Social Work, 37*, 322–328.

Tracy, E. M. (1990). Identifying social support resources of at-risk families. *Social Work, 35*, 252–258.

CHAPTER 10

Eugene Kinckle Jones

A Statesman for the Times

Felix L. Armfield
Iris B. Carlton-LaNey

Eugene Kinckle Jones (1885–1954) grew up in an integrated environment in Richmond, Virginia. This was unusual, given the entrenchment of Jim Crow segregation. Both of Jones's parents were well educated and taught in African American institutions of higher education. His father taught theology at Virginia Union College for Negroes, and his mother was a music teacher at Hartshorn Memorial College for African American women. As a youth, Jones witnessed his parents' peer interactions with White intellectuals in and about Richmond.

Upon the completion of his studies at Virginia Union College in 1905, Jones enrolled at Cornell University in Ithaca, New York, to pursue a master's degree in mathematics and engineering. After one year, however, he refocused and instead completed his studies in economics and social science, graduating with a master's degree in 1908. With his impressive credentials in hand, Jones confronted the color line that he found limited his employment options to teaching in the private and public schools for Negroes in Louisville, Kentucky (Kinckle Jones Report, 1932). There he met the prominent social worker and sociologist, George Edmund Haynes, who proposed that he come to New York and work for the newly formed League on Urban Conditions Among Negroes (Jones, 1940, p. 7), which Haynes cofounded.

When Jones arrived in New York City in 1911 to accept the position of field secretary for the League on Urban Conditions Among Negroes (renamed National Urban League [NUL] in 1920), he became an energetic advocate for African American migrants; he began his lifelong commitment to legitimize the African American social worker's professional authority. Jones's first major task involved assessing and reporting on the conditions of African American life in New York City. He assumed the responsibility for helping migrants to become acculturated to their new urban environments, often meeting new arrivals at the train depot and assisting them in finding housing and employment. Equal access to employment opportunities was denied to African Americans, a phenomenon that Jones had experienced. In an effort to deal with employment discrimination, Jones met with personnel in industries and business firms to discuss and arrange for expanded employment opportunities. Many firms had quotas for hiring African Americans, and other employers used them only as strikebreakers, a practice that fueled the flames of hostility among White workers (Weiss, 1974). Jones also intervened with employment bureaus on behalf of juveniles and adults. He helped to negotiate contracts for African American men, placed personnel workers in industrial plants, and generally tried to raise the visibility of "Negro" workers.

By 1916, Jones had been officially appointed executive secretary of the NUL. Over the next four years, the northward migration of African American men and women increased rapidly. Jones recognized the need for more professional social workers to serve this growing population. He, along with other African American social workers, tried to convince white social workers of the need to address the race question. Jones devised a plan of action for the African American social work movement based upon the ideals of interracial cooperation. Jones believed that basic racial misunderstanding was the source of many problems. He was convinced that "the development of harmonious relations between the races by getting the best elements of the two races to work together" would address the problems of racial disharmony. He also believed that forming "joint committees of white and [C]olored people to attack the social problems of Negroes and of the community at large" was a strategic solution (Jones, 1923/1978, pp. 417–418). The notion of African American and White social workers working together as colleagues was not a comfortable one for many White social workers, and the fear that any long-range alliance with African American social workers might weaken their goals of professional recognition was a pervasive one.

The decades of the 1920s and 1930s proved to be extremely active years for Jones. As the spokesperson for the NUL, he found his duties constantly expanding. The 1920s were a decade of constant political, social, and economic change for African Americans. In spite of the major cultural awakening of the Harlem Renaissance, African Americans continued to find themselves politically and economically marginalized. During this time, many African Americans migrated north to escape the oppression of the South, but upon their arrival, they found mounting racial discrimination in housing, jobs, and education. The Great Depression only made these already bad conditions worse for the newly arriving urban migrants. In the midst of these economic hard times, Jones was always working to further the goals of the NUL, with fundraising responsibilities claiming a major part of his time. Fundraising was a continuing challenge, and Jones noted that many White philanthropists were rather stingy with their financial giving to African Americans, especially during the late 1920s and 1930s. Nonetheless, the NUL received some of its operating funds from noted philanthropists such as J. D. Rockefeller, Julius Rosenwald, and Andrew Carnegie. Feeling the strain of keeping the NUL afloat, Jones confided to Gunnar Myrdal in 1940 that even leading philanthropists

> will give small sums to Negro causes seemingly as balm to their consciences. They frequently will give to *one* Negro cause only as evidence of their "interest in the Negro" while contributing to as many different white organizations as are represented by phases of social work in which they are interested. (Jones, 1940, pp. 3–4)

Coupled with the already demanding duties of the day-to-day operation of the NUL, Jones's schedule of appointments and appearances around the country on behalf of the League were ever-expanding. During this decade, Jones was instrumental in laying the foundation that moved the NUL into national prominence. *The New York Times* "Editorial" on April 27, 1932, reported that "the name The National Urban League does not convey to many the purpose of this organization. But when it is known that KINCKLE JONES is its administrative secretary, its identity is better recognized" (Jones, 1932). Jones was polished, sophisticated, and naturally conservative with a no-nonsense approach to dealing with the social problems confronting African Americans.

Through a host of activities, Jones was able to cultivate the national image of the League. Soft-spoken and non-confrontational toward the status quo, he quickly became the noted, handsome, refined, and skillful leader of the NUL. Jones was also non-threatening, a trait that made him acceptable to a varied audience. He was highly sought after for public speaking engagements such as radio broadcasts, commencement speeches, and addresses to local branches of the NUL. Jones also worked on special councils, committees, and boards, including the Durham Fact-Finding Conference, the Lincoln House Social Settlement Board in New York, and the NUL's Committee on Race Relations, which developed strategies for appealing to prospective employers for jobs for African Americans.

Historical Outreach

Involved in many aspects of the life of the community, Jones, like many other members of the African American intelligentsia, also played a significant role in the African American intellectual movement of the 1920s—an aspect of his career not generally noted. He was perhaps the most instrumental participant in helping to establish a permanent repository for Arthur A. Schomburg's collection of African American historic artifacts. In 1926, Schomburg approached Jones; L. Hollingsworth Wood, who was the NUL President; and Charles S. Johnson, editor of *Opportunity*, the literary organ for the NUL, to discuss turning over his massive collection of African American memorabilia to the NUL. Schomburg was informed that the NUL was not in a position to take on such a collection, nor could their facilities accommodate the project. Jones, along with Wood and the Director of the New York Public Library, Edwin H. Anderson, decided to approach the Carnegie Foundation. The Carnegie Foundation agreed to purchase the collection for the sum of $10,000 (Sinnette, 1989). A year later, in 1927, the 135th Street Branch Library of the New York Public Library received the collection.

In later years, Jones worked with Schomburg and a group of other notable intellectuals to establish the Associates in Negro Folk Education located in New York City and

Atlanta. The Associates later published the Bronze Booklet Series (from 1935 to 1938) that chronicled African Americans' history in their own words. Through this effort, Jones was involved with many prominent figures, including Charles S. Johnson; Mary McLeod Bethune, founder of Bethune-Cookman College; Franklin Hopper; and Lyman Bryson of Teachers' College, Columbia University (Sinnette, 1989). These activities increased Jones's personal and political powers and further publicized and supported the NUL's agenda.

Jones maintained contact with an impressive list of philanthropic organizations and frequently called upon their officers. These funding sources included institutions and individuals such as the Laura B. Spelman Rockefeller Memorial, the Carnegie Foundation of New York, the Phelps Stokes Fund, Friends of Mrs. Ella Sachs Plotz, and Mrs. L. Hollingsworth Wood. Jones also maintained regular contact with the pioneering schools of social work across the country, including the New York School of Philanthropy, the University of Chicago School of Social Administration, the University of Pittsburgh, and Ohio State University. In addition to the financial concerns of the League and its agenda, Jones was continually promoting the training of African American social workers (Jones, 1928/1971c).

Other NUL affiliates also promoted the ideal of formal training for African American social workers. For example, NUL fellow and director of the Armstrong Association of Philadelphia, Forrester B. Washington (1926/1978), extolled the virtues of the trained social worker, saying "our training in social work has taught us that we live in a changing world and that this change is taking place at a faster rate all the time" (p. 449). The scientific method, he further indicated, "has prepared [social workers] to live in this world of change and to deal with it. It has kept them from accepting any fixed idea of an established system of social work. It has taught them that at the very time they are using methods that have been tested by experience in the past, to be critical of these methods as applied to this changing world." He also noted that the trained social worker is capable of work that "accelerate[s] human progress" and facilitates "the process by which social change takes place" (Washington, 1926/1978, p. 449). A product of the League's training program, Washington's career exemplified the success of the program. The early schools of social work were critical players in the League's long success in producing well trained and committed social workers.

Jones was pleased with the success of the League's training program and spoke of these trained social workers at every opportunity. He worked to further the League's mission and to communicate a message of self-help and education. The radio was fast becoming a popular means of public mass communication. Jones took advantage of the public demand for radio broadcasts. On Sunday, May 16, 1926, he delivered a radio address entitled "Go-To-High School, Go-To-College" and sponsored by Alpha Phi Alpha Fraternity. This broadcast provided an opportunity for Jones to inform young African Americans of the numerous options available to them if they pursued an education. He also claimed in this address that "the past ten years have proved to be the banner period of this age" (Jones, 1926a). Perhaps in an effort to build on African American community strengths, Jones did not focus on the race riots and economic dislocation of African Americans after World War I; instead, he emphasized the accomplishments of the race. Furthermore, Jones declared that "competent teachers, social workers, clergymen and other community leaders are far too few in numbers, and should be augmented from the ranks of the Negro students of today" (Jones, 1926a). Jones always promoted social work as an exciting and meaningful career choice for young African Americans. He lobbied for a greater expansion of secondary and collegiate institutions for African Americans, noting that "the more liberal support of organizations working to secure larger civic and industrial opportunities for the Negro like the National Association for the Advancement of Colored People and the National Urban League" had had tremendous success (Jones, 1926a).

Jones's web of affiliations gave him greater opportunities for effectiveness. He used his fraternity, of which he was a founding member, to provide a forum for presenting issues of national interest to the African American community. Through this coalition, Jones and the Alpha Phi Alpha Fraternity together worked toward the ideals of community uplift (Wesley, 1929). In a 1925 speech delivered at the New York State Conference of Charities and Corrections, Jones stated his mission and challenged the social work profession when he proclaimed:

> The opportunity for statesmanship service to humanity is ours. The obligation is ours. We cannot pass on to posterity the responsibility for work which we should assume. The challenge of democracy is before us. The Negro is probably the real test of democracy in America. (Jones, 1925)

By the mid-1920s, Jones had achieved national prominence. His speaking engagements had grown well beyond the exclusive purview of the social work audience. In 1924, Virginia Union University named Jones one of its distinguished alumni and awarded him an honorary degree of LLD. Jones never broke ties with the university nor the state of Virginia (B. Jones Dowling, personal communication, June 15, 1995). In June 1926, he delivered the commencement address "The Negro's Opportunity Today" at West Virginia Collegiate Institute. Jones read a "Who's Who" list of African Americans, never failing to include the accomplishments and contributions of African American social workers. He proclaimed in a self-referential note, "A colored man is a member of the National Conference of Social Work elected to this Board of fifteen persons by a membership of 4,000 social workers—the overwhelming majority of whom are white" (Jones, 1926b). Jones had been elected the previous year to the executive board of the National Conference of Social Work (NCSW) and served as the organization's treasurer. Essentially, Jones spoke of the numerous achievements of African Americans—always mindful of the distance most had traveled to reach any level of accomplishment. Perhaps one of the most cogent points of the speech was when he boasted:

> Even in America, the Negro brought in as a slave was not introduced into the economic life of the country as a competitor to the white man, but as an aid. I

> doubt whether any statesmen of the periods in which Negroes were brought to America as slaves would have continued the experiment if they had known that 1865 would have recorded Negroes to the number of four million on American soil, eventually to become economic competitors of white men. (Jones, 1926b)

Undoubtedly, such speeches were a source of empowerment for his listeners and brought additional political power to both Jones and the NUL.

Between 1915 and 1930, social workers, African American and White, strove to construct a distinct professional identity. Jones had a direct impact upon the development of this identity through his affiliation as the first African American member of the NCSW's executive board. The NCSW served as the umbrella organization for all other social work entities. It was the parent organization of the American Association of Social Workers (AASW). Established in 1921, the AASW was the most important body of the NCSW throughout the 1920s. One of the organization's objectives was to define and secure professional standards for social work (Chambers, 1971). Throughout the 1920s, academic training institutions became more prominent in the evolutionary process of the social work profession.

During Jones's seven-year stint on the NCSW executive board (1926–1933), he addressed and interpreted the social and economic concerns of the African American community to an integrated national audience. He eventually was elected vice president of the main body of social workers—the NCSW (Jones, 1940). This platform enabled Jones to espouse the concerns of African American social and economic welfare. He was often able to place those concerns on the national agenda of social work activity. For example, Jones continuously argued before the conference the issues of health, economics, and housing as they adversely affected the African American population.

Social work was one of the few professions, at that time, that accepted African Americans and Whites into the same professional organizations. Although it is arguable to what extent this practice was one of equity, Jones and other African American social workers embraced the White social work organization. Jones insisted in 1928 that "there is probably no profession in which Negro members are on as cordial relationships with White members as is that of the social worker" (Jones, 1928/1978, p. 463). His participation with this group supported his opinion that the best people of both races could address the community's problems in intelligent and beneficial ways.

Most other more established professions, for example, medicine, nursing, science, law, and history, practiced segregation or discrimination within their professional memberships during the early twentieth century (Hine, 1989; Manning, 1983; McMurry, 1981; McNeil, 1983; Meier & Rudwick, 1986; Thoms, 1929). In response to this exclusion and in recognition of their unique needs, African Americans created their own professional organizations: African American physicians created the National Medical Association in 1895, attorneys established the National Bar Association in 1925 (McNeil, 1983), and professional nurses created the National Association of Colored Graduate Nurses in 1908 (Hine, 1989).

While African American social workers may not have confronted blatant discrimination within NCSW, their everyday experiences were fraught with Jim Crow practices and insulting behavior from colleagues. This was a grave concern for many African American social workers of the era. Jones often attempted to address these concerns. On one occasion, he wrote to an associate in Boston:

> In our great America, relations between the various elements making up our population—native Protestants, Catholics, Jews, foreigners, Negroes, Indians—need constantly to be watched, that no disturbing propaganda may work havoc to the improving conditions. (Jones to S. A. Allen, July 28, 1926c)

Other problems confronted Jones and the cadre of approximately 500 college-trained African American social workers on the eve of the Great Depression in 1928. The depression had begun to make its way through the African American community long before it hit the masses; the economic hardship forced African American men and women to the fringes of the labor force. Jones worried that there were not adequate numbers of African American social workers to meet the demand. The increasing number of trained African American social workers reflected the efforts of several northern White social service training schools in cooperation with Jones and the League Fellowship Programs. The slow, but steady, progress that the League made in training African American social workers and the seemingly inclusive policies of NCSW toward African American social workers were not enough to make Jones pause in his pursuits. He was convinced that more needed to be done. Following George Haynes's lead, Jones put the training of African American social workers at the top of the NUL's agenda.

In the South, there were only two social work schools by the 1920s that had been established for African Americans—the Atlanta School of Social Work and the Bishop Tuttle Memorial Training School of Social Workers at St. Augustine College in Raleigh, North Carolina. The Atlanta program, established in 1920, offered a general social work approach. The Bishop Tuttle School of Social Work, begun in 1925, specialized in training social workers in conjunction with religious education (Gary & Gary, 1994). In spite of the massive efforts to train African American social workers, the results did not meet the growing demands of a burgeoning urban African American population.

Pushing Ever Forward

Jones continued to push the NUL's agenda forward, although his efforts did not always meet with success. In fact, Jones's proposals met with particular resentment in many parts of the South. Certain southern cities, such as Savannah and Augusta, Georgia; Charleston, South Carolina; Louisville, Kentucky; Richmond, Virginia; Charlotte, North Carolina; and Jacksonville, Florida; were places where Jones's proposals were met with disdain. Jones (1940) stated, "There [the South] in many instances, the proposals I made for Negro welfare had not been considered seriously for Whites. The excuse given for rejecting proposals was frequently frankly stated: 'We are not doing that for white people. Surely you would not expect us to discuss such an undertaking for Negroes'" (p. 4).

Not only were Jones's efforts met with rejection from southern Whites, but also his attempts were often perceived as erroneous or misguided by some African American communities. Jones stated near the end of his career in 1940:

> On the other hand, I often was met with rebuffs from prominent Negroes in the communities where we wished to establish Urban League branches for Negroes. Especially was this true in northern communities where the Negro leadership was based upon fights against segregation. Any social welfare effort in the interest of Negroes was immediately branded as an attempt to segregate them. (Jones, 1940, p. 4)

Migration had already made relations between home people and old settlers in many urban centers uncertain. Recent African American urban population and migration scholarship reveals that the growing tensions between the two groups were not unique to any urban city in particular. However, each city tended to have its own unique situation. For instance, Gottlieb (1991) revealed that with Pittsburgh, "tensions that arose from growing differences of class and culture within the African-American population were not overcome by the rising awareness of a common racial identity" (p. 74). Grossman (1989) stated that "Chicago's black middle-class residents assumed that the migrants had to be guided and controlled from the moment they stepped from the train." Grossman further argued that, "by inculcating restraint, the Old Settlers hope to protect the migrants' souls and pocketbooks, while preserving the community's honor" (p. 145). Chicago's established African American middle-class structure oftentimes resented the idea of segregation; the resentment grew more apparent with the arrival of African American migrants from the South. Kusmer (1976) discovered that the NUL's efforts in Cleveland in the early twentieth century were also slow to gain acceptance in the African American community because residents thought of their type of social work practice as paternal and punitive. They were seen as having "fostered the view that poverty and economic dislocation resulted, in many instances, from the failure of the lower class to adopt bourgeois goals and standards" (Kusmer, 1976, p. 256). Essentially, the organization was viewed as blaming the victim and ignoring systemic influences. Somewhat in line with the Cleveland community's impression, Simon (1994) noted that early social workers were often less inclined toward empowerment and instead sought to establish societal protection for vulnerable people. The NUL also took the paternal role and negotiated for their clients instead of with them in many instances. This type of practice could garner resentment which, on occasion, it did.

In 1925, the Neighborhood Union of Atlanta refused to become affiliated with the NUL. The Union had done an enormous job of aiding the downtrodden African American community of Atlanta since its inception in 1908 and had aligned itself with the Community Chest in Atlanta. African American women's clubs and other welfare leaders there had worked hard to establish "free kindergartens, day nurseries, and orphanages" (Rouse, 1989, p. 118). The NUL recognized the Neighborhood Union's success and, wanting to use the organization as a model, requested that the Union turn its records over to NUL headquarters in New York. Atlanta's established African American community caretakers were not willing to cooperate with Jones and the NUL in this joint venture (Neverdon-Morton, 1989). The wife of Atlanta University's President John Hope, Lugenia Burns Hope, who was nationally recognized as an African American southern reformer, led the battle against the efforts of the NUL. "She made it clear . . . that the union would neither merge with the league nor totally turn over its community work in Atlanta to the league" (Rouse, 1989, p.118). Though Jones's motives were well intended, they revealed a level of arrogance and paternalism that was not completely surprising for an organization that pioneered African American social work practice and considered itself the gatekeeper of social work among its people.

Each city presented a unique challenge to Jones and the NUL, and Detroit was no exception. Strictly divided along ethnic lines, Detroit began to receive migrants by the time of the Civil War. As with most other northern urban areas, these migrants came in search of educational and employment opportunities. By the late nineteenth century, a small group of southern African American business and professional men had settled in Detroit (Katzman, 1973). Other northern cities had experienced similar settlement patterns; however, Detroit was the more challenging northern city. "The NUL accepted the challenge with vigor. The pressing needs of both industry and migrants transformed Detroit into a social laboratory demonstrating the role of the Urban League in aiding southern migrants' adjustment to urban-industrial life" (Thomas, 1992, p. 53). This was largely due to the fact that by then the automobile industry was the city's main employer.

The Detroit branch of the League was established in 1916, and, in 1918, John C. Dancy, Jr., became its "conservative spokesman" (Dancy, 1966; Thomas, 1992). Prior to Dancy, Forrester B. Washington had been the Detroit Urban League's (DUL) executive secretary. Washington had become a "prominent national authority on black urban problems" while he was with the DUL. This organization was the main supplier of African American workers for such companies as Chrysler, Dodge, Studebaker, Briggs, and Cadillac (Meier & Rudwick, 1979). Washington was a strong advocate of African American economic empowerment through jobs that were available in the industries of Detroit and laid the foundation for strong and effective League work. However, it was Dancy who established the long-term relationships with the auto industry of Detroit.

Dancy's relationship with the automobile tycoons was cemented over two decades. In the 1920s "industrialization created the dependency relationship between key black leaders and Henry Ford" (Thomas, 1992, p. 277). A host of African American ministers and business owners aligned themselves with Ford and the industrial establishment (Katzman, 1973). By the 1930s, growing dissension over the labor movement had created a major source of friction between the Urban League's national office and the DUL. By this time, the NUL had endorsed collective bargaining and the Congress of Industrial Organizations (CIO; Meier & Rudwick, 1979; Thomas, 1992). Detroit's industrial African

American workers were trapped between the growing union movement by White autoworkers and the often violent hostility of the companies.

The issue of unionism was a much larger issue than what was going on with the NUL. African Americans had been a major concern in the American labor movement from as early as the 1870s, as evidenced by the founding of the Knights of Labor in 1869 (Foner, 1974; Harris, 1982; Weaver, 1946). As the growing concerns of American industrialization and world market imperialism became more entrenched in the American work place, so too did the attendant concerns of Jones and the NUL with securing permanent employment for African Americans. On the eve of the Great Depression in May 1929, the *Opportunity* reported "no real advance in the attitude of organized labor toward the colored workers and sentiment in labor circles is still set against Negro participation" (Foner, 1974, p. 174).

The hostility of African Americans to some unions and unionization in general was nothing new. Their only involvement was often as strikebreakers. They commonly did not trust unions and furthermore did not understand the nature of collective bargaining. Moreover, after strikes ended and agreements were reached, African American workers were dismissed and White union strikers returned to work. By the time of the Great Depression (1929–1941), African American workers in the American work force were even more displaced. Jones was a much sought after expert on the economic conditions of the African American community as early as the mid-1920s. By the later 1920s, he was someone from whom governments, sociologists, and economists sought advice. Karl F. Phillips, Commissioner of Conciliation in the U.S. Department of Labor, constantly communicated with Jones and sought his recommendation for nearly every African American applicant that came before him seeking federal employment (Phillips, 1924–1926). Jones obliged him with the necessary information or referred him to more appropriate individuals. No doubt this contact assisted Jones in being appointed the Advisor of Negro Affairs in the Department of Commerce during the New Deal from 1933 to 1936.

Jones accomplished an enormous amount through his work with the NUL and his active role with the NCSW during the 1920s. On the eve of the Great Depression, he was a national figure of major prominence. Jones's national prominence is significant to the development of the social work profession, yet his contributions to social work have been ignored. The following discussion provides a framework for understanding his contributions to the American social work profession.

Implications for Practice

Kinckle Jones, as he was known, worked to empower the people he served. He engaged in empowerment-based practice as he attempted to ensure a better quality of life for African Americans who were migrating to urban centers in the North and South. Simon (1994) has identified nine essential guidelines for empowerment-based practice that are applicable to Jones's work.

Guideline 1: *Shape programs in response to the expressed preferences and demonstrated needs of clients and community members.* Jones was committed to listening to the migrants' needs as he developed programs and services. Under Jones's authority, the NUL's Department of Research and Investigation engaged in scientific inquiry to understand the meaning and scope of the problems that confronted urban African American migrants in various cities. For example, Jones (1923/1978) described one report as "a survey of the Negroes of Hartford, Conn. This report covers the school life, industrial activities, housing, crime and recreation. In fact, it is a complete study of nearly 65 percent of the total Negro population of that community" (p. 419). Jones further noted that the report was completed to aid in the "construction of social service programs for the Negroes in Hartford." Jones felt that "giving facts concerning Negroes to the public [was] . . . one of the most important acts to be performed" because it dispelled "false opinions concerning alleged deficiencies" (Jones, 1923/1978, p. 418).

Guideline 2: *Make certain that programs and services are maximally convenient for and accessible to one's clients and their communities.* The programs that Jones administered focused on those large urban communities in which social problems and racial oppression made the lives of migrating African Americans difficult. The NUL established local League affiliates in major cities to make certain that professional social services were accessible to those most in need. Since cultural receptivity is part of accessibility, the NUL also focused on training African American social workers to provide the needed services. Jones (1928/1978) felt that any social agency or organization that brought its work into the African American community should hire trained "Negro social workers" with a plan of "placing them in strategic positions with these organizations so that the most effective work may be done" (p. 458). The NUL Fellowship Program was a vital part of the League's mission. This program, designed to select, train, and place young scholars with a propensity toward social work, was quite successful. Scholars such as Inabel Lindsay, Abram Harris, and Ira de A. Reid entered the social work profession with training acquired through the Fellowship Program (Carlton-LaNey, 1994).

Guideline 3: *Ask as much dedication to problem solving from one's client as from oneself.* Jones demanded a great deal from himself, as evidenced by his limitless work schedule. He also requested that others be as actively involved in helping to find solutions to the many problems facing the African American community. As he spoke of the tasks that lay before the African American community, Jones (1928/1971b, p. 64) said, "We must keep on our toes from the word go!" He felt that the "easy life" was a deterrent to progress and that "general apathy" was the greatest enemy to the human family (p. 65). While Jones asked as much from others as he was giving, he was nonetheless somewhat paternal in his approach to problem solving on behalf of vulnerable individuals. Part of this could be attributed to his orientation as a member of the "Talented Tenth," which mandated that the educated and privileged provide leadership for those outside that elite group.

Guideline 4: *Call and build upon the strengths of the clients and communities.* This guideline requires that social workers configure services that use the wisdom and experience of clients and community to problem-solve. For example, DUL regularly sponsored a 10¢ newcomers' community dance. This dance introduced newly arrived immigrants, many of whom moved to the North alone without family or friends, to "more desirable people" who had been in Detroit longer. This served to entertain, educate, and provide an opportunity for people to network and establish relationships (Washington, 1917).

Simon (1994) noted that groups that have been marginalized often need contributions from a larger whole, as well as from themselves, to survive and cohere. Jones recognized this and noted in 1928 that social work among African Americans would "bring into closer cooperation White and colored leaders who are concerned about community welfare and [would] have the effect of making Negroes an articulate group in the community" (Jones, 1928/1978, p. 463).

Guideline 5: *Devise and redevise interventions in response to the unique configuration of requests, issues, and needs that a client or client group presents. Resist becoming wedded to a favored interventive method.* Essentially, a broad range of methods is needed for empowerment-based practice. Jones and the NUL employed a diverse range of methods to meet their goals, which included efforts to "promote, encourage, assist and engage in any and all kinds of work for improving the industrial, economic and social conditions among Negroes" (Jones, 1928/1978, p. 456). Their services and programs ran the gamut from employment bureau management to health fair promotions to war camp activities. Conducting a wide range of services required a range of skills and methods to be effective.

Guideline 6: *Make leadership development a constant priority of practice and policy development.* Jones (1928/1971b) said that "the first requisite in the development of leadership in the Negro, possibly even more important than his general training, is self-confidence and belief in his own racial capacity" (p. 65). He often recalled for audiences the "splendid accomplishment of Negroes" and the need for more well qualified and well trained young men and women to "deliver high class, dependable, thorough, and efficient technical service" (Jones, 1928/1971b, p. 66). Furthermore, the NUL Fellowship Program engaged in both social work education and leadership development.

Guideline 7: *Be patient, since empowerment takes substantial amounts of time and continuity of effort.* Clearly, this guideline was also part of what drove Jones's work. He realized that these changes would be slow and that "time [was] the solver of problems" (Jones, 1928/1971a, p. 146). Jones was meticulous and encouraged thorough preparation for success. He was convinced of the need for the talented of the race to make the necessary sacrifices for thorough preparation. He did not urge quick solutions, but encouraged patient, well thought out approaches to social work practice.

Guideline 8: *Take ongoing stock of social workers' own powerlessness and power at work.* Jones sometimes listed himself as one of the success stories among African Americans. He used his role with the leading national social work organization as evidence that he was among the elite leadership within the profession. Yet, he did not have illusions about his position and the position of the race. Jones was never allowed to forget that while he enjoyed some degree of privilege and a good reputation among social workers, politicians, and others, he was still African American and there were numerous obstacles in the way of his success. It is not surprising, therefore, that he identified prejudice against the race as the first obstacle to success. Jones felt that "man's spirit" was the most potent weapon against racial prejudice.

Guideline 9: *Use local knowledge to contribute to the general good.* The ninth and final guideline for empowerment-based practice highlights how the NUL specialized in gathering and sharing information about the African American community. Jones indicated that the League maintained a "clipping bureau and files for assembling data of all kinds having a bearing on Negro life." The files, he noted, were "available for preparing lectures, articles and discussions on the Negro for students, professors and lectures on social work" (Jones, 1923/1978, p. 419).

Finally, E. Kinckle Jones, social worker, politician, and statesman, should be remembered as one who worked to ensure a place for African Americans within the social work profession. As Jones indicated, he accepted the "opportunity for statesmanship service to humanity" (Jones, 1925) and worked to pass on to posterity a lifetime of responsible activity that targeted social problems affecting all of America.

References

Carlton-LaNey, I. B. (1994). Training African American social workers through the NUL Fellowship Program. *Journal of Sociology and Social Welfare*, *21*, 43–53.

Chambers, C. A. (1971). *Paul U. Kellogg and the survey: Voices for social welfare and social justice.* Minneapolis: University of Minnesota Press.

Dancy, J. C. (1966). *Sand against the wind: The memoirs of John C. Dancy*. Detroit: Wayne State University.

Foner, P. S. (1974). *Organized labor and the Black worker, 1619–1973.* New York: Praeger Publishers.

Gary, R. B., & Gary, L. E. (1994). The history of social work education for Black people, 1900–1930. *Journal of Sociology and Social Welfare, 21*, 67–81.

Gottlieb, P. (1991). Rethinking the Great Migration: A perspective from Pittsburgh. In J. Trotter. *The Great Migration in historical perspective: New dimensions of race, class, and gender* (pp. 68–82). Bloomington and Indianapolis: Indiana University Press.

Grossman, J. R. (1989). *Land of hope: Chicago, Black southerners, and the great migration.* Chicago: The University of Chicago Press.

Harris, W. H. (1982). *The harder we run: Black workers since the Civil War*. New York: Oxford University Press.

Hine, D. C. (1989). *Black women in white: Racial conflict and cooperation in the nursing profession, 1890–1959.* Bloomington: Indiana University Press.

Jones, E. K. (1925, December 11). *Negro migration in New York State*. Speech delivered at the New York State Conference of Charities and Corrections, Hotel Roosevelt, New York City, National Urban League Papers.

Jones, E. K. (1926a, May 16). Go-to-high school, go-to-college, urged by Alpha Phi Alpha Fraternity. Delivered over Radio Broadcasting Station WMCA (Hotel McAlpin, NY), NUL Papers, Series IV, Box 3, Manuscript Division, Library of Congress, Washington, DC.

Jones, E. K. (1926b, June). *The Negro's opportunity today*. Commencement Address at West Virginia Collegiate Institute, NUL Papers, Series IV, Box 3, Manuscript Division, Library of Congress, Washington, DC.

Jones, E. K. (1926c, July 28). Letter to S. A. Allen, Boston, Massachusetts. NUL Papers, Series IV, Box 3, Manuscript Division, Library of Congress, Washington, DC.

Jones, E. K., (1932, April 27). Editorial. *The New York Times.*

Jones, E. K. (1940). Abridged autobiography of Eugene Kinckle Jones. Dictated for Gunnar Myrdal. NUL Papers, Library of Congress, Washington, DC.

Jones, E. K. (1971a). Negroes, north and south—A contrast. In J. Sochen (Ed.), *The Black man and the American dream* (pp. 142–146). Chicago: Quadrangle Books. (Original work published 1928)

Jones, E. K. (1971b). Negro youth goes out into life. In J. Sochen (Ed.), *The Black man and the American dream* (pp. 63–67). Chicago: Quadrangle Books. (Original work published 1928)

Jones, E. K. (1971c). The Negro's opportunity today. In J. Sochen (Ed.), *The Black man and the American dream* (pp. 196–203). Chicago: Quadrangle Books. (Original work published 1928)

Jones, E. K. (1978). Building a larger life. In E. Ross (Ed.), *Black heritage in social welfare, 1860–1930* (pp. 417–422). Metuchen, NJ: Scarecrow Press. (Original work published 1923)

Jones. E. K. (1978). Social work among Negroes. In E. Ross (Ed.), *Black heritage in social welfare, 1860–1930* (pp. 456–464). Metuchen, NJ: Scarecrow Press. (Original work published 1928)

Katzman, D. M. (1973). *Before the ghetto: Black Detroit in the nineteenth century*. Chicago: University of Illinois Press.

Kinckle Jones Report. (1932, April 27). *New York Times*.

Kusmer, K. L. (1976). *A ghetto takes shape: Black Cleveland, 1870–1930*. Chicago: University of Illinois Press.

Manning, K. R. (1983). *Black Apollo of science: The life of Ernest Everett Just*. New York: Oxford University Press.

McMurry, L. O. (1981). *George Washington Carver: Scientist and symbol*. Oxford, England: Oxford University Press.

McNeil, G. R. (1983). *Groundwork: Charles Hamilton Houston and the struggle for civil rights*. Philadelphia: University of Pennsylvania Press.

Meier, A., & Rudwick, E. (1979). *Black Detroit and the rise of the UAW*. New York: Oxford University Press.

Meier, A., & Rudwick. E. (1986). *Black history and the historical profession, 1915–1980*. Chicago: University of Illinois Press.

Neverdon-Morton, C. (1989). *Afro-American women of the south and the advancement of the race, 1895–1925*. Knoxville, TN: The University of Tennessee Press.

Phillips, K. R. (1926). Letters from Karl R. Phillips, Commissioner of Conciliation, Correspondence, December 1924–March 1926. RG-138, No. 1400, National Archives, Washington, DC.

Rouse, J. (1989). *Lugenia Burns Hope: Black southern reformer*. Athens: The University of Georgia Press.

Simon, B. (1994). *The empowerment tradition in American social work*. New York: Columbia University Press.

Sinnette, E. (1989). *Arthur Alfonso Schomburg: Black bibliophile and collector*. Detroit: The New York Public Library and Wayne State University Press.

Thomas, R. (1992). *Life for us is what we make it: Building Black community in Detroit, 1915–1945*. Bloomington: Indiana University Press.

Thoms, A. B. (1929). *Pathfinders: A history of the progress of colored graduate nurses*. New York: Kay Printing House.

Washington, F. (1917). The Detroit newcomers' greeting. *The Survey, 38*, 333–335.

Washington, F. (1978). What professional training means to the social worker. In E. Ross (Ed.), *Black heritage in social welfare, 1860–1930* (pp. 445–449). Metuchen, NJ: Scarecrow Press. (Original work published 1926)

Weaver, R. (1946). *Negro labor: A national problem.* New York: Harcourt, Brace and Company.

Weiss, N. (1974). *The National Urban League, 1910–1940.* New York: Oxford University Press.

Wesley, C. H. (1929). *The History of Alpha Phi Alpha: A development in college life.* Chicago: The Foundation Publishers.

CHAPTER 11

Mary Church Terrell and Her Mission
Giving Decades of Quiet Service

Sharon Warren Cook

In the African American community, education and activism frequently coexist. As an African American woman at the turn of the twentieth century, Mary Church Terrell was embarking upon a voyage of advocacy for "women of color" and emerging as a prominent civil rights leader. From its inception, her work was branded by the relationship between gender and race. The pairing of the two proved paramount in examining African American women's place in history. Often racism and sexism are motivated by similar economic, social, and psychological forces. Consequently, many people who sought to oppress African Americans were also antifeminists (Giddings, 1984).

In responding to the struggles of racism and sexism, Mary Church Terrell positioned herself to become a change agent in two of the most important social reform movements in American history: the fight for the rights of African Americans and the fight for the rights of women. Terrell and many other women argued that the African American woman's experience under slavery, her participation in the work force, her political activism, and her sense of independence combined to make her more of a woman, not less (Giddings, 1984). The title of her autobiography, *A Colored Woman in a White World* echoed the two threads that would weave together her missions of inclusion, education, equality, access, and empowerment.

As she was born during the Civil War in 1863 and died in 1954 just after the *Brown v. Board of Education* decision, Terrell's life spanned the steadfast toil for emancipation. She was born on September 23, 1863, in Memphis, Tennessee, to Louisa (Ayres) and Robert Reed Church, who were both former slaves. Her father was a successful businessman and a millionaire real estate owner. Her mother, who divorced Robert Church when their daughter was three years old, was a hairdresser who owned and operated a hair piece shop in New York (Sheppard, 1959).

Robert Church was able to afford luxuries for his daughter that were uncommon for most "colored girls" of her day. At the age of six, she was sent to Yellow Springs, Ohio, to attend the Model School conducted by Antioch College. She then attended Oberlin College, which was one of the few integrated institutions of higher learning in the United States (Oberlin opened its doors to African Americans in 1835). After graduation in 1884, Mary Church returned to Memphis to keep house for her father. Before long, she grew dissatisfied because she wanted to put her education to better use. At the end of the year, when her father remarried, she felt free to leave. Her father was so angered by this decision that he threatened to disinherit her (Andrews, 1986).

In 1887, Mary Church obtained employment in the public school system in Washington, DC, as a Latin teacher in the Preparatory School for Colored Youth (named the M Street High School in 1891). From 1889 to 1890, she traveled in Switzerland, Germany, and Italy, where she quickly learned several languages, including German and Italian. She relished both the cultural opportunities available in other countries and the freedom from racial tensions that she experienced there. While abroad, she refused several invitations to marry European men because she felt that such a marriage would cause her to relinquish her African American identity. In 1891, after her return to the United States, she married Robert Terrell, a Harvard graduate and an attorney, whom she had met while teaching in Washington, DC. Robert Terrell was prominent in Washington and eventually became a judge in the municipal court (Robinson, 1970).

Terrell's return to the United States brought a quick reminder of the racial injustices and brutalities that permeated the lives of African Americans. In Memphis, just one year after her marriage, there were 255 documented lynchings in the city, but one death in particular gripped her as no others had and spurred her to fight for social justice. The victim, Thomas Moss, had been one of Terrell's childhood friends. Terrell received notice that he had been murdered by a mob of White men who were outraged by the success of Moss's grocery store. Never before had such a blatant injustice struck her so personally, ultimately propelling her into new social and political arenas.

Moss's murder prompted Terrell to seek out an old family friend, the famous abolitionist Frederick Douglass. Together they secured an appointment with President Benjamin Harrison at the White House for the explicit purpose of requesting that he condemn lynching in his annual address before Congress. Terrell later wrote that, like every President before Franklin Roosevelt, Harrison refused to take a public stand against lynching (Giddings, 1984; Sterling & Quarles, 1965). Terrell believed that the greatest obstacle preventing the end of lynching was the public's attitude toward such a crime. In her exasperation and sorrow, she admitted that it was "impossible to comprehend the causes of the ferocity and brutality which attend the average lynching-bee without taking into account the brutalizing effect of slavery" (Terrell, 1904/1972b, p. 209).

The lynching of her close friend was followed by the death of her newborn infant in a segregated, poorly equipped hospital (Giddings, 1984). These events forever erased any ideas that Mary Church Terrell had of leading a more traditional life as a married gentlewoman. Subsequently, she began her life of activism and agitation for civil rights launching a lifelong career that touched the lives of the wealthy, the poor, the prominent, and the meek alike.

In 1892, Terrell, along with Anna Julia Cooper and Mary Jane Patterson, organized the Colored Women's League of Washington, DC. Terrell was elected the first president. The guiding principle behind this club, like most others, was racial uplift and empowerment through self-help. According to White (1999), the club women believed that an intensive, well targeted social service delivery system could help to solve the race problem. The Women's League established a night school where Terrell taught several evenings a week. The league was more focused on educational concerns than issues of women's suffrage and sexual oppression, which were issues of paramount importance to Terrell at the time.

In 1895, Congress empowered the commissioners to add three women to the city's all-male school board. Believing that one of these positions should have been offered to an African American woman, Terrell called the commissioner in charge of school affairs to tell him of her convictions. As she outlined the qualifications of a woman she knew, the commissioner listened thoughtfully. When she had finished, he questioned her about her preparation and credentials. The commissioner decided not to accept Terrell's recommendation; instead, he appointed her (Dannett, 1964).

It now seemed that Mary Church Terrell was blossoming into a reformer and activist for which her uncharacteristic upbringing had not fully prepared her. In 1896, African American women met in Washington, DC, to form the National Association of Colored Women (NACW). Mary Church Terrell became the organization's first president as the NACW resulted from the merger of the National Federation of Afro-American Women and the Colored Women's League. Choosing as its motto, "Lifting As We Climb," the association founded kindergartens, day care centers, schools for nurses, and a home for the elderly. Additionally, the organization fought for better schools, worked with delinquent youngsters, and taught sharecroppers who resided on large plantations in the South (Smith, 1992). The success of women's club activities provided an impetus for the further development and growth of other women's groups.

The Role of Women's Clubs

The proliferation of self-help groups pushed issues of African American women to the forefront (Knupfer, 1996). From 1890 to 1895, the propensity of African American women to support and develop coalitions permeated the country. It is speculated that the merger of clubs was directly linked to the common denominator of sexual oppression that these women suffered from both African American and White men. Essentially, the "defense of Black womanhood united them as did no other single cause" (White, 1999, p. 52).

African American women used their club movement to draft policies and resolutions essential for inclusion and elevation. They used their literary organs to educate and inform women of relevant issues, problems, and opportunities. Through various media and forums, the African American club women's movement evoked multiple ideologies, discourses, motifs, and images of womanhood, motherhood, and home life (Knupfer, 1996). Women like Terrell adhered to the notion of a web of affiliation. In addition to the NACW, Terrell was also a member of the Delta Sigma Theta Sorority. The self-help work of African American women's sororities was very similar to that of women's clubs, and indeed many modeled their social service systems after those of the NACW (White, 1999).

In 1925, Terrell wrote the official oath for Delta Sigma Theta Sorority, a sisterhood of college-educated African American women. The oath read in part:

> We feel deeply the need for protection against the growing prejudices of all kinds in the United States of America. The time has come when we feel deeply called upon to give voice for the first time to the strong feelings which have possessed us. (Giddings, 1984, p. 86).

She further stated that their claim to justice and equality was the general claim of all Americans and the specific claim of a race that has made its contribution to the development of the life of this country (Giddings, 1984). Terrell's sorority oath differs very little from the requiem that she offered to any audience of African American women.

During the Progressive Era, hundreds of African American Women's Clubs flourished (Knupfer, 1996). Women created a vibrant social world of their own, as they sought to achieve social, spiritual, and political uplift. They battled institutional discrimination, advocated for antilynching laws, and fought for suffrage. Terrell, in her advocacy, espoused respectability and behavioral standards for African American women. Club women reshaped their language, rituals, and practices to correspond to historically and culturally veritable expressions of motherhood and womanhood (Perkins, 1983). Terrell affirmed this historical continuity in her declaration, "Nothing lies nearer the hearts of colored women than the children" (Jones, 1982, p. 23). The dual pictures of motherhood and home spoke of a community ethos nurtured through singular and group activities.

Mamie Garvin Fields, a community activist and one of Terrell's contemporaries, recalled the power that Terrell brought to the women at the Mt. Zion A.M.E. Church in Charleston, South Carolina, in 1916. According to Fields (1983), Terrell spoke on the topic "The Modern Woman." Fields described the scene at the church on that hot sultry evening as crowded and intense. Such an enormous group of women occupied pews in such close proximity that they had to put even the smallest purse between their toes. The pasteboard fans had to be "worked back and forth in front of you [otherwise] you were liable to elbow your neighbor" (p. 189). Fields said that "[we] sat in the heat, dresses clinging to us, ladies' hats almost touching, fans just a-going" (p. 189) to hear the powerful speech from the NACW president from Washington, DC. Terrell was regal, eloquent, and elegant. "She wore a pink evening dress and long white gloves with her beautifully done hair"(p. 190). Terrell spoke to the women of their "social debt," which required them to share their education with the less fortunate of the race, to go into the communities to improve them, and to go out into the nation to change it (Fields, 1983, p. 190). She noted that above all they must organize and work together.

While many were impressed with Terrell's eloquence and elegance, others did not share these opinions. Essentially, the activities, beliefs, and rhetoric of club women were not without scrutiny and criticism. Many club women were thought to hold themselves to "higher ideals" than ordinary women (Jones, 1982). In some cases, there was a tendency to distance and disassociate themselves from poorer, less respected African American women. Such stratification was evident in Terrell's statement, "Even though we wish to shun them and hold ourselves entirely aloof from them, we cannot escape the consequences of their acts" (Jones, 1982, p. 26).

Organizations such as the NACW attracted a heterogeneous band of elite female educators, doctors, and social status personages. Hamilton's (1978) typology of 108 club women from 1896 to 1920 revealed interesting characteristics of their members. Of the 49 women for whom a date of birth was available, 36 had been born between 1860 and 1885. This period was marked by the optimism of emancipation and reconstruction. These women had long histories of activism in the abolitionist movement and the women's rights movement. Seventy-five percent of the leaders were married. Finally, 70 women for whom information on a place of birth was available had been born in the South, but migrated North in the early twentieth century (Hamilton, 1978).

Essentially, Terrell was among a group of women who shared her history, values, and ideologies. Furthermore, these women were elitist, high achievers who themselves were among the "talented tenth" of the African American intelligentsia. Yet, White (1999) concluded that the characteristics that ensured group cohesion were also to mark their virtual decline. While in their heyday, nonetheless, women's clubs made a significant impact on the quality of life in the African American community. These women rallied together to bring about systemic, planned change while simultaneously embracing the tradition of home and hearth.

The NACW: Advocating and Strengthening

Reflecting the NACW's strong belief in the significance of home life, Mary Church Terrell stated:

> Believing that it is only through the home that people can become really good and truly great, the National Association of Colored Women had entered a sacred domain hoping to inculcate right principles of living and to correct false views of life. (Knupfer, 1996, p.12)

In a Victorian vein, her advocacy of the domestic role of women indicated a nonfeminist nature of the organization. In fact, many of these women were quite traditional in their idea of the role of wife and mother. Giddings (1984) noted that, on one hand, they agreed with the fundamental notion of the Victorian ethic, but on the other, they opposed the racist and classist implication of the cult of true womanhood. Terrell likewise felt the push and pull of her convictions on the cult of true womanhood. While embroiled in a struggle to maintain a clerkship position with the federal government in 1918, Terrell recalled that she had to temper her response to racist treatment, otherwise she would "never have submitted to the outrage without waging a righteous war against it" (p. 168). But she did not want to embarrass her husband and fearing a vehement response "might easily hurt his standing as a judge in Municipal Court" (p. 73), Terrell relented. She concluded that she had "always believed that a wife has no right to injure her husband's career by what she says or does" (p. 73).

In addition to its avowed objective, the NACW, with Terrell at the helm, succeeded in shifting the interests of its leaders from the home to a national social spectrum (Knupfer, 1996). Terrell was especially interested in the establishment of mothers' clubs. These clubs functioned as depositories and disseminators of pertinent information on the "best" child rearing practices and strategies for maintaining successful homes. An analysis of the effectiveness of these clubs would call for speculation about the effects of the elite cast of members and the organizations' abilities to attain goals (Jones, 1982). Terrell and other leaders were aware that the support of the masses was essential for efficacy of NACW's programs. The NACW's motto, "Lifting As We Climb," reflected this awareness. In 1901, Terrell declared:

> In no way could we live up to such a sentiment better than by coming into closer touch with the masses of our women. So that if the call of duty were disregarded altogether, policy and self preservation would demand that we do go down among the lowly, illiterate and even the vicious to whom we are bound by the ties of race and sex, and put forth every possible effort to uplift and claim them. (Terrell, 1940, p. 235)

In honest admissions, Terrell frequently not only indicated the reasons that the NACW concerned itself with elevating the less fortunate members of the sex, but also revealed the biases of elite women. Implicitly, she maintained that the leaders who were not genuinely concerned with the welfare of the masses pursued the elevation of these women as a vehicle for enhancing their own positions in society (Dannett, 1964). Because of her leadership in the NACW, Terrell received many opportunities to serve the African American community and to speak before White women's suffrage groups. In 1898, she delivered a speech before the National American Women's Suffrage Association entitled, "The Progress of Colored Women." Terrell spoke of "the cruel and unreasonable prejudices" (Knupfer, 1996) that neither the merit nor necessity of African American women seem to be able to undo. She went on during the speech to reference the energy and eager zeal of African American women to assist and support each other since emancipation.

Political Savvy: The Route to Resources and Opportunities

As Terrell recounted the progress that African American women had made, she encouraged further progress in every aspect of community life. For Terrell, the care of children was a major area of the NACW's agenda. Terrell used her access into mainstream America to petition on the behalf of the "voiceless victims" of injustice—the children. In her appearance at the National American Women's Suffrage Association, she stressed the necessity of free kindergartens in every city if America were "to allow the children to receive from us what it is our duty to give" (Giddings, 1984). She advocated the establishment of a Mothers' Congress to enlighten others of appropriate child rearing practices. Terrell lobbied for funding to open a sanatorium to allow African American medical students an opportunity to gain practical knowledge and to serve as an alternative to the charity wards of public hospitals. She constantly prodded her audiences with questions about the legal status and vulnerabilities of African Americans. Terrell was also persistent in petitioning the legislators of Louisiana and Tennessee to repeal the obnoxious "Jim Crow Laws." Terrell spoke against the Convict Lease System of Georgia. She used her popularity abroad to shed light on the atrocities occurring in America.

Perhaps her most celebrated speaking engagements, albeit not the most inspiring, were in 1904, 1919, and 1937. In 1904, she spoke at the Berlin International Congress of Women. As the lone African American woman at the Congress, she felt a deep sense of responsibility to perform well. She had memorized her speech in English, but decided to deliver it in German—although she had not spoken German in 15 years (Smith, 1992). In 1919, she addressed the delegates of the International League for Peace and Freedom that met in Zurich. In 1937, she represented African American women at the World Fellowship of Faiths in London. Meeting and participating with groups at home and abroad afforded her the privilege of having a support network that included Booker T. Washington, educator and national African American spokesman; W. E. B. DuBois, scholar and founder of the National Association for the Advancement of Colored People (NAACP); Susan B. Anthony, feminist and suffragist; and Jane Addams, Hull House founder. In addition to being involved with prominent leaders and reformers, Terrell was also recognized as someone deserving of public accolades and deference.

Celebrations of a Pioneer

In 1934, the Oberlin Alumnae Association voted unanimously to request that the president of Oberlin College confer an honorary degree on Terrell for services rendered to her race and for the efforts she had made to create a better understanding between the races in the United States (Ham, 1980).

In 1940, the culmination of Terrell's writing career led to the publication of her autobiography, *A Colored Woman in a White World.* In this work, she emphasized her experiences as an African American female who had grown up in "white dominated America." She was careful not to reveal much of her personal and emotional life as a woman, but as White (1999) noted, African American women were reluctant to put their private lives and histories in the public's hand because of a history of abuse and slander. A lifetime of guarded public presentation of self could not be so easily undone by the presumed prerogative to pen an autobiography.

In 1950, Terrell entered a segregated Washington, DC, restaurant with an interracial group. After the African Americans were refused service, members of the group filed affidavits against the restaurant. Three years of protest and legal battles ended in the protesters' favor. At the age of 90, in the court case of *District of Columbia v. John Thompson*, Terrell saw the desegregation of eating facilities in Washington, DC.

A Pillar of Strength

Terrell, the daughter of former slaves, amassed a lifetime of accomplishments that spanned the period from the Emancipation Proclamation to the Supreme Court's decision in *Brown v. Board of Education*. She spent her life seeking greater freedom as an African American and as a woman. Transcending rites of passage customarily reserved for White women, she refused conventional roles and became the voice for millions of silent victims. She used her talents to teach, to lecture, to organize social welfare services, and to empower women. She fought for racial equality and suffrage for women. Although she could have easily "passed" for White and did on occasion when the chains of racism became unbearable, she generally accepted and responded to the larger society's views of her as an African American woman. Terrell felt a strong sense of race pride, yet she knew that her light skin made her more acceptable to Whites. She used this to leverage and to strengthen her "race work." In her writings, she referenced social gatherings to which Whites invited her as a way to "give the color line a good rub" (Sterling & Quarles, 1965, p. 81). Until her death in 1954, she used her attributes to advance her people. In one of her last documented speeches, it was clear that Terrell understood that the fight for social justice was immutable when she said, "Keep on going, keep on insisting, keep on fighting injustices" (p. 81).

Implications for Social Work

American social psychologist Gordon Allport (1958) hypothesized that contact between the races will not necessarily make relations better, but will often make them worse, depending on the circumstances in which contact takes place. Allport formulated the *contact hypothesis,* which maintains that prejudice will decrease if two groups with equal status have contact, but will increase or intensify if contact occurs under conditions of inequality. While Terrell was well educated, wealthy, and politically connected, she nonetheless understood and experienced racial prejudice.

As a student at Oberlin in the early 1880s, Terrell used her position as editor of the school's magazine to voice her views of the injustices that existed between the races at that time. Using the media and speaking engagements, she tried to bridge a gap between the African American community and the White world. She saw maps of future political and social journeys being drawn by the lack of access to resources that burdened her race. Building on Terrell's legacy, today's social workers must work with a sense of urgency to help motivate communities to unite, strengthen, and organize around various issues. The profession of social work is linked to communities through a history of oppression. Terrell's advocacy for African Americans contributed to the development and advancement of a more independent and empowered citizenry. The realities of injustice serve to ground social work education, practice, and research.

Terrell's struggles illustrate a willingness to nurture, support, teach, and uplift others. During her life, she demonstrated an understanding of the connections between privilege and social debt. She encouraged both professional and personal involvement with persons in need of assistance. Historically, achieving economic and educational success has carried a moral, monetary, and service obligation (Carlton-LaNey, 1999). This is a tradition worth reconsidering. Social workers can facilitate this by encouraging every member of society to allow others an opportunity to benefit from their skills, wisdom, experiences, and access to resources. Terrell believed that African Americans had a social responsibility to assist each other. She demonstrated her convictions by helping to establish kindergartens, schools, training programs, and neighborhood clubs.

Understanding systems, their linkages, and their interdependence was fundamental to Terrell's work. Today, social workers' efforts are harmed by a failure to similarly understand system interconnectedness and to secure adequate community, political, and legislative support. In order to meet the increasing needs of the most vulnerable persons in today's society, dialogue concerning social policies and practice must improve. In the 1940s, Edvard Lindeman asked social workers what role they were playing in determining the direction in which the United States was moving. He was attempting to engage social workers in a debate over policies in health care, racism, education, employment, and the democratic tradition of citizen participation. In order for our profession to make an impact, it is imperative that social work practitioners have a working knowledge of how to influence the development of social welfare policy (Segal & Brzuzy, 1998).

All social workers must take into account the vast amount of stratification in America. Quantifying the devastation is only part of the solution. Social workers must humanize those adversely impacted by the institutionalized racism that permeates the country. Individuals in the upper echelons of society control an inordinate amount of the nation's wealth. The privilege of the upper class contrasts sharply with the poverty of millions of poor people who struggle daily. It is paramount to understand the clear cause-and-effect relationship between the unequal distribution of resources and a limitation of choices. Whether race continues to be correlated with poverty will remain a topic of debate as the new century begins.

References

Allport, G. (1958). *The nature of prejudice*. Garden City, NY: Anchor Books.

Andrews, J. (1986). Mary Church Terrell. In W. Trattner (Ed.), *Biographical dictionary of social welfare in America* (pp. 95–99). Westport, CT: Greenwood Publishing Group.

Carlton-LaNey, I. B. (1999). African American social work pioneers' response to need. *Social Work*, *44*, 311–321.

Dannett, S. (1964). *Profiles of Negro womanhood*. Yonkers, NY: Educational Heritage.

Fields, M. (1983). *Lemon Swamp and other places*. New York: The Free Press.

Giddings, P. (1984). *When and where I enter*. New York: Bantam Books.

Ham, D. (1980). *Notable Black American women: The modern period* (Vol. 4, pp. 1115–1119). Cambridge, MA: Harvard University Press.

Hamilton, T. (1978). *The National Association of Colored Women, 1896–1920*. Unpublished doctoral dissertation, Emory University, Atlanta, GA.

Jones, B. (1982). Mary Church Terrell and the National Association of Colored Women. *Journal of Negro History*, *67*, 20–33.

Knupfer, A. (1996). *Toward a tenderer humanity and a nobler womanhood*. New York: New York University Press.

Perkins, L. (1983). The impact of the 'Cult of True Womanhood' on the education of Black women. *Journal of Social Issues*, *39*, 17–28.

Robinson, W. (1970). *International library of Negro life and history*. New York: Publishers Company.

Segal, E., & Brzuzy, S. (1998). *Social welfare policy, programs, and practice*. Itasca, IL. F. E. Peacock Press.

Sheppard, G. (1959). *Mary Church Terrell—Respectable person*. Baltimore: Human Relations Press.

Smith, J. (1992). *Notable Black American women*. Detroit, MI: Gale Research.

Sterling, D., & Quarles, B. (1965). *Lift every voice: The lives of Booker T. Washington, W. E. B. DuBois, Mary Church Terrell, and James Weldon Johnson*. Garden City, NY: Doubleday & Company.

Terrell, M. (1940). *A colored woman in a white world*. Washington, DC: Ransdell.

Terrell, M. (1972). Lynching from a Negro's point of view. In G. Lerner (Ed.), *Black women in white America* (pp. 205–211). New York: Vintage Books. (Original work published in 1904).

White, D. (1999). *Too heavy a load*. New York: W.W. Norton & Company.

Williams, F. (1972). The club movement among the colored women. *The Voice of the Negro* (pp. 99–102). New York: Vintage Books.

CHAPTER 12

Thyra J. Edwards

Internationalist Social Worker

Elmer P. Martin and Joanne M. Martin

Heralded in 1944 as "one of the most outstanding Negro women in the world," Thyra J. Edwards is virtually unknown today even in her chosen field, social work. Yet she was one of the most important Black social work pioneers of the twentieth century ("Thyra Edwards Coming to Buffalo," 1944, p. 1).

Edwards was a journalist, world traveler, lecturer, and labor organizer, but she saw her journalistic work, her travel seminars, and her speaking engagements as part of her practice as a professional social worker.[1] She even saw her work as a union organizer as social work. Edwards believed that social work should not be limited to a narrow focus or single discipline, such as psychoanalysis or sociology, but should also encompass such areas as political economy, social history, women's issues, race relations, labor issues, and world affairs, particularly since these areas significantly affected people's lives.

Having studied psychology, psychiatric social work, and psychoanalysis, Edwards could have easily followed the popular trend in the social work profession during her time, psychoanalysis. However, she believed that social workers should broaden their scope if they were truly going to promote social welfare. In this sense, Edwards not only anticipated the ecological systems approach so pervasive in social work today, she went beyond it to include what modern sociologists call "world system theory." Edwards's life and the forces that shaped her dynamic world systems perspective of social work are the focus of this analysis.

Social Work Education

Edwards was born December 25, 1897, in Houston, Texas, to Horace and Anna Bell Edwards. A few years after she graduated from the Houston Colored High School in 1915, the Edwards family, which included Thyra and her three sisters, Anna, Thelma, and Bell, moved to Gary, Indiana, where Thyra Edwards trained in the relatively new profession called social work.

During the summer of 1920, Edwards took courses in family casework, child welfare, and labor problems at the Chicago School of Civics and Philanthropy; over the next several years, she took additional courses in psychiatric social work, psychoanalysis, the social sciences, literature, and forensic science at Indiana University, Kent College of Law, and the University of Chicago. Edwards noted that the Chicago-Gary area was a virtual battleground between labor and capital, and her interest in labor problems led her to study labor relations and economic history at Brookwood Labor College, a trade union school sponsored by the American Federation of Labor (AFL) in Brookwood, New York. In addition, Edwards took two other courses at Brookwood that were to have a profound influence on her professional life: journalism and public speaking.

Child Welfare and Study Abroad

Edwards's main area of interest was child welfare. From 1920 to 1928 she took various positions working to improve the quality of life of children. In 1920, she became a playground supervisor for the Gary, Indiana, public schools. She next served as a probation officer for the Lake County Juvenile Court from 1921 to 1925, moved up to the position of "child placing agent" for the Lake County Board of Children's Guardians, and in 1928 founded and became director of her own home for children, the Lake County Children's Home. Convinced that the problem of children in poverty was a problem of labor, she also served as a lecturer in the Educational Department of the Brotherhood of Sleeping Car Porters headed by A. Philip Randolph.

Although Edwards had achieved her dream of founding and running her own home for children, her increasing disillusionment with the child care system in America led her to explore the child welfare policies and practices of other countries, particularly the ones that she had studied in her courses on labor. By 1931, Edwards was ready to give up the security of her position and seek answers abroad. Therefore, she applied for and received a fellowship from the AFL to study at the International People's College in Elsinore, Denmark. This first of many trips to Europe was to become the single most important influence on shaping her thoughts on social work, social action, women's issues, and race. For six months Edwards took courses in workers' education, social welfare legislation, modern European political thought, and economic consumer cooperatives. She also took numerous field trips to labor union meetings, workers' schools, consumer cooperatives, political rallies, women's organizations, and youth groups. After her stay in Denmark, Edwards spent an additional 6 months exploring England, Sweden, Finland, the Soviet Union, Austria, Germany, and France.

Edwards was fascinated by the diverse group of people she had met abroad. She was particularly interested in the "darker people of the earth" (Edwards, 1945, p. 11). She compared their situation under the "powerful league of white people" with the conditions of Black people in America. Her conclusion that the colonial policy of European powers "is not one whit less ruthless, violent and prejudiced toward their dark subjects than that of America toward the Negro" had a deep impression upon the way Edwards viewed the American race problem (Edwards, 1936a, p. 140). She was no longer convinced that the Negro problem was a particular malady that must be cured by isolationist remedies. Instead, she believed that the Negro needed "to adjust his outlook to a global scale" (Edwards, 1944b, p. 233).

Edwards returned from Europe in 1937 and her return, like the trip itself, caught the attention of the Black press. She herself had sent stories to the Associated Negro Press detailing her experiences in Europe. Upon her return, one Black newspaper reported:

> Thyra Edwards, vivacious and vital, returned Monday on the SS Normandie. Yes, she's been to Paris. But if she brought any Chanel or poiret models back home with her, she failed to mention it during a packed hour of conversation on the day of her arrival. What she did bring home with her, money couldn't buy—exciting experiences with leaders of women's and youth movements, vivid pictures of life in the Soviet Union; sharp impressions of life under the several fascist regimes ... Of all the countries she visited—England, Denmark, Sweden, Finland, the Soviet Union, Germany, Austria, Poland, Switzerland and France—Miss Edwards declares Germany and Poland are the most wretched, degenerating rapidly under fascist dictatorship. (Cooke, 1936, p. 6)

The article went on to say:

> But most of all, she brought back with her a passionate desire to mobilize Negro women in this country and to acquaint them with such burning problems as social legislation for women, the organization of domestic workers and the lowering of living standards. (Cooke, 1936, p. 6)

Organizing of Black Women

While in Europe, Edwards not only had gained a worldwide perspective of the plight of the darker people of the Earth, but also she had viewed firsthand the conditions of women. She believed that Black women, like women in the rest of the world, were generally abused and exploited as workers, and when they suffered, the children of the world suffered. Black American women, Edwards maintained, represented one of the most unorganized groups of workers of the world. Edwards said that being Black, being female, and being workers made them thrice abused, thrice exploited, and thrice underpaid.

Therefore, Edwards became a labor organizer for the International Ladies Garment Workers Union (ILGWU, an affiliate of the AFL) and targeted for change the largest employer of Black women garment workers in Chicago, the Ben J. Sopkins Apron Factory. The factory had a rich history of being extremely reactionary and antagonistic toward union organizers. A few years earlier the 800 women in the Sopkins shops had gone on strike. It had lasted for only what Edwards called "two heroic weeks" before the police were called in and "kicked, mauled, and slugged and cracked . . . heads" until the women gave in (Edwards, 1935b, p. 173). According to Edwards, conditions had not changed for the better since the strike. Most of the Black women received only five cents an hour for a 52-hour week, and some had weekly take-home pay of less than one dollar and ninety cents.

To serve as a bulwark against legitimate trade unions such as the ILGWU, the owner had created his own company union. Its chief role was to keep out the so-called communist agitators and to convince workers that "employer and employee have a common rather than a contra-interest" (Edwards, 1935a, p. 72). Edwards (1935a) took specific aim at the company union's chief program of propaganda, a program called "loyalty week." During "loyalty week" the company union shamelessly forced its workers to carry large placards printed in bold legend that read:

> We are satisfied with our jobs
> We are satisfied with our wages
> We are satisfied with our working conditions
> We are satisfied with our employer
> DOWN WITH AGITATORS
> (Edwards, 1935a, p. 72)

The workers were also forced by the threat of losing their jobs to wear armbands that read "I am a loyal employee of Mr. Ben J. Sopkins" (Edwards, 1935a, p. 72).

Edwards was particularly perturbed at what she dubbed "misguided Uncle Tom Negro leaders" who were hired during "loyalty week" to come in and talk to the Black workers. Edwards (1935a) wrote:

> For the noon hours Negro preachers were brought into the shops to preach to the Negro workers on their lunch period—white workers might go outside to enjoy the sunlight or puff at a cigarette, and the text was 'loyalty to Mr. Sopkins, who for 25 years has been like a father to the Negro women on the South Side letting them work in his factories on his machines.' Well, so did 'ole massa' in slavery. What of it? (p. 72)

Edwards (1935b) wrote that "the girls in the Sopkins shop did not love Mr. Sopkins anymore than Negroes down South love to ride in Jim Crow cars" (p. 174). These women, she held, carried the signs because they were intimidated and because they represented "the great uninformed mass of unskilled labor caught between the nether stones of unscrupulous employers and uninformed and unscrupulous race leadership" (1935a, p. 82).

Edwards's usual persistence and militancy so antagonized officials at the Sopkins factory that they targeted her for their most scathing and vociferous attacks. One article expressing the company's view stated:

> When Miss Edwards can show us a sound reason for choosing the man who collects fifty cents a week because we work rather than the man who pays us for working; when Miss Edwards can demonstrate her theory that union leaders are white-armored Galahads self-dedicated to our protection, then we will submit—maybe! But until that day, Miss Edwards, we are going to remain very militantly and very shamelessly opposed to anything smelling of unionism. (Evans, 1935, p. 114)

Edwards's ILGWU continued to apply the pressure, and Edwards saw her role as a labor organizer as social work par excellence. She carried her business cards to prove it; her cards did not read "Thyra J. Edwards, labor organizer," but "Thyra J. Edwards, social worker." She believed that few things affected people's quality of life more than their economic or employment circumstance and that organizing women, the most abused, exploited, underpaid, and unorganized workers, definitely fell within the parameters of social work.

Relief Work

Believing that social workers needed to work outside and inside institutions that affect the lives of the people, Edwards combined her work as a union organizer with work in relief administration. While she did not believe that America's social welfare legislation had reached the political maturity that such legislation had reached in countries such as Sweden, Denmark, and the Soviet Union, she did believe that Roosevelt's New Deal policies, as flawed as they were, represented the most progressive social legislation in the nation's history. Edwards chose relief work because it affected more intimately the lives of poor, ordinary working class people. From 1931 to 1933 she served as a supervising caseworker and intake supervisor for the Joint Emergency Relief Commission and the Illinois Emergency Relief Commission in Chicago. In 1935, she became an assistant supervisor for the Housing Division of the Public Works Administration, and in 1936, she became the assistant district administrator of the Chicago Relief Administration.

Within these relief agencies, Edwards (1932) felt that she and the social workers under her charge had two main roles: to see that justice, fair play, and equity were administered to all clients, regardless of color; and to serve as advocates on behalf of the poor. Edwards (1936b) was well aware that "there is a prevailing sentiment [among white relief officials] that Negroes should not be hired as long as there are white men without jobs" (p. 213). Edwards was also well aware that there was a prevailing notion fostered among right-wing reactionaries that Black people would rather receive a handout than go to work. She felt that since "professional social workers have been in intimate daily contact with large segments of the unemployed population," they were "in possession of the facts to expose and explode these hair trigger conclusions branding the unemployed as maligners, chiselers and indolent and hopeless parasites" (1936b, p. 215).

Edwards's social work in labor unions and in relief agencies was consistent with her idea that progressive social workers had an obligation to radicalize, humanize, reform, direct, and eventually lead even the most conservative and reactionary social welfare agency or societal institution. She believed that social workers must become politicized, and this thought kept her constantly on the picket line for one cause or another. This idea is key to understanding her philosophy of social work, social action, and social change.

World Tours

The cornerstone of Edwards's theory of social work was that social workers must develop an international focus. With fascism rising, with the darker people of the world crying out for freedom, with the women of the world seeking their place in the sun, and with America continuing its racist treatment of its own colored colonial subjects, Edwards felt Black social workers had a special obligation to "take the lead in directing Negroes from their parochial introversion to some grasp of their relations on a world scale" (Edwards to C. Barnett, May 18, 1944). Since she was one of the most well traveled women in America, in 1936 she took upon herself the responsibility of conducting what she called "travel seminars," taking Black groups on extensive educational and cultural tours of Europe. Her new job as a director at the Abraham Lincoln Centre, a Black settlement house in Chicago, allowed her to lead these travel seminars during the summer months. Edwards took college students, teachers, social workers, and union members on a seven-week tour of France, Italy, Belgium, Denmark, Austria, Germany, the Soviet Union, Switzerland, Sweden, Finland, and England. She said that initially her travel groups were "very critical," for they had expected the typical tour of the typical tourist attractions and sites. "You know how the race is," she joked (Edwards to C. Barnett, October 26, 1936). But, Edwards maintained, after a few days even the most critical of them could see that "our group had visited more institutions, been entertained in private homes and by groups and altogether had a more thorough view of the countries and people visited" (Edwards to C. Barnett, October 26, 1936).

Edwards's group attended seminars conducted by European scholars, visited with African and West Indian students, met with world leaders, had dinner in the homes of friends that Edwards had made on her personal trips to Europe, and attended receptions in their honor at various colleges throughout Europe. Edwards found upon their return home that her tour group was her best form of advertisement for the next year's tours. She said, "If the groups are lecturing and showing movies that's a big help . . . I think it's good business to let them have the stage. The satisfied customers are important factors" (Edwards to C. Barnett, October 26, 1936).

By 1938, Edwards's tours to Europe had grown so popular that she also added a travel seminar to Mexico. She had written that although "Mexico has no race problems as we know it," Black Americans "should know and be known by Mexico" not only because they can find a "comfortable sense of security and warm friendliness," but also because

Mexicans, Haitians, Virgin Islanders, Hawaiians, Filipinos, and Puerto Ricans are all the colonial subjects of the United States of America (Edwards, 1940, p. 10). Edwards (1944b) believed Black Americans should recognize their common struggle with Mexicans and other American colonial subjects and jointly press their case before "the forum of world opinion" (p. 219).

Edwards saw no contradiction or inconsistency in the need for Black people to operate on the world stage and their need also to build and strengthen Black institutions at home. In fact, she (1944a) held that Black people, along with working with progressive interracial and international groups, needed "their own independent pressure groups composed, financed and controlled by themselves" (p. 3).

Journalistic Work

Edwards's journalistic work, like her travel tours, was a mechanism for helping people to see the common connections of the peoples of the world. On her first trip abroad, she sent stories to her longtime friend, Claude Barnett. Barnett fed the stories, through the Associated Negro Press, which he founded, to Black newspapers around the country. Edwards literally served as a foreign correspondent. She had press cards from the Associated Negro Press, the *Chicago Defender Press*, and the Federated Press (the news service bureau for American labor). She was also on the editorial board of the *Soviet Russia Today*, a prominent Russian newspaper, and *The Woman Today*, an American trade union magazine.

Edwards wrote long, detailed, descriptive stories, particularly on the impact of capitalism, imperialism, and colonialism on the lives of ordinary struggling peoples. Barnett often chastised her for sending stories with 2,000 and 2,500 words, instead of the 500 words he required, and her sister, Thelma, told her that she had "too fullsome a style." But while pleading guilty "to forgetting that stipulation of 500 words," she told Barnett that "just saying 500 words isn't enough. Which 500 words?" (Edwards to C. Barnett, December 7, 1936).

Lecture Tours

Edwards's stories gained wide popularity among Black readers in America, but her lectures were popular among people of all colors. She was a much sought after speaker, carving out a grueling schedule for herself. She would take Black people on tour to Mexico during July and then tour Europe during August and September. She would come back to the Chicago-Gary area and take a month to recuperate from her tours and journalistic work; then her season on the lecture circuit would begin and go on until it was time for another travel seminar.

Edwards's chairpersonship of the Women's Section of the National Negro Congress, a Black left-wing civil rights organization, her position as executive director of the Congress of American Women, and her membership in the American Association of Social Workers and several other professional groups kept her going back and forth across

America for speaking engagements. In addition, she "conducted seminars on labor and social action for the Foundation of Religion and Labor at numerous colleges and universities, including Kentucky State A&M, Duke, North Carolina State University, Gammon Theological Seminary, and Florida A&M. She also lectured widely abroad" ("Thyra Edwards Coming to Buffalo," 1944, p. 1).

Edwards's strength as a speaker was that she was highly competent in speaking on a wide range of important subjects and, as one reporter put it, "in her own graphic style" (Cooke, 1936, p. 6). She loved talking just as much as she loved writing and traveling, and she did so with a kind of clarity, confidence, and eloquence that generally left her audience dazzled.

The Spanish Civil War

The outbreak of the Spanish Civil War in 1936 meant to Thyra J. Edwards, the political activist with leanings to the left, a worldwide drive to halt the spread of fascism and, hopefully, to prevent World War II, but it also was a test case of the major social work ideas she had been trying to teach throughout most of her professional life. She had said to Black Americans all along that there are "no geographical escapes for the race. For the individual Negro—yes. He can find those anywhere, even in America. But for the mass man, the group, the race, no. He has to fight the issue out on all fronts" (Edwards, 1936a, p. 140).

"Just now," she wrote, "the Spanish people happen to be symbolic of all the rest of us. And certainly there isn't going to be any freedom and equality for Negroes until and unless there is a free world" (Edwards to C. Barnett, October 15, 1937). Therefore, she felt that Spain was the major front on which the progressive peoples of the world were called to do battle, and she wasted little time heading for Barcelona, Spain, as a delegate of the leftist-oriented Social Workers' Committee to Aid Spanish Democracy. Traveling, working, and living with Constance Kyle, a White Chicago social worker whom Edwards described as "a splendid type," Edwards declared that "we are not on an international save the Negro crusade but rather on an international commission concerned with freedom and democracy for all kinds of people" (Edwards to C. Barnett, October 15, 1937).

In Barcelona, Edwards found herself in the midst of air raids, which she said "we've had nightly since we've been here" (Edwards to C. Barnett, October 15, 1937). Nevertheless, she threw herself into her characteristic "give-it-all-you've-got." She resumed her journalistic work, and in the face of machine gun fire and bombs, she went in search of other famous Black people, such as Langston Hughes, Paul Robeson, Claude McKay, and the Cuban poet Nicholas Guillen, who were serving in Spain. Most important, she tried to track down the hundred or so Black Americans who served in Spain under the Lincoln and Washington Battalions of the Fifteenth Brigade. The Moors, who were being used as shock troops by fascist Franco to overthrow Spanish democracy, were also subjects of her stories (Edwards, 1938).

Edwards wanted to be the eyes through which Black America could see close up what was happening in Spain and its relevance to the darker people of the world, but her main concern was the plight of the Spanish children. She worked tirelessly in the children's colonies, organizing homes and relief stations for the thousands of innocent children who had been left homeless, motherless, maimed, and terrified by the ravages of war. Edwards also set up psychiatric units to deal with the psychological and emotional effects of war on children; she was probably one of the first social workers to treat war trauma in children. (Anna Freud and others did this several years later during World War II.) While Edwards's work with the children was pioneering, her hopes for freedom for the Spanish people proved to be in vain. Madrid fell into the hands of the fascists, and in 1939, the bitter, bloody Spanish Civil War came to an end.

Many Black and White American leftists had given their lives in the Spanish conflict. Many others walked away depressed, discouraged, and disillusioned. Edwards, however, shifted her battle to yet another front. She went to Mexico and set up the Spanish Relief Campaign. This campaign helped over 40,000 Spanish refugees to gain political asylum and resettle in Mexico. She also went to the Soviet Union to study the plight of women and children there and to understand the implications for child welfare and women's struggles in America.

Personal Life

Since Edwards's brand of social work embraced the world, her life was busy and full; she lived at an exhausting pace. She was so serious, determined, and committed to struggle for social change that even her personal life was generally associated with her personal growth as a social work professional. She once told a lover: "How I hunger for your touch. Please don't let me go away from you so long again. . . . Never again will it be my doing that six months separate us. Life is too soon over" (Edwards to Phillip, January 5, 1934). But Edwards would go away for long stretches time and time again because she loved meeting people and making friends in faraway places. Of course, her main reason for traveling abroad was to study socioeconomic and political conditions with a view toward showing Black Americans the parallels between their plight and the condition of the oppressed peoples of the world. She said, "It is really quite interesting when you go after it. Europe becomes only another USA . . . with people . . . just as eager to be friends as we are" (Edwards to C. Barnett, August 25, 1936). Making friends abroad helped her to strengthen her perspective of worldwide social welfare issues.

Edwards enjoyed entertaining her friends in America and abroad and being entertained by them. She particularly enjoyed having friends over to her place for lavish meals. She had such a great reputation for being an excellent cook that she had even proposed doing a weekly newspaper column featuring her menus and recipes. Edwards's reputation for being a fine dresser equaled her reputation as a cook. She designed many of her own clothes and some for her friends as well.

Edwards learned much about the issue of race and color while entertaining or being entertained by friends abroad. For example, in the Soviet Union on the Black Sea Riviera, she enjoyed bathing in the nude with her friends and found her skin color to be an asset. She wrote:

> There are some splendid specimens—as well as some pretty flabby numbers. Many sunburned blacker than I. And I was trying to bake a few shades darker. It's more popular here. I'd love to be one of those velvety black gals. I could tuck this end of the world in my breast pocket. And even a mere brown skin has no cause to complain. (Edwards to C. Barnett, October 30, 1936)

But, sometimes her skin color put her and her friends in danger:

> I went over to Germany to visit my little family. They were both happy and frightened to see me. For things are more tense in Germany and people who entertain foreign guests are immediately subject and liable to police raids. And to entertain a Negro? That was enough to put you in jail for six months. (Edwards to C. Barnett, August 25, 1936)

Meeting and knowing personally some of the world's leading musicians, artists, actors, actresses, and writers helped Edwards to cultivate an interest in the arts. She also enjoyed attending world fairs, festivals, and exhibitions. For example, she was excited as she wrote Barnett that the Russians were "getting ready for a Pushkin jubilee next year. Also, a great agricultural exhibition. Then there's the Paris exhibition. I shall build my tours around these" (Edwards to C. Barnett, October 20, 1930).

Even with her greatest love, her family, Edwards tended to mix play with learning and teaching. She wrote long letters to her mother detailing her experiences at home and abroad, and she often took her sisters with her on travel seminars. It was only during the Christmas holiday that Edwards seemed not to mix her professional life with her social life. No matter where she was in the world, she always tried to return to the United States in time for Christmas with her family. She said, "Christmas is my birthday and my family has always made much of it in quiet family fashion. My aunt Anna is a miracle and makes me feel like a cream puff" (Edwards to C. Barnett, March 22, 1944).

Besides her family, children were Edwards's greatest love. She never bore any children of her own, but she considered all children, not just her nephew, Billie, to be her children. She loved being in the presence of and working tirelessly on behalf of them wherever she was needed in the world. Child welfare was to be her main area of interest from the beginning to the end of her professional career as a social worker.

Final Years

Edwards's international perspective of social work kept her working on three major fronts: the welfare of children, the struggles of women, and the outcries of the darker people of the world. All this required high-level activity and exhausting work, but her seemingly boundless energy belied the fact that she had severe health problems for much of her life. Low blood pressure, she said, "simply knocks me down," and a bronchial condition often kept her bed-ridden (Edwards to C. Barnett, April 2, 1934). Edwards herself often said that she was doing too much, and her family and friends agreed.

World War II slowed Edwards down somewhat; it brought an abrupt end to her travel seminars (she took her last group to Europe and to Mexico in 1940); meanwhile, the American government tried to put an end to her political activities at home. By 1942, Edwards, still working at the Lincoln Centre, was interviewed by the Subversive Personnel Committee of the Federal Security Agency. The interviewer asked her, "Are you now, or have you ever been a member of the communist party?" She answered, "I am not now and have never been a member of the communist party." She was even asked, "Is there, to your knowledge, a unit of the communist party in Chicago, or elsewhere, known as or called 'The Thyra Edwards Unit'?" To this she replied, "I have never heard of a so-called 'Thyra Edwards Unit'" (Edwards to P. H. Lowrey, Executive Secretary, Subversive Personnel Committee, Washington, DC, December 12, 1942).

In 1943, Edwards left her beloved Chicago and went to New York to work as managing editor for *The People's Voice*, a newspaper founded by the flamboyant politician, Adam Clayton Powell, Jr. That same summer, Edwards, then 45 years old, married Murray Gitlin, an official of the United Jewish Appeal. In November of that year, she underwent major surgery, resulting in several months of inactivity.

The following year, 1944, was an equally challenging one. She became assistant director of the Education and Public Relations Department of the National Maritime Union. Her father's death that year left her devastated, and although she had recovered from the major surgery, she said that a problem that developed subsequently "still holds me to the house, unable to walk" (Edwards to C. Barnett, March 22, 1944).

By April 1944, Edwards was able to walk well enough to attend the International Labor Conference in Philadelphia to discuss post-war planning for the colonized peoples of the world. Edwards was disappointed that the Black governments of Haiti, Ethiopia, and Liberia had not sent delegates to the conference, particularly since she said these countries had such "backward labor policies" (1944b, p. 233). She was even more dismayed that Black American leaders and the Black press did not take the conference seriously enough to attend. After all, she had spend a good portion of her life trying to convince Black Americans that they needed to develop an international focus, and she felt certain that they needed to be present at any world body that was seeking to plan the future of the world's people of color.

At the end of World War II, in 1945, Edwards, who was the executive director of the Congress of American Women, served on an international committee investigating post-war conditions in Germany. Here again, her concern was basically with the plight of women and children. In 1948, she followed her husband to Italy where he became director of a branch of the American Joint Distribution Committee. There in Italy, Edwards learned to speak Italian, took up painting, developed friendships, mingled with peasants and the clergy, and became "an active participant in Jewish community life" (Ades, 1953). Also, in accordance with her nature, she organized the first Jewish child care program in Rome, assisting Jewish children who had been victims of the Holocaust (Ades, 1953). This was a remarkable feat in itself, an African American woman creating homes for Jewish children in Italy, yet it was thoroughly consistent with Edwards's international approach to social work.

After five years in Italy (1948–1953), Edwards's health began to deteriorate again, and the Gitlins rushed back to New York City in the winter of 1953 where Edwards underwent another surgery. Sensing that her life was about to end, Edwards outlined several books that she had wanted to write, and she sketched out topical information for her autobiography to be entitled *A Thread from Every Man in the Village*. The theme was that if each adult gave a thread, then every child in the village could be clothed. All of her life Edwards had given thread, but she would never live to see her autobiography completed. She died on July 9, 1953. Memorial services were held at the St. Phillip Episcopal Church in Harlem. One of her longtime friends, Bernard Ades (1953), delivered the eulogy, in which he said:

> Our friend, Thyra, was a well-rounded large soul, who knew how to combine all the softer virtues with the hard struggle for the rights of humanity. She not only knew how to do it, she did it. In her last days she said that she was satisfied that she had led a full, rich life and has no regrets. We agree.

Thyra J. Edwards Gitlin was cremated, and her ashes were scattered over the Atlantic Ocean that she had crossed time and time again throughout her adult life.

Edwards as a Model Social Worker

In many regards, social work is just beginning to catch up to where Thyra J. Edwards was years ago. She emphasized that a chief role of the social worker was to fight against oppression in all forms and to promote social justice and equality. She urged social workers to become advocates on behalf of disadvantaged and at-risk populations. She believed that social workers should address issues and problems specifically affecting the well-being of women. Edwards stressed cultural diversity or the need of social workers to be able to work with many diverse populations. These are all key areas that the Council of Social Work Education is emphasizing today in the training of social workers for both the bachelor's degree and the master's degree.

Years ago, she believed that Black people should use their own history and culture to inform their ideas about social work. While she believed that Black people should join interracial organizations and lead them, she also believed that they should build their own institutions, just as she had created the children's home. Only recently has social work given some attention to a Black experience–based social work practice (Martin & Martin, 1995).

In international social work, Edwards was far ahead of social workers today. Contemporary social workers emphasize micro, mezzo, and macro systems, but Edwards, realizing how small capitalist expansion had made the world, was operating on the levels of what modern sociologists (thanks to the pioneering Black sociologist, Oliver C. Cox) call "world systems theory." The idea that the plight of Black Americans and the American worker is linked to the destiny of the people of Europe, Africa, Asia, and South America is just as foreign to social workers today as it was to them several decades ago. Yet this idea was the cornerstone of Edwards's social philosophy and the guide to her social work praxis. Martin and Martin (1985) wrote that "as black social workers become increasingly conscious of the plight of blacks throughout the world, coming face to face with such stark realities as the daily death of thousands of Africans by starvation, they will strive for greater globalization of social work" (p. 89). In her pioneering work with children made refugees and children traumatized by war, Edwards was trying to catapult social workers into the twenty-first century as far back as the 1930s and 1940s.

If Edwards was ahead of social workers today in her emphasis on internationalism, then she was definitely ahead of her contemporaries on many fronts. At a time when it was practically unheard of for Black people to rise to the level of a supervisory or administrative role, Edwards played that role consistently. At a time when White social workers were reluctant to work alongside Black social workers for fear of being accused of the racist taboo of "fraternization with niggers," Edwards not only worked well with White people, but also felt comfortable in positions where she was in charge. At a time when White social workers thought that Black social workers should help only Black clients, Thyra J. Edwards worked with clients of all races and nationalities, whether they were Jewish survivors of the Holocaust, Spanish refugee children, or White Americans down-and-out from the Depression. At a time when women's issues were hardly a consideration—even for social workers practicing "the woman's profession"—Edwards was making the welfare of women a top agenda item. As the executive director of the Congress of American Women, she led American women, Black and White, toward linking their struggle to that of the women of the world.

Edwards believed that one fought wherever oppression, inequality, and social injustice were, whether local, national, or international, and that each advance anywhere was an advance everywhere for democracy, equality, and justice. She believed that whether working inside the establishment or outside or both (as she generally did), one was obligated to seek to radicalize, humanize, and reform the system. She believed that right-wing reactionary thinking ideologically impeded progressive social change and should always be challenged vociferously. Nowhere is this thinking more relevant than with the right-wing domination of social welfare discourse today; many social workers are growing more conservative and reactionary in scope by the minute. Edwards's dynamic theory of social action, her sensitivity to human suffering, and her willingness to give her fullest energy and attention to making life better for every person on the planet make her a great role model of commitment and compassion to be emulated by social workers now and in the future.

Note

1. For the correspondence, autobiographical sketches, travel itinerary, and so forth on Thyra J. Edwards, see the Thyra J. Edwards Papers Society, Chicago, Illinois, and the Claude Barnett Papers at the Chicago Historical Society. The professional profile of Thyra J. Edwards and all the letters cited in this work are from those papers.

References

Ades, B. (1953, July 12). Eulogy of Thyra Edwards Gitlin. Delivered at Saint Phillips Church, New York City. Thyra J. Edwards Papers, Chicago Historical Society.

Cooke, M. (1936, December 12). She was in Paris and forgot Chanel. *Amsterdam News*, pp. 6, 11.

Edwards, T. J. (1932, May). Chicago in the rain: Relief for Negro homeless men on the south side. *Opportunity*, *10*, 148, 149.

Edwards, T. J. (1935a, March). Let us have more like Mr. Sopkins. *Crisis*, *42*, 72, 82.

Edwards, T. J. (1935b, June). Who is disinterested? *Crisis*, *42*, 173–174, 187.

Edwards, T. J. (1936a, May). Negro literature comes to Denmark. *Crisis*, *43*, 140, 141, 146.

Edwards, T. J. (1936b, July). Attitudes of Negro families on relief. *Opportunity*, *14*, 213–215.

Edwards, T. J. (1938, March). Moors in the Spanish War. *Opportunity*, *16*, 84–85.

Edwards, T. J. (1940, January 6). Unprejudiced Mexico. Thyra J. Edwards Papers, Chicago Historical Society.

Edwards, T. J. (1944a). Are "race relations advisors" helping or hindering the advance of the Negro? Claude Barnett Papers, Chicago Historical Society.

Edwards, T. J. (1944b, July). The ILO and post-war planning for the colonies. *Crisis, 51*, 217–220, 233.

Edwards, T. J. (1945, January). A new deal for French Africa. *Crisis*, *52*, 10–13, 29.

Evans, J. W. (1935, July). Thumbs down on unions. *Crisis*, *42*, 103, 114.

Martin, E. P., & Martin, J. M. (1985). *The helping tradition in the Black family and community*. Washington, DC: NASW Press.

Martin, E. P., & Martin, J. M. (1995). *Social work and the Black experience*. Washington, DC: NASW Press.

Thyra Edwards coming to Buffalo with Captain Mulzac. (1944, October 27). *Amsterdam News*, p. 1.

CHAPTER 13

Sarah Collins Fernandis and Her Hidden Work

Huguette A. Curah

The career of Sarah Collins Fernandis so clearly epitomizes the social work concept of *service* that its omission from social work history leaves social work education incomplete. Fernandis's work is of importance to social work, African American history, and American history. Her work spanned the period from the early 1890s to her death in 1951 (Randolph & Roses, 1990), and her contributions as a social worker included the following: pioneering the African American settlement house movement (Peebles-Wilkins, 1995); participating in post-Civil War reconstruction work from Pennsylvania to Vermont; teaching school in several states; improving the housing conditions for poor African Americans in Maryland, Washington, DC, Pennsylvania, and Rhode Island; organizing waste disposal in the African American neighborhoods of Washington, DC, and Baltimore; establishing daycare centers for African American working mothers; initiating the school lunch program in Baltimore's African American public schools; and advocating for public health for African Americans on the local and national levels (Fernandis, 1917, 1924; Moore, 1923; Peebles-Wilkins, 1995). The work that Sarah Collins Fernandis performed nearly a century ago in the settlement house movement is consistent with today's philosophy of family support social work practice.

Sarah A. Collins was born on March 8, 1863, to Caleb Alexander and Mary Jane Driver Collins of Port De Poset, Maryland, now called Port Deposit (Mather, 1915; Randolph & Roses, 1990). At the age of fourteen, she enrolled at the Hampton Normal and Agricultural Institute for Negroes and Indians, where she graduated salutatorian in 1882 (Randolph & Roses, 1990). Between the years of 1882 and 1890, she attended the New York School of Social Work (now known as New York University), after which she taught for 3 years at the Hampton Institute. General Armstrong, founder of the Hampton Institute, then recommended her for another teaching position. This first position outside Hampton was with the Women's Home Missionary Society of Boston, a teaching assignment that took her to Florida, Georgia, Tennessee, and other southern states. This teaching position gave Collins a close look at the plight of post-Civil War African Americans in that part of the country. These recently emancipated African Americans believed that migrating to the North was the answer to the joblessness, poverty, and hatred that faced them in the South. During this experience, Fernandis caught a glimpse of the enormous amount of work that was needed to improve the lives of these former slaves, with whom she closely identified and empathized. These early teaching years preceded her teaching and social work career in Baltimore, Maryland (Collins, 1893; Moore, 1923).

Collins taught in Philadelphia in the middle to late 1890s, then returned to her native Baltimore in the late 1890s or early 1900s, where she taught in the public school system for a few years. While teaching, she began performing casework as a volunteer Friendly Visitor with the Charity Organization Society of Baltimore. It was during this time that she met John Fernandis whom she married in 1902 (Moore, 1923). The scant information provided on John Fernandis indicates that he was a barber and something of a social worker himself. It is documented that John Fernandis worked with male youths and was actively involved in the "mission," at least in the Colored Settlement of Washington, DC (Moore, 1923).

Soon after their marriage, the Fernandis couple moved to Washington, DC, where they set up housekeeping and became involved with the Washington branch of the Associated Charities. The general secretary of the Washington Associated Charities had met Fernandis during her teaching years in Baltimore and requested that she come to Washington to establish the Colored Department of the Associated Charities. Fernandis accepted, attending the biweekly conferences and meetings held by the Associated Charities whose topics for discussion included "The Moral Standards of the Alleys," "Intermittent Husbands and Lax Family Ties," and "Colored Offenders and the Police Courts." These biweekly meetings were planning sessions where members of the Colored Conference Class formulated analyses of and remedies to the social problems of the inner city Negro (Fernandis, 1904). The meetings included visits to the inner city neighborhoods identified as most in need of social work services. According to Fernandis, this is where plans were made for the first African American social settlement in the United States (Fernandis, 1904).

The Colored Social Settlement

In October 1902, Fernandis and her husband relocated to an area described as the worst Black neighborhood in the District of Columbia and began their settlement house, the Colored Social Settlement. The neighborhood was called "Bloodfield," after its reputation for violence and bloodshed, and Fernandis was determined to change its reputation by changing the state, habits, and attitudes of its inhabitants. Fernandis believed that the substandard living conditions of the poor African Americans in Bloodfield were the result of social and economic deprivation inflicted on disenfranchised people by the larger society. Fernandis also believed that it was her duty to empower her people in order to improve their standard of living. Using a strategy that can be seen as a prototype for today's family support approach to social work practice, Fernandis worked toward and achieved enormous gains for the poor African American families of the Colored Social Settlement of Washington, DC.

The family support approach to social work practice identifies several important concepts that are critical to working with families and communities. For example, it stresses the need for restoring to the family or community the responsibility of articulating its service needs to the social worker, rather than allowing the social worker's assessment to be the main determinant for service provision. Family support philosophy also requires that the program provide clients with an atmosphere designed to make them feel at home (Batavick, 1997). The typical family support program maintains as its focal point for intervention the family or community unit. The typical family support program works toward empowerment of the unit through the promotion of community "helper" relationships, as well as through an emphasis on unit strengths. The work of Sarah Collins Fernandis in the Colored Social Settlement embodies all of these family support concepts, with the additional feature of her actual residence in the settlement house. Essentially, Fernandis became a "settler" (Simon, 1994), residing in the settlement house and becoming a neighbor to those whom she served.

Fernandis's achievements while at the Colored Social Settlement included establishing a branch of the public library in the settlement; teaching the community to save money through a stamp savings program; establishing a milk distribution station; providing day and evening care services for the children of working mothers; providing free kindergarten classes; providing homemaking classes for women and girls, teaching such subjects as sewing, cleaning, and cooking; providing food to those without; providing clubs for all ages, male and female; providing public bathing facilities for those in need; establishing the first playground open for African American children in Baltimore; successfully lobbying for compulsory school attendance legislation and better housing conditions for the poor African American community; establishing trade classes for male youth; establishing the strong and effective "Neighborhood Association"; providing volunteer opportunities for willing college students at the settlement; conducting home visits and family counseling; providing job referral services; and sharing information on property beautification (Fernandis, 1905, 1906, 1907, 1910; "Personal Notes," 1904; Woods & Kennedy, 1970). Many of the preceding service endeavors would today fall under the general heading of family support social work practice, indeed embodying the very framework of this approach to social work.

Fernandis placed great emphasis on teaching her neighbors skills from which their families and community would reap a lifetime of benefits. These skills were deemed essential to alleviate economic and social depravity. Some of these life skills included financial savings, trades, housekeeping, and child rearing. Fernandis did not limit the teaching of these skills to one venue, alternately teaching in classrooms at the settlement house, during home visits, in the street, during club meetings, and in the example of her own actions. The teaching of these life skills, and the choices they represented for African Americans at that point in American history, exemplify the family support (and social work) value of client empowerment. By teaching skills such as thrift and saving money through the stamp savings program, Fernandis provided economic empowerment to neighboring families within the community. This empowerment was not limited to the ability to save and the choice of how to spend their saved money, but included the psychological benefits that accompanied a family's newfound ability to plan for its own future. Through this type of concrete social service, Fernandis was also giving the individuals and families hope, a rare commodity in the slums and tenements of Washington, DC, and Baltimore (Batavick, 1997; Fernandis, 1904, 1905; "Founder's Day," 1910).

Building a Neighborhood Network

Another way in which Fernandis's work typified family support social work practice was in her use of home visiting to establish relationships with her neighbors, conduct informal needs assessments, and provide services. The philosophy of the family support approach includes the notion of social workers assuming roles resembling those of family members (Batavick, 1997). This concept of a worker being part of the family was familiar to Fernandis who became intimately involved with the lives of those she served, believing that close proximity would enable her to provide comprehensive services. Fernandis, for example, visited the home of "Baby Ben," whose teen-aged mother was not able to adequately care for him due to a lack of resources. Fernandis described this home visit in rich detail and identified the services that she provided to the family as a result of the informal needs assessment gleaned from the home visit. Those services included referring Ben's mother to the appropriate agency to obtain employment services, providing her with affordable daycare services, providing Ben with milk, and teaching the young mother how to care for the baby's skin ailments as well as how to meet his general physical needs (Fernandis, 1905).

Fernandis's success as a social worker was due not only to her ability to reach those in need of services, but also to her ability to engage those privileged members of society whose resources could benefit her neighbors at the Colored Social Settlement. Fernandis matched the disenfranchised African American families with better off African American students, teachers, and wealthy White philanthropists through the use of volunteers, program sponsors, and political advisors and agitators. She recruited college students, as well as teachers, to provide direct services as volunteers. The list of volunteers included students from the Colored Normal School, Howard University, and the Armstrong Manual Training School. Local schoolteachers and at least one local school principal also volunteered their time and expertise. These volunteers were employed as mentors to the settlement's youth, as classroom instructors, as after-school tutors, and as facilitators at club meetings. One such volunteer took over as director of the Colored Social Settlement when Fernandis moved on to begin another settlement house (Fernandis, 1904, 1905, 1906, 1907; Simkovitch, 1908).

Utilizing her connections with the (White) Associated Charities and "some of the best white citizens of the city," Fernandis advocated for habitable housing for the families in the settlement community while she initiated proceedings to have old, uninhabitable shacks torn down and new, low-income housing built for the African American families. Again, using her personal and political power within both the Black and White communities, Fernandis was instrumental in securing the Congressional funding of the first playground for African American children in Washington, DC. This use of available and influential human capital is yet another example of how Fernandis's work is illustrative of what is now known as family support, fitting in with the philosophical notion of building new and improving existing helper relationships (Batavick, 1997; Fernandis, 1907).

Historical Accord

The incredible work and vision of Fernandis clearly have historical significance. First, Fernandis's work constitutes necessary measures taken to achieve a modicum of decency in the lives of African Americans in her era. Second, Fernandis performed tasks in the *tradition* of African American social workers across the country, with perhaps more visible results in that day. Third, Fernandis achieved amazing results and recognition at a time when being an African American, as well as assisting African Americans, was of no interest to the majority of the nation's citizens.

Fernandis's accomplishments at the Colored Social Settlement did not go unnoticed by her contemporaries. The success of Fernandis's Colored Social Settlement was recognized by the National Conference of Charities and Corrections, the American Institute of Social Service, and The Charity Organization of New York; articles about her settlement work were published in the journals *Social Service* and *Charities*. The Colored Social Settlement was visited by "experienced settlement workers from other cities, notably one from London's East End" (Fernandis, 1906, p. 48) indicating that, among settlement workers, Fernandis had attracted *international* attention. This international interest inspired visits from other pioneer settlement house workers from Oxford's Toynbee Hall (Carson, 1990; Fernandis, 1906).

Mary White Ovington also visited the Colored Social Settlement and expressed a deep respect for Fernandis's settlement work and for the way in which she did the work. Ovington's published comment was "You could not anywhere find a settlement carried on upon finer, more practical, and sympathetic lines" (Moore, 1923, p. 322). Ovington's comment implies that Fernandis's work was at least equal to that of White settlement workers and superior to that of many.

Fernandis's work was all the more remarkable because the societal norms of the Progressive Era included legalized discrimination based on race. It was legal to keep African Americans segregated and legal to deny their educational, social, medical, and environmental "betterment." This made it much more difficult to solicit funds for efforts to assist the poor African American communities than it was to obtain monies for efforts to assist the White immigrant communities. Furthermore, the American version of the settlement movement was specifically aimed at alleviating the distress of the growing immigrant population, not that of the African American migrant population. This spirit of discrimination pervaded the social service field, facilitating the exclusion of African Americans in service provision efforts, even by the settlement workers. According to Trolander (1975), "many settlement workers shared the prejudices of the period and either ignored the black or sought to relegate him to an inferior place" (p. 24). Ovington was, in fact, part of a small minority in her belief that African Americans could benefit from a social settlement. Apart from a select few, the general belief among White settlement workers was that African Americans "could best progress on their own, through separate self-help or racially oriented organizations, but not through the settlement movement" (Lasch-Quinn, 1993, p. 5).

Fernandis believed, as did other settlement workers, that the existing societal structure was responsible for the poverty of those she served and that African Americans had no choice but to live as they did. The chasm between the ideology of Fernandis and that of her White contemporaries lies in Fernandis's belief that this was true for African Americans and her work to address this truth. The majority of White settlement workers believed that poor African American people were in as dire need of assistance as immigrants, but that African Americans were so inferior socially and intellectually that they were beyond White help. This is illustrated by Davis's (1967) quote of a worker in a settlement for Blacks, who stated, "Our settlement has its unique problem for it deals not with a race that is intellectually hungry, but with a race at the *sensation* [italics added] stage of its evolution and the treatment demanded is different" (p. 95).

The aforementioned existing structure as it related to African Americans consisted of enforced racial segregation, scarcity of work for African American farm workers who had recently migrated to the North, lack of social welfare assistance, scarcity of educational opportunities for poor African Americans, and a studied neglect of the living conditions and needs of African Americans by the majority population. Fernandis believed that societal norms forced the inner city African American into poverty and despair. Describing her neglected African American neighborhood in the District of Columbia in 1907, Fernandis said, "It seems but natural that the class of Negro segregated here should be notoriously self-expressed by a prevalence of lazy lounging on saloon corners, a general appearance of slovenly unkemptness and oft-recurring petty offenses . . . " (p. 704). Fernandis believed that both society (as much of it as she could reach) and the poor, "delinquent Negro" would have to work at a remedy for their current plight.

Education Matters

Fernandis believed that education and social activism were the keys to improving the condition of poor African Americans. Moreover, she believed that African Americans needed political knowledge to agitate for needed changes, but that this would be impossible without formal education. To this end, she advocated for compulsory school attendance legislation that would affect the neglected African American communities, and she set out to educate and organize the settlement community in the District regarding needed social changes. Fernandis believed that people could and would work together toward the mutual goal of betterment of the social conditions of African Americans, and she was not afraid of enlisting the aid of organizations and individuals. Far from being naive about the racist barriers to cooperation, Fernandis became an expert negotiator, maneuvering the potholes of racial hatred by using her network of supporters in places such as the Associated Charities to obtain audiences with those who may otherwise have been opposed to aiding the African American. Fernandis was able to convince reluctant philanthropists that they would receive returns on their investments and that these were not simply donations, but investments in human capital (Fernandis, 1924; Moore, 1923).

Fernandis disliked the separation of neighbors by fences, and as part of her work she taught unified neighborhood by example, initiating conversations with all who passed through or by the settlement. This approach sent the message that the settlement belonged to the community and that Fernandis and her team were accessible, regardless of the need or the time. Yet, Fernandis saw this as "among the most touching features of the work" (Fernandis, 1906, p. 47). Essentially, she believed in being a living example and in speaking her mind, telling the neighborhood drunks to save their money instead of drinking it, showing "careless but not unheeding" mothers of neglected children how to care for their children, and showing neighbors with neglected yards how to beautify by gardening (Fernandis, 1905). Fernandis liked to talk to neighbors where yards adjoined, exchanging recipes, seeds, news, and advice. She vehemently advocated for African American property ownership, even by the very poor; Fernandis was instrumental in the creation of special housing programs that assisted African Americans in leasing with the intention of buying their homes.

It is impossible to give an adequately descriptive picture of Fernandis without giving many more examples of her work beyond the Colored Social Settlement. That pioneer social settlement for African Americans exemplifies Fernandis's contribution to social work and its true meaning to practice frameworks, such as family support. The Colored Social Settlement further illustrates how easily racism changes history, simply by the omission of facts. Femandis's accomplishments in that social settlement alone ought to have earned her a place not only in social work history, but also in American history. Hers was the first official social settlement for African Americans in the United States.

A Career Expands

Fernandis was not limited to settlement work, although she responded to another request and went on to form a second African American social settlement in Greenwich, Rhode Island. Fernandis was asked to organize efforts in Pennsylvania, and then she was asked by the National League of Women Voters to be part of a lecture tour aimed at garnering financial support and "a sympathetic fellow-feeling for the colored woman worker" (Moore, 1923, p. 324). Fernandis was also asked to begin the "Colored" branch of the Women's Civic League, called the Cooperative Women's Civic League in Baltimore; invited to serve on the Women's Advisory Council to the U.S. Public Health Service in Washington, DC; and appointed as the first African American social investigator in the first African American public health clinic at Baltimore's racially segregated Provident Hospital (Moore, 1923; "Graduates," 1922; "Negro Housing," 1916).

Sarah Collins Fernandis led a remarkable professional life. Her life was all the more remarkable because she was African American and female. All of Fernandis's achievements and appointments attest to the breadth and depth of her contributions to social work and to the fact that she had eventually gained some degree of acceptance among some of her White contemporaries. Her life's work and professional acceptance have historical implications and could not have gone unchronicled except by deliberate exclusion. This is unfortunate, as her contributions to social welfare and to the practice of social work are significant, although their significance is limited to those who are now deceased: her contemporaries and her community. Fortunately, Fernandis was not as limited in life as she has been in death.

References

Batavick, L. (1997). Community-based family support and youth development: Two movements, one philosophy. *Child Welfare, 76*(5), 639–664.

Carson, M. (1990). *Settlement folk: Social thought and the American settlement movement, 1885–1930.* Chicago: The University of Chicago Press.

Collins. S. A. (1893, September). Sidelights on the "other half." *The Southern Workman.*

Davis, A. F. (1967). *Spearheads for reform: The social settlements and the progressive movement, 1890–1914.* New York: Oxford University Press.

Fernandis, S. C, (1904, June) A colored social settlement. *The Southern Workman,* pp. 346–350.

Fernandis. S. C. (1905, October 7) A social settlement in South Washington. *Charities,* pp. 64–66.

Fernandis, S. C. (1906, April). Neighborhood interpretations of a social settlement. *The Southern Workman,* pp. 46–49.

Fernandis, S. C. (1907, September 14). In the making. *Charities and the Commons,* pp. 703–705.

Fernandis, S. C. (1909, May). The children's open door. *The Southern Workman,* p. 272.

Fernandis, S. C. (1910, April). Hampton's relation to the constructive needs of the Negro. *The Southern Workman,* pp. 202–205.

Fernandis, S. C. (1917, October). Social service work in Baltimore. *The Southern Workman,* pp. 537–542.

Fernandis, S. C. (1924, November). A more excellent way. *The Southern Workman,* pp. 526–528.

Founder's Day Services. (1910, February). *The Southern Workman,* p. 77.

Graduates and Ex-Students. (1922, August). *The Southern Workman,* p. 391.

Lasch-Quinn, E. (1993). *Black neighbors: Race and the limits of reform in the American settlement movement, 1890–1945,* Chapel Hill: University of North Carolina Press.

Mather, F. (Ed.). (1915). *Who's who of the colored race.* Reprint. Detroit: Gale Research. 1976.

Moore, R. H. (1923, July). A pioneer settlement worker. *The Southern Workman,* pp. 320–324.

Negro housing in Baltimore. (1916, April). *The Southern Workman,* p. 208.

Peebles-Wilkins, W. (1995). Fernandis, Sarah A. Collins. In *Biographies Encyclopedia of Social Work,* (19th ed., Vol. 3, p. 2584). Washington, DC: NASW Press.

Personal notes. (1904, July). *The Southern Workman,* p. 412.

Randolph, R. E., & Roses, L. E. (1990). *Harlem Renaissance and biographies: Literary biographies of 100 Black women writers, 1900–1945.* Boston: G.K. Hall & Co.

Simkovitch, M. (1908, July). Colored settlement work. *Charities and the Commons,* p. 507.

Simon, B. (1994). *The empowerment tradition in American social work.* New York: Columbia University Press.

Trolander, J. (1975). *Settlement houses and the Great Depression.* Detroit: Wayne State University Press.

Woods, R. A., & Kennedy, A. J. (Eds.). (1970). *Handbook on settlements.* New York: Arno Press and The New York Times.

CHAPTER 14

E. Franklin Frazier and Social Work

Unity and Conflict

Susan Kerr Chandler

I really don't know what will become of you.
Why don't you give up and conform and be comfortable?

Gustavus Steward ("Dock") to
E. Franklin Frazier, July 31, 1927

E. Franklin Frazier, director of the Atlanta School of Social Work from 1922 to 1927, is probably the best known of the African American pioneers in social work. He is scarcely *well* known—the *Encyclopedia of Social Work* did not include his biography until 1987 and schools of social work rarely note and less often study his contributions to the field. Still, his name is recognized, and his face appears on posters celebrating the profession's centennial where he is described as an "author," a "scholar noted for his studies of the black family," and as someone who "promoted training for social workers."

There is some irony in Frazier's recent emergence as a "social work pioneer." First, it was sociology, not social work, that brought Frazier to prominence. Frazier was the first African American president of the American Sociological Association and the author of eight books and over 100 articles in that field. The books include his widely read polemic, *Black Bourgeoisie* (1957a), and two important texts, *The Negro Family in the United States* (1939) and *The Negro in the United States* (1957b). Social work was late in claiming Frazier as its own. Second, the designation "pioneer" implies a relationship of mutual support, even pride, which Frazier and social work rarely enjoyed. Although Frazier worked with enormous energy during the 1920s to establish and accredit the first African American school of social work—the Atlanta School of Social Work—his relationship with the profession was as much characterized by conflict as it was common purpose.

Three of Frazier's intellectual and social commitments united him in part with social work and at the same time led to significant disjunctures with the profession. These are (1) a worldview that included socialism and the empowerment of the African American community through economic cooperation; (2) a radical commitment to racial justice, including an intense dedication to the kind of rigorous and scientific education that would "[fill] the Negro's mind with knowledge and [train] him in the fundamental habits of civilization" (Frazier, 1924d, p. 144); and (3) a controversial effort to use the combined tools of psychoanalysis and social inquiry to probe the internal operation of race prejudice and racial oppression in both Whites and Blacks. These commitments, combined with an irreverent sense of humor and a personal unwillingness to compromise, defined Frazier's achievements, enriched his energetic work on behalf of social work, and eventually contributed to his decision to draw away from the profession.

Six Years in Social Work[1]

E. Franklin Frazier was professionally associated with social work for 6 years during the 1920s. He was a student at the New York School of Social Work from 1920 to 1921, after earning an undergraduate degree from Howard University and a master's in sociology from Clark University. At the New York School, Frazier took a full round of courses and completed a major study of African American longshoremen. After a year's sojourn in Europe studying Danish cooperatives as a fellow of the American-Scandinavian Foundation, Frazier returned to the United States and took a position as professor at the Atlanta School of Social Work. A year later, he became its director, a position he held until 1927.

Frazier came to social work in 1920 at age 26 with a worldview already well formed. The son of a highly conscious race man and part of a remarkable generation of African Americans destined to lead the race through a period of intense social, political, and economic change, Frazier had a head start. At the age of 20, Frazier later wrote, he was already committed "to take an intense interest in the Negro problem. I was militant in my opposition to the existing race relations and urged young Negroes to assume a militant attitude toward discrimination and oppression" (1951, p. 234). He was deeply familiar with the emerging radical African American movements through work on his master's thesis, *New Currents of Thought Among Negroes in America* (1920). Frazier had vehemently opposed World War I, and he had spent the war years teaching and working for the Young Men's Christian Association in a kind of conscientious objector status (Platt, 1991). "I resented," he said, "being drafted in a war which, in my opinion, was essentially a conflict between imperialistic powers, and in view of the treatment of the Negro in the United States, the avowed aim, to make the world safe for democracy, represented hypocrisy on the part of America" (1951, p. 234).

It is not surprising that social work should be both enriched and threatened by the arrival in the profession of this brilliant, energetic, ideologically sophisticated, and well traveled young African American man. He would have had difficulty in any social work position. That he took up his career in the South at a time when Ku Klux Klan membership was soaring and at a fledging African American school of social work controlled mainly by a board of White liberals sealed his fate. Leaders like W. E. B. DuBois and William Robinson, a Georgia school superintendent, said when he was finally forced to resign, "[we] have felt from the beginning that Frazier was in . . . an impossible position" (Robinson to C. Adams, February 14, 1927).

When Frazier accepted the faculty position at the Atlanta School of Social Work, the school had been in existence just two years (Frazier, 1927a; Platt, 1991; Thomas, 1967). From his arrival in 1922, Frazier worked tirelessly to publicize the Atlanta school, to make it independent economically, and to attract qualified students (Davis, 1962; Platt, 1991). There is no evidence that he was not entirely successful in his efforts. It was impossible to read the Black press in those days without encountering the Atlanta School of Social Work and its young director. Frazier published 28 articles in both White and Black journals (see Edwards, 1968, for a bibliography of Frazier's works), won several prizes, and brought considerable attention to the school in exactly those circles that would be most likely to support a school of social work. He also made original contributions to social work education, practice, and theory, encouraging self-help and cooperation at a time when most of social work was turning toward individualized casework. He was a tireless chronicler of Black community life and set an example of militant activism against racism (Platt & Chandler, 1988; Platt, 1991).

Despite all of Frazier's successes, the board of directors "gently and politely" informed Frazier in February 1927 that they would "accept [his] resignation in June," a "strange climax," he wrote, "to my work in Atlanta" (Frazier, 1927a, p. 1). Frazier's departure will be examined after a closer look at those three intellectual and political commitments that defined his work, shaped his contributions to social work, and went beyond what the profession was ever prepared to handle.

A Lifelong Socialist

In 1915, E. Franklin Frazier joined the Howard University Socialist Club and began a lifelong commitment to socialism, economic cooperation, and documentation of the work lives of African Americans. Frazier shared these ideological commitments to a greater or lesser extent with social work contemporaries like Florence Kelley, Jane Addams, Edith Abbott, Mary Van Kleeck, and Eduard Lindeman.

Frazier's growing interest in socialism is apparent in his master's thesis, *New Currents of Thought Among Negroes in America* (1920), a survey of the "new radicalism" that Frazier wrote in the context of the enormous class and race militancy that followed World War I. *The Messenger,* a socialist magazine published by A. Philip Randolph (later president of the Brotherhood of Sleeping Car Porters) and Chandler Owen, clearly captured Frazier's attention. Frazier was already thinking about economic cooperation, which, he noted, was a significantly different strategy for attaining economic independence than that advocated by Booker T. Washington and the Tuskegee forces:

> [Washington] emphasized individual enterprise and initiative while [*The Messenger*], recognizing the growing tendency towards cooperative enterprise, urges the establishment of collective undertaking. This advice is sound for few Negroes possess sufficient capital to undertake business careers. (Frazier, 1920, p. 28)

Cooperation so interested Frazier that he applied for and won a fellowship from the American-Scandinavian Foundation to study Danish folk high schools and the well developed cooperative movement in Denmark. He was struck by the economic well-being and high cultural level of rural Denmark, "which offers such a contrast to rural life in the South" (1922b, p. 428), and during his tenure at the Atlanta School of Social Work, he repeatedly wrote on the advantages of cooperation (1922a, 1922b, 1923a, 1923b, 1924e, 1925b, 1927c). Frazier was alarmed at the low level of business acumen among Blacks and also at the tendency for wealth to be accumulated and ostentatiously displayed by a few (1923b). Frazier's experience in Denmark convinced him that there was another, better way to develop economically, and the articles he wrote on his return were meant to be a practical help in establishing cooperatives in African American communities. Cooperative enterprises, he wrote, were practical and simple; grew naturally from the economic situations in which rural African Americans found themselves; and could succeed. Most important, they would provide a context in which rural residents might learn organizational and business skills, the building blocks of democracy. Frazier, for his part, never assumed an automatic or easy progression from one social and legal status (for example, slavery) to another (for example, democracy) and felt leaders were obligated to construct the opportunities for "moral activity in society"—like schools, trade unions, and cooperative enterprises (Frazier, 1922b, p. 428).

Danish folk high schools, which served the children of the rural peasantry and were supported by the pledges of local citizens, particularly absorbed Frazier. "While in most countries, the days of idleness wear heavily on farmers' sons," he wrote, "the sons of Danish farmers congregate in these high schools . . . and their view of life is broadened and its meaning deepened" (1922a, p. 328). Frazier thought similar schools in the South could develop "broad and intelligent" rural community leadership and "stem the tide of artificial migration to cities of youths seeking a more varied environment," something he worried about (Frazier, 1922b, p. 429). He wrote about schools like Fort Valley High and Industrial School, a rural Georgia high school distinguished not only by the achievements of its graduates, but also by its community program. Six workers "go out among the Negro people" and organize farm demonstrations, community clubs, home demonstrations, educational lectures, and social service programs (1925b, p. 461), all of which he saw as critical to the building of a skilled and knowledgeable populace. This is precisely the kind of collective, community-based program in which Frazier hoped social work would engage itself.

Not only was Frazier ideologically drawn to socialism and cooperation, he also clearly took pleasure in being out among working people, talking with them, and uncovering the details of their lives. In 1921 at the New York School of Social Work, he launched a project sponsored by the Urban League in which he investigated the work and home lives of African American longshoreman (1924b). This was Frazier's first experience as a "social investigator," and he was painfully self-conscious. In order to acquire the information, he wrote, "it was necessary for the investigator to visit docks, piers, saloons, the homes of the men, union meeting places, and chance assemblages of the men" (Frazier, 1924b, p. 198). The study, finally published in 1924, was of high quality, quite in contrast with the limited and sentimental accounts of African American life in most social work journals. Frazier combined statistics with excerpts from the wide-ranging interviews to produce a clear picture of a large group of Black industrial workers attempting to survive in the face of discrimination from employers and unions, wretched housing, lack of any social or recreational outlet except an occasional church service, and a general depression in the industry.

Of the 82 longshoremen Frazier interviewed, 80 answered "yes" unconditionally when asked, "Do you favor the unions?" despite the discrimination that they had experienced (for example, the failure of the union to provide an African American organizer). Frazier, too, supported unions and felt if the "struggle between capital and labor becomes intensified the Negro may become an integral part of the proletariat and the feeling against his color may break down in the face of a common foe" (1924b, p. 223).

In Georgia, Frazier continued to study both rural and industrial workers and was a keen observer of economic processes and their relation to the prospects of African Americans. He investigated the lives of Black sharecroppers, conditions in small towns, the cotton economy, the physical and mental health of Black Georgians, lynching and the Ku Klux Klan, superstitions regarding the cause and care of illness, Black schools, the emerging middle class, and more during his years in Atlanta.

Frazier's interest in socialism, economic cooperation, and the lives of working people united him with social workers like Florence Kelley and Eduard Lindeman, but in general it isolated him (and them) from the profession that was emerging. Although the New Deal would see a resurgence of progressive social work, in most cases, those in dominant positions in social work put their hopes in class collaboration, not in socialism and programs rooted in the activities of the working class.

A Radical Commitment to Racial Justice

If Frazier's commitment to socialism complicated his relationship with social work, his uncompromising stance on racial justice did so even more. Frazier's friend and colleague St. Clair Drake wrote in 1967, "A man of Frazier's temperament could not survive in a Negro educational institution of Georgia in the 1920s, for he was as proud of his reputation as a fighter as he was his status as a scholar and he was always forthright and outspoken" (1940/1967, pp. ix–x). Frazier's outlook and energy quickly brought him into conflict with both White racists and Black intellectuals ready to accommodate the status quo.

In 1920, social work had at best a mixed record vis-à-vis race. On the positive side, the National Urban League had been included in the national meetings of the National

Conference of Social Work since 1912, and Jane Addams, Mary White Ovington, and others had helped found the National Association for the Advancement of Colored People. But African Americans could not help but notice that the governing bodies of the profession from the national boards to city directorships were exclusively White; coverage of African American issues in social work journals and conferences was sparse and often inaccurate; liberal paternalism, sometimes less toxic, sometimes more, dominated the profession ideologically; and worst of all, nearly all settlements and social service agencies were segregated (Chandler, 1994, 1995).

Frazier held out hope for the profession, however, primarily based on his enthusiasm for social work's case method and commitment to scientific inquiry. Frazier had enjoyed his education at the New York School of Social Work, and he maintained connections with professors Bernard Glueck, Porter Lee, Mary Van Kleeck, and Kate Cleghorn for many years. Arriving in Atlanta, he threw his considerable youthful energy into the School of Social Work, determined to build up the school and enrich the program with his perspectives on case work, economic cooperation, and scientific investigation. He was determined to make the Atlanta school a "first class school of professional social work" (1924a, p. 252). Arthur Davis, Frazier's colleague at Howard, wrote of his work, "Frazier did yeoman and pioneer work in building up the institution and making it standard. The matter of standards had not been important prior to his directorship. It was thought that a Negro social worker needed the 'right attitude' much more than he needed academic preparation. The school was, therefore, inclined to take almost anybody who applied. But the young director insisted on standards, and he traveled throughout the south, selling the idea of an adequately trained social worker" (1962, p. 430).

Frazier hated segregation and always commented when he encountered it in social work. In an account he wrote for Gunnar Myrdal's *An American Dilemma,* he described arriving at an Atlanta meeting of social workers and discovering it was to be segregated. He was furious and left the conference, saying, "I have told you white people not to invite me to any meeting where you are going to place the Negroes to themselves as if they were roaches or fleas and unfit for human association" (Frazier, n.d.). The test of social work, he felt, would come in its attitude toward segregation. "Now what will be the attitude of such agencies as the societies for family welfare?" he wrote in a 1924 article. "Are they going to tack on an inefficient colored branch so as to appear sincere before the world? And then turning their back upon the stepchild of charity, devote their energies to work among whites? The availability of well-trained colored social workers will check to some extent such hypocrisy" (1924a, p. 254).

Frazier's refusal to attend segregated meetings, his outspoken articles on the subject of race, his criticism of the "deceit and fawning" of the "so-called Negro leaders" who in pretending to "emulate the meekness of the Nazarene" conveniently forget to "follow his example of unrestrained denunciation of injustice and hypocrisy," all contributed to a growing tension between the Atlanta School of Social Work board of trustees and Frazier (Frazier, 1924c, p. 213). In 1925, that tension increased when Frazier published a review of Thomas Woofter's book, *The Basis of Racial Adjustment* (1925c). Woofter, a board member, was a prominent White liberal and had designed *The Basis of Racial Adjustment* as a text for college courses on race relations. Frazier was under considerable pressure to write a favorable review, but he instead used the occasion to indict the position of southern liberals. "There is in the book," Frazier wrote, "too much of a rationalization of the southern position" (Frazier, 1925c, p. 443). He concluded that the book might "offer consolation to a group willing to remain serfs because these are men who will protect them from the grosser forms of injustice and violence." But it would not give hope, he went on, "to the growing number of self-respecting and intelligent Negroes who want to be treated as other people. . . . I do not know one intelligent young Negro who intends to stay in the South longer than to accumulate and get a start in life" (p. 444).

By 1927, Frazier's relationship with the board of trustees was in shambles, and they suggested that he "ought to resign and let someone else take his place who might prove more effective as Director" (Board of Trustees, 1927, p. 5). Frazier's "ideas of racial adjustment" clearly did not conform either to those of the segregated South or to those of the social work establishment. The last chapter in his association with social work and the South was not yet finished, however. It involved a third commitment, Frazier's determination to probe the internal dynamics of race prejudice.

The Psychology of Race Hatred

Inabel Burns Lindsay, first dean of the Howard University School of Social Work, studied at the New York School of Social Work at the same time as Frazier. Remembering her classes there, she laughed, "[We] just got soaked in the Freudian approach" (1970, p. 33). Frazier, too, studied Freud and spent the decade of the 1920s thinking and writing about the psychology of race hatred in a series of innovative articles (1924a, 1924b, 1924d, 1924f, 1925a, 1926, 1927b) that foreshadow the work of Algerian psychologist Frantz Fanon. Frazier wanted, first, to examine the *internal* constraints that kept African Americans tied to the patterns of the past and, second, to explore the "pathology of race prejudice," a complex that produced exaggerated, uncontrolled, indeed insane, behavior in White southerners (1927b, p. 856).

His work in this area is especially fascinating in terms of Frazier's pull and push with social work. Frazier was drawn to social work because it worked in the conjuncture of three fields or commitments that particularly captivated him: psychology, social investigation, and connection with working people. Theoretically at least, social work should have welcomed groundbreaking work that used the tools of both psychology and social investigation to explore human prejudices. But probing White southerners' racism for "characteristics ascribed to insanity" (Frazier, 1927b, p. 856) took social work's enthusiasm for Freud in a direction for which few were prepared and threatened the uneasy balance between segregationists and others in the profession. Social work declined the opportunity to use Freud's insights in any but a remarkably conservative way.

When Frazier went out to talk with African American longshoremen or families in the South, he was attentive to their mental status as well as the physical conditions of their lives. It always fascinated him intellectually and often disheartened him as well. For example, in studying African American longshoremen, Frazier was frustrated by the men's reaction to him, the social investigator, and to his Urban League–sponsored study. After a month of effort, he wrote that he had been able to complete only 82 surveys "due primarily to suspicion on the part of the men, as well as a stubborn indifference" (1924b, p. 197). Frazier thought their suspicions—that the investigation was a scheme devised by White owners or White union men against African American workers—"absurd." "Two hours of explanation failed to dispel these misgivings and suspicions," he wrote in exasperation, "especially when it was learned that some of the personnel of the Urban League were white." Greater often than these fears were the men's "deep-seated and in some instances ineradicable distrust of their own people." "What white man do you want to sell me out to now?" the workers asked Frazier (1924b, p. 199).

Further, the men in Frazier's view lived under the "domination of fear and hopelessness." They had no hope in anything; he reported, "They feel that their fate is adverse because they are colored and colored people in America are impotent and cannot strike back at their oppressors except at the price of annihilation" (Frazier, 1924b, p. 200). These "unique psychological reactions" troubled and angered Frazier because he felt the fears locked the workers in a kind of passivity. Frazier called this the psychology of negation or the psychology of people in subjection (1924f), and he felt it was part of the enormous invisible legacy of oppression that represented the success of "the deliberate and calculated plan of the South to inculcate in Negroes diffidence and self abasement" (p. 201). Frazier did not contradict the wisdom of the workers' view of power relationships, but he puzzled over how, given that, one could move oppressed people to action. It is one reason, of course, why he thought so carefully about cooperative enterprises and their ability to engage rural African Americans in productive, democratic activity.

Later, after he had moved south, Frazier speculated on the effect of the southern social environment on African Americans' physical and mental health (1924f, 1925d). Here, fear was critical. "Negroes are constantly afraid that they will overstep the bounds set for them by white people," Frazier wrote, noting that "no human organism in which the fear instinct is constantly aroused can function properly." Frazier recounted how rural southerners would tell him that they felt "right poorly," even when examination showed they were not sick in an insight related to theories regarding somatization, now widely accepted among those who work with refugees, Frazier concluded, "To the extent that the Negro lives under the domination of fear, he is unhealthy" (1924f, p. 239). Any improvement in African Americans' health, he thought, depended on a change in attitude among White southerners—they must be taught "to valuate the Negro as any other human being"—and on education for rural African Americans (1924f, p. 239).

More controversial, in fact volatile, was Frazier's use of the new psychology to analyze race prejudice in Whites. From the time of his arrival in the South, Frazier had carefully observed Whites and their mental processes relative to African Americans. In an early article on health care, Frazier wrote, "It has been well nigh impossible in the South to get communities to adopt health programs when it was thought that the Negro would share the benefits. This has been part of the psychosis of the White South in which fear of the Negro has dominated" (1924f, p. 239). Frazier developed his thoughts on the psychosis of the White South in an article, "The Pathology of Race Prejudice," which he wrote in 1923 and finally got published in *Forum*, a leftist liberal journal, in June 1927 (Frazier, 1927; Platt, 1991). Frazier questions why White men and women, who are normally kind and law-abiding, are capable of "revolting forms of cruelty" when African Americans are involved? How is it possible to explain the behavior of a school board member who "jumps up and paces the floor, cursing and accusing Negroes, the instant the question of appropriating money for Negro schools is raised" (Frazier, 1927b, p. 857)? What accounts for these exaggerated reactions? Frazier's answer was a "Negro complex." Like other complexes, the Negro complex makes itself known in various ways. One way is by dissociation; "southern White people write and talk about the majesty of law, the sacredness of human rights . . . and the next moment defend mob violence, disfranchisement, and Jim Crow treatment of the Negro" (p. 857). Another is by projection; White women, experiencing desire for Black men, project their feelings onto Black men and report advances by them "when no such thing existed" (p. 861). Frazier was being a bit outrageous in this article, but it was a deadly serious business to southerners. Unlike most social workers, who tiptoed around their colleagues' racism (Chandler, 1994), Frazier not only did not keep quiet, he sought out—with a clinician's precision—the volatile places like sexual attraction between the races.

"The Pathology of Race Prejudice" was published in *Forum* in June 1927, shortly after the board of trustees had asked Frazier to resign from the Atlanta School of Social Work, and its appearance set in motion a small storm remembered for years in the African American community. Sam Small, the editor of Atlanta's largest paper, the *Constitution*, discovered the article and launched a diatribe against it and Frazier in his popular column, "Looking and Listening." Listing Frazier's diagnoses and accusations, Small disparaged them all as unimportant, circumstantial, and unscientific: "Scarcely believable to one who was born here in the south on premises swarming with negro slaves, who grew up in daily contact with them, saw them emancipated . . . and whose only prejudice against the negro is that he prefers not to eat and sleep with him" (1927, p. 6). As for Frazier's comments about White women and Black men, Small considered them "revolting, . . . in fact the vilest that this writer has encountered in a lifetime" (1927, p. 6).

"The Pathology of Race Prejudice" marked the end of Frazier's association with Atlanta and social work. Receiving what he interpreted as a threatening telephone call, Frazier put a gun in his belt and called friends who spirited him out of town. From Atlanta, Frazier fled to Baltimore. The June 25th edition of the *Baltimore Afro-American* carried multiple front page headlines: "Oust Frazier from Atlanta Social School," "Ideas on Race Equality Too Advanced for Dixie Says Director," "Whites Threatened Him with

Lynching," and "E. Franklin Frazier Has Been Forced Out of the Principalship of Atlanta School of Social Service after Five Years." Frazier, the article reported, had been forced to leave the Atlanta School as a result of his article, "The Insanity of Race Prejudice." It continued, "Action by the school trustees took place two weeks ago, but is just becoming known as every effort was made to keep quiet the fact that every school of social service does not welcome progressive ideas." Frazier was pictured under the banner, "Flees Atlanta Lynchers" ("Whites," 1927, p. 1).

Not surprisingly, the trustees of the Atlanta school were enraged and shot off a letter to the *Afro-American* protesting Frazier's and the paper's chronicling of the events. "If the Atlanta School of Social Work had been disposed to remove Mr. Frazier because of any of his magazine articles or his personal views," they wrote, " it could have done that a long time ago, but he has been allowed perfect freedom of speech . . . during his entire five years as Director. . . . As a matter of fact, Mr. Frazier was asked to resign because he did not prove effective as an administrator" (Board of Trustees, 1927, p. 5).

Charles Johnson, editor of the Urban League journal *Opportunity,* wrote Frazier a week later to tell him that he had been in Atlanta a few days after "Sam somebody" in his column in the *Constitution* "went into hysterics over your *Forum* article. Everywhere I went the colored populace was asking, 'Have you read Frazier's farewell to the South?' I understand the news stands have been exhausted of the issue" (Johnson to E. F. Frazier, June 29, 1927, p. 1).

Frazier's best friend from childhood, the satirist Gustavus Adolphus Steward ("Dock"), penned a number of bitter letters to Frazier that summer. "I am glad you are out of it," he wrote, "I think that deep down in Atlanta has always been the thought that you were an 'uppish nigger,' wanting to associate with White women—'associate with' meaning in the language of *Atlanta Constitution* editors, 'go to bed with.'" Later, he laughed at Frazier for failing "once again" to "get back into the uplift and good graces of the philanthropic trust." "I see that your good friend, John Hope [the first Black president of Atlanta University], has been given another one of those jaunts to Europe," he went on.

> The good nigger is always rewarded, I hope you see. While bad niggers like E. Franklin Frazier are simply kicked out of their jobs. It serves them right, too. They should do the proper amount of bootlicking... keep the good white folks believing that they are heaven-sent guardians of creation and the best friend of American Negroes, simply making the utmost sacrifices to bring them up to the level of human beings. . . . Now if you would just follow John Hope, or J. O. Thomas, or Eugene Kinckle Jones, you would find your path blooming with roses and free trips to Europe thrown in occasionally.

"I really don't know what will become of you," he chided Frazier. "Why don't you give up and conform and be comfortable?" (Steward to E. F. Frazier, July 31, 1927).

Conclusion

The bitterness and debate unleashed by Frazier's departure from Atlanta and social work can be understood only in the context of race relations in the South and of Black social work's nearly impossible position within it. Frazier, a brilliant scholar who was drawn to social work's potentially liberating role, found himself in the end unable to accept the "conditions of racial adjustment" that not only the South, but also his social work sponsors demanded. Frazier hated paternalism and the limitations it placed on African Americans. Nor would he tolerate African Americans who accommodated to the status quo. Others in social work, both Black and White, did not agree with his position. They found him unwise and difficult. His tactics, for them, could lead only to a split between African Americans and the White support that African American social service programs, in their judgment, so desperately needed to survive. In general, this limited vision of social work won the day, and individual militant social workers found themselves, like Frazier, fighting both a racist society and an accommodationist profession.

One can imagine that beyond the grave Frazier and Dock still correspond and still enjoy skewering self-satisfied professionals. They are having a laugh, no doubt, about Frazier's recent poster status. "Please," Frazier would say, "if you use my face, include some ideas, especially those that speak to the core of racial and class injustice." And to those serious students whom he liked he would add, "Do not let go of your ideas and your activist commitments; they are what you have to fight with—to lose them is to lose any chance of making a mark on the world."

Note

1. For a full view of Frazier's life, see Anthony Platt's authoritative biography, *E. Franklin Frazier Reconsidered* (1991).

References

Board of Trustees of the Atlanta University School of Social Work. (1927, July 8). Letter to the *Baltimore Afro-American*, 5.

Chandler, S. (1994). 'Almost a partnership': African Americans, segregation and the Young Men's Christian Association. *Journal of Sociology and Social Welfare, 21*, 97–111.

Chandler, S. (1995). 'That biting, stinging thing that ever shadows us': African-American social workers in France during World War I. *Social Service Review, 69*, 498–514.

Davis, A. (1962). E. Franklin Frazier (1894–1962): A profile. *Journal of Negro Education, 31*, 430.

Drake, St. C. (1967). Introduction to E. Franklin Frazier, *Negro youth at the crossroads.* New York: Shocken Books. (Original work published 1940)

Edwards, G. F. (1968). *E. Franklin Frazier on race relations.* Chicago: University of Chicago Press.

Frazier, E. F. (1920). *New currents of thought among Negroes in America.* Master's thesis: Clark University.

Frazier, E. F. (1922a). The folk high school at Roskilde. *Southern Workman, 51*, 325–328.

Frazier, E. F. (1922b). Danish people's high schools and America. *Southern Workman, 9*, 425–430.

Frazier, E. F. (1923a). The co-operative movement in Denmark. *Southern Workman, 52*, 479–484.

Frazier, E. F. (1923b). Cooperation and the Negro. *Crisis, 25*, 228–229.

Frazier, E. F. (1924a). Social work in race relations. *Crisis, 27*, 252–254.

Frazier, E. F. (1924b). A Negro industrial group. *The Howard University Review, 1*, 196–232.

Frazier, E. F. (1924c). The Negro and non-resistance. *Crisis, 27*, 213.

Frazier, E. F. (1924d). A note on Negro education. *Opportunity, 2*, 144.

Frazier, E. F. (1924e). Cooperatives: The next step in the Negro's business development. *Southern Workman, 53*, 508.

Frazier, E. F. (1924f). Discussion. *Opportunity, 2*, 239.

Frazier, E. F. (1925a). Social equality and the Negro. *Opportunity, 2*, 165–168.

Frazier, E. F. (1925b). A community school: Fort Valley High and Industrial School. *Southern Workman, 54*, 459–464.

Frazier, E. F. (1925c). Review of *The basis of racial adjustment* by Thomas Woofter. *Social Forces, 4*, 442–444.

Frazier, E. F. (1925d). Psychological factors in Negro health. *Journal of Social Forces, 3*, 488–489.

Frazier, E. F. (1926). Family life of the Negro in the small town. *Proceedings of the National Conference of Social Work*, 384–388.

Frazier, E. F. (1927a). My relations with the Atlanta School of Social Work. Frazier Archives, Moorland-Spingarn Research Center, Howard University.

Frazier, E. F. (1927b). The pathology of race prejudice. *Forum, 70*, 856–861.

Frazier, E. F. (1927c). The Negro in the industrial south. *The Nation, 125*, 84–85.
Frazier, E. F. (1939). *The Negro family in the United States.* Chicago: University of Chicago Press.
Frazier, E. F. (1951). Autobiographical notes. In C. Odum, *American sociology* (p. 234), New York: Longmans, Green, and Company.
Frazier, E. F. (1957a). *Black bourgeoisie.* Glencoe, IL: Free Press.
Frazier, E. F. (1957b). *The Negro in the United States.* New York: Macmillan.
Frazier, E. F. (n.d.). Memoranda submitted to Dr. Guy B. Johnson embodying stories of experiences with whites particularly in the South, for Gunnar Myrdal's *An American dilemma.* (Myrdal, G. [1996]. An American Dilemma: The Negro Problem and Modern Democracy. Somerset, NJ: Transaction Publishers.)
Johnson, C. (1927, June 29). Letter to E. Franklin Frazier. Frazier Archives, Moorland-Spingarn Research Center, Howard University.
Lindsay, I. (1970). *Oral History.* Bancroft Library, University of California, Berkeley.
Oust Frazier from Atlanta Social School. (1927, June 25). *Baltimore Afro-American,* pp. 1, 10.
Platt, A. M., & Chandler, S. K. (1988). Constant struggle: E. Franklin Frazier and Black social work. *Social Work, 33*, 293–297.
Platt, A. M. (1991). *E. Franklin Frazier reconsidered.* New Brunswick, NJ: Rutgers University Press.
Robinson, W. A. (1927, February 14). Letter to Charles Adams. Frazier Archives, Moorland-Spingarn Research Center, Howard University.
Small, S. (1927, June 10). An Atlanta Negro's diagnosis of the insanity of race prejudice. *Atlanta Constitution*, 6.
Steward, G. (1927, July 31,). Letter to E. Franklin Frazier. Frazier Archives, Moorland-Springarn Research Center, Howard University.
Thomas, J. O. (1967). *My story in black and white.* New York: Exposition Press.
Whites threatened him with lynching. (1927, June 25). *Baltimore Afro-American*, pp. 1, 10.

CHAPTER 15

Historical Development of African American Child Welfare Services

Vanessa G. Hodges

Throughout history, African American children have suffered greatly from a combination of factors, including the ravages of slavery, institutionalized discrimination, and racial oppression. Infants and children, obviously unable to take care of themselves, have been systematically excluded from traditional private and later public child welfare services. From the old auntie or granny in the slave community to the fresh air societies and kindergartens of the settlement movement, African American children's care and ultimate survival were dependent on the sacrifice and dedication of individuals and organizations committed to the children's proper upbringing.

Status of African American Children in the Early Twentieth Century

Child welfare services experienced significant changes in the early twentieth century. Services were professionalized, and public funding assumed greater prominence. Reformers advocated change in child labor laws and compulsory school attendance (Stadum, 1995). Institutional care in the form of orphanages and settlement houses was predominant, although foster care was beginning to emerge as a viable alternative. The prevailing philosophy remained one of child rescue (Billingsley & Giovannoni, 1972), with little recognition of the role and value of the family as a unit (Stadum, 1995).

Despite the positive shift in child welfare services as a result of additional public funding and professionalization, African American children still fared poorly—facing discrimination and exclusion from public services. According to census data summarized by Billingsley and Giovannoni (1972), there were 1,060 public, sectarian, and private child care institutions in 31 northern states. Of these, just 35 admitted only Black children, 254 would admit both Black and White children, 60 admitted all (White, Indian, Japanese, Chinese) but Black children, while 711 admitted only White children.

In 17 southern states, there were a total of 388 child-serving institutions. Of these, 44 admitted only Black children, eight admitted all children, 28 admitted all but Black children, and the remainder, 308, admitted only White children.

Infant mortality rates were high in the early 1900s. Significant numbers of African American children died at birth or soon after. For example, African American children born in areas such as Montgomery, New Orleans, Alexandria, and Norfolk were twice as likely as White children to die prematurely. In Atlanta, between 1882 and 1895, one-third of all deaths of African Americans were children under the age of five (Jones, 1985). Though the overall infant mortality rate started a slow decline in the early 1900s, the death rate of African American children remained extremely high, substantially higher than that of White children. Unfortunately, the current infant mortality rate in the Black community remains high, more than 100 years later.

Developing Systems of Care for African American Children

Because of historical neglect and exclusion from the mainstream child welfare system, the African American community was required to develop its own system of care for children. These systems were influenced by churches, schools, secret organizations, women's clubs, and individual African American philanthropists.

Churches. Churches played major roles in meeting many needs in the African American community. In addition to meeting spiritual and moral needs, the church was heavily involved in developing and supporting child welfare services, including orphanages, kindergartens, and schools. Church congregations helped to clothe, feed, house, teach, nurture, inspire, and socialize children who were not amply cared for by their families (Billingsley & Giovannoni, 1972).

The church had an important role in child welfare. Churches sponsored many mission projects, often focusing on families and children. These mission projects had a dual purpose. One purpose was for conducting Bible classes and teaching the scriptures. The First Congregational Church in Atlanta sponsored missions at the Carrie Steel orphanage to the children who were residents of the home (Russell, "The Institutional Church in Transition: A Study of First Congregational Church in Atlanta," as cited in Ross, 1978).

Schools. Many African Americans viewed education as the way to social advancement and betterment. Churches played a large part in helping to organize, establish, and finance grade schools and institutions of higher education. In addition to teaching academics, schools served an important social work role in the African American community. School facilities served as meeting places for community residents. Classes sponsored by the YMCA, church (Sunday school and Bible classes), and social organizations such as women's clubs were all located in the community. Programs such as home visiting, night schools for working girls, and conferences for teachers and farmers were held at schools (Billingsley & Giovannoni, 1972). The Calhoun Colored School and Social Settlement was an excellent example of this type of child welfare endeavor.

Founded in Lowndes County, Alabama, in 1892, the Calhoun School integrated industrial training and academic education. The school, for example, offered a home nursing class designed to inform students about the causes and prevention of disease, first aid, bandages, lifting and bathing patients, care of babies, and other skills that women were believed to need in order to care for their families' health (Lasch-Quinn, 1993). The mothers' club at the school ended its meetings with a renewal of a mutual vow that participants referred to as the Neighborhood Covenant. Reciting the covenant in unison, the mothers stated, "We promise, with God's help, to live for our children, to do everything we can to put down all that is unfriendly to the life of a little child, and to try in every way to build up the things which will help the children" (Sixteenth Annual Report, Calhoun, pp. 17–18, as cited in Lasch-Quinn, 1993).

Colleges. African American colleges also served a dual role in the African American community. In addition to teaching and research, many of these institutions sponsored an "annual social betterment conference" that was instrumental in increasing social work resources. Many colleges also housed and sponsored kindergartens, settlement houses, night schools, traveling libraries, home-visiting programs, and amusement activities for children (Billingsley & Giovannoni, 1972).

Lodges and Secret Organizations. Lodges and secret organizations served as resources to children and to the African American community. Organizations such as Masons, Odd Fellows, and Knights of Pythias sponsored activities and fundraising for benevolent causes. While membership to these organizations was limited to men, women's auxiliaries complemented the fraternal organization (Billingsley & Giovannoni, 1972).

Women's Clubs. Started in the North, women's clubs offered assistance to children and families by helping to establish settlement houses (Lasch-Quinn, 1993) and to support hospitals, homes for orphans and the aged, reformatories, kindergartens, and other much needed institutions (Billingsley & Giovannoni, 1972).

African American women's organizations subscribed to the traditional female roles of the times. Women were expected to bear and raise children, take care of the home, uphold religious and class morals, and raise children as good stewards and citizens (Lasch-Quinn, 1993). Through organizations, women extended these "caretaking" responsibilities to society in their efforts to care for society's children. In 1895, Josephine St. Pierre Ruffin, president of the New Era Club of Black women, stated:

> We need to talk over not only those things which are of vital importance to us as women, but also the things that are of especial interests to us as colored women, the training of our children, openings for boys and girls, how they can be prepared for occupations and occupations may be found or opened for them, what we especially can do in the moral education of the race with which we are identified, or mental elevation and physical development, the home training it is necessary to give our children in order to prepare them to meet the peculiar conditions in which they shall find themselves, how to make the most of our own, to some

> extent, limited opportunities. (Ruffin, "An Open Letter to the Educational League of Georgia," as cited in Ross, 1978, p. 164)

The National Association of Colored Women (NACW) was founded in 1896. It represented a collective of African American women across 40 states. The mission of the organization, as promoted by the first president, Mary Church Terrell, was dedicated to the "uplifting" of children (Peebles-Wilkins, 1995).

> . . . we must build the foundation of the next generation upon such a rock of integrity, morality, and strength, both of body and mind, that the floods of proscription, prejudice, and persecution may descend upon it in torrents, and yet it will not be moved. (Terrell, "The duty of the National Association of Colored Women to the Race," as cited in Peebles-Wilkins, 1995, p.138)

Individual Philanthropists. There were a number of African American philanthropists who supported child-and family-related services. For example, at his death, Thomy Lafon bequeathed the majority of his estate to support the orphanages for boys, hospitals, and homes for the aged. In another example, an African American born into slavery, George Washington, left money in his estate to support African American youth in college. Eartha Mary Magdalene White amassed an estate that was estimated at more than $1 million during her lifetime and donated both time and monies to establishing services for children and the elderly. Residing most of her life in Jacksonville, Florida, she started the Boys' Improvement Club in 1904 by using her own money to hire recreation workers. Later, recognizing the need for child care for working mothers, she started the Milnor Street Nursery, which was supported by a combination of public funds and her own money (Johnson, 1994). Another philanthropist, famed hair care mogul Madam C. J. Walker, donated thousands of dollars to African American schools, numerous orphanages, retirement homes, and the YWCAs and YMCAs.

Types of Child Welfare Services Developed by African Americans

Orphanages. While many of the orphanages for African American children, particularly in the North, were organized and operated by Whites, African Americans did establish and manage orphanages. These orphanages were run in homes and survived based on the hard work of the women who ran them, charitable gifts, small tokens from parents when possible, and the help of the children themselves. Children were trained in "washing, ironing, cooking, sewing (such as plain sewing), embroidering, hemstitching, etc" (DuBois, 1909, p. 54). Many of the orphanages that were established through individual efforts did not survive the death of the owner.

There were a few orphanages that were conceived by individuals and supported by churches and other organizations, such as the Masons and the Federation of Colored Women's Clubs. These orphanages tended to have a more formal structure, with administrative boards and more secure funding. The purpose of these orphanages was to provide a safe, nurturing environment and to "save" children who were destined for poverty, homelessness, and despair (Billingsley & Giovannoni, 1972).

Carrie Steele, a laborer at the Atlanta Union Depot, started the Carrie Steele Orphan Home in 1890. At the Union Depot, Steele observed many children who were homeless, abandoned, begging for food, and wandering the streets. She was quite saddened and moved by the plight of these children and dedicated her life to saving them by providing them with a safe home. Steele was very industrious. She was able to purchase land and build a small cottage. In order to finance the home, Steele, who had been educated during slavery, wrote a story of her life and used the profits for her orphanage. She also solicited funds and donations from others, both Blacks and Whites (Carter, "Mrs. Carrie Steele Logan," as cited in Ross, 1978).

Steele opened her home to the homeless children whom she had seen at the Union Depot. In her petition to establish the home, she wrote that she planned a place

> . . . where such children may be cared for and educated, and taught to sew, cook, etc., that they may be prepared to earn an honest living and have instilled into their minds while young sound principles of integrity and industry. (Carter, "Mrs. Carrie Steele Logan," as cited in Ross, 1978, p. 145)

Steele housed over 50 children whom she trained to read and care for themselves. Older girls assisted with the housework and care of younger children. Boys worked on the farm. Although the home was nondenominational, religion was an important part of the activities in Steele's orphanage. Children were taught to pray. Sunday school was held each week, and all children participated, even younger ones. A board of directors managed the home (Carter, "Mrs. Carrie Steele Logan," as cited in Ross, 1978).

Combined Facilities. There were a few facilities that addressed the needs of both elders and children. For example, Memphis, Tennessee, had an Old Ladies and Orphans' Home and an Old Folks and Orphans' Home. Combined homes were started by both individuals and organizations. In general, homes sponsored by organizations were on sounder financial bases than those initiated and supported by individuals (Billingsley & Giovannoni, 1972). Orphanages and combined institutions for children and the aged survived as the primary residential institutions providing care for African American children well into the twentieth century (Billingsley & Giovannoni, 1972).

Kindergartens. African American children were excluded from traditional child care and educational opportunities. Community members, therefore, tried to develop a similar system for African American children (Billingsley & Giovannoni, 1972).

The need for kindergartens was identified as a result of the Atlanta University Conferences of 1896, 1898, and 1905. Surveys conducted in 1896 and 1897 revealed that children were not receiving consistent and appropriate child care while mothers were at work. The goal of these centers was to provide a safe and loving environment for children while their mothers were working. Children were believed to be very impressionable:

> It is a daily experience to find a child of tender years left to tend the baby with but a scant meal of meat and bread, while the widowed mother is out at work, who returns at night tired and exhausted to feed and care for the children. Such a state of constant activity exhausts her vital force and she dies at an early age leaving little children in the hands of chance to be brought up among the weeds of vice and sin. If there has been a day nursery with good conscientious persons at its head, in which these children have had their physical, mental and moral natures properly cared for at a small cost to the mother, they would have developed into characters with sufficient magnitude to lift humanity to a higher plane, instead of degrading it, and the mother who would no doubt have lived out her three score years and ten. (Russell, "The Institutional Church in Transition: A Study of First Congregational Church of Atlanta," as cited in Ross, 1978, p. 259)

The Gate City Kindergarten was organized and opened in the fall of 1905. Women primarily organized such efforts. Gertrude Bunce, Mrs. David T. Howard, Mrs. J. W. E. Bowen, Mrs. George Burch, Mrs. A. Graves, Mrs. John Hope, and Mr. and Mrs. A. F. Herndon, and others were among the organizers. Two kindergartens were opened initially, and by 1908, five centers were open. The locations were selected according to the neighborhoods in Atlanta that had the highest need. These centers were free to the children and financed through churches as mission projects or through donations of real estate and money. The financial responsibilities were assumed by the Atlanta Community Chest (Russell, "The Institutional Church in Transition: A Study of First Congregational Church of Atlanta," as cited in Ross, 1978). Launching the kindergartens required effort and donations from many individuals and organizations. Some donated money, others fuel, still others property (houses) at very low rental rates; organizations donated money for teachers' salaries; others paid for milk for the children.

The Atlanta Community Chest partially funded the kindergartens for over 30 years. However, the most important and significant development of these kindergartens was the unselfish dedication of the women who served on the board and who solicited donations and made contributions and donations to meet the needs of children whose mothers were working. These women assumed responsibility for the operations of these kindergartens based on faith. They earned no salary and had no dependable funding source. Through their own fundraising efforts, they were able sustain these organizations. Many hours of time were donated to ensure the safety of the children. Colleges, churches, public schools, individuals, and organizations were all solicited to keep these kindergartens open (Russell, "The Institutional Church in Transition: A Study of First Congregational Church of Atlanta," as cited in Ross, 1978).

Women of the board also solicited support for the kindergartens through other means. For example, soap was donated, and extra soap was sold for fundraising. Women's circles also helped to finance the kindergarten by raising money through bazaars where food and handmade clothing were sold. Colleges contributed by sponsoring sporting events and donating admissions fees. Other fundraisers included baby contests, lawn parties,

Easter egg hunts, and candy and rummage sales. Women in the association paid monthly dues, and these funds were also donated. Teachers were the only paid employees, and their salaries were minimal (Russell, "The Institutional Church in Transition: A study of First Congregational Church of Atlanta," as cited in Ross, 1978).

The kindergartens were established so that

> the underprivileged might start on life's journey of good citizenship unhandicapped, with horizon, that mothers might be enabled to work more efficiently, by being relieved of anxiety, because the nursery had cared for their children during the day. Thus nurseries aided in building the health and character of these underprivileged children, and sheltered them from the influence of "curbstone education." (Russell, "The Institutional Church in Transition: A study of First Congregational Church of Atlanta," as cited in Ross, 1978, p. 263)

Homes for Working Girls. Homes for African American Working Girls were established to assist girls and young women who had migrated to the North for work. Many of these girls came seeking "a better life" and were without family or a support system. These homes, such as Victoria Earle Matthews's White Rose Home and Industrial Association for Working Girls (as discussed in chapter 1) provided the girls with safe housing and helped them to locate employment. Started by women's organizations, as well as by individuals, these homes also helped to socialize women and provided emotional support and, in some cases, financial support (Billingsley & Giovannoni, 1972).

Homes for Wayward Children. Services for delinquent juveniles were established as early as 1899, although African American children were often remanded to jails or reform schools; this was true even for children who were not in legal trouble because of the lack of orphanages and homes to care for homeless, indigent children. One option for wayward girls was the Virginia Industrial School for Colored Girls in Richmond, Virginia.

The Virginia Industrial School for Colored Girls, a residential program for wayward or delinquent girls, was opened in 1915 in Hanover County, Virginia. Started by Janie Porter Barrett, a social worker seasoned by establishing a Child Welfare Department at the Locust Street Settlement, the Industrial Home for Colored Girls aimed to prepare these girls for independent community living. In addition to academic and job skills training, the curriculum included religious training, crop harvesting, household management, and cultural and recreational activities. Value-based learning was also emphasized by modeling and encouraging honesty, open communication, cooperation, pride, and service (Peebles-Wilkins, 1995).

The Industrial Home (discussed fully in chapter 9) was a highly structured environment. Girls adhered to a behavior system that included demerits for such infractions as escaping, insubordination, stealing, lying, disrespecting authority, quarreling, inattention, laziness, fighting, and uncleanliness. The girls worked on an honor system, striving to reach the highest level, "honor girl," which enabled them to wear the "white dress" and to be moved to a higher level cottage. The girls were "paroled" following two years of satisfactory performance. Paroled girls were placed with families who were responsible for their continued education and support. These families were both Black and White and occasionally included the girls' birth families, although home placements were rare (Peebles-Wilkins, 1995).

Children-Focused Programs. The First Church organized the first Boy Scout troop for Negro boys in Atlanta. The church applied for a charter in 1910, but it was not granted until 1931 under the leadership of a new minister who pleaded for the charter. The Scout troop was very successful, and both the boys and Scout leaders were awarded many honors. Another example of children-focused programs was developed in New York's Lincoln House Settlement for Colored Americans during the early 1900s. Birdye Haynes, headworker at the settlement, described the "Home and Babies" components at the settlement when she noted that the aims of the house were to "secure a more scientific care of homes and of children, through the work of its mothers' clubs and visiting nurses" (Haynes, 1919, p. 124). Through this program, the Lincoln House Settlement held a "baby show" each October. In addition to the show of healthy babies, lectures on child welfare–related subjects, such as nursing, infant mortality, disease prevention, and housing issues, were given at the house. Both parents and their children attended the lectures. The "baby shows" were successful and eagerly anticipated events at Lincoln House and other settlements including Janie Porter Barrett's Locust Street Settlement in Hampton, Virginia.

Conclusion

Mutual aid is a recurring theme in the history of child welfare. This type of aid was the only support available to most African American families, as they were excluded from the traditional welfare system. Incredible generosity and donations of time, talent, skills, and love characterized mutual aid. Sacrifice was another component of aid. Families with very little material and few financial resources were still willing to donate and share their assets through taking in relatives and family members, donating to organized efforts, or assuming the care of foster children in their own homes.

> Mutual aid manifested itself in many forms. Grandmothers cared for their children's children and all three generations benefit; the elderly women gained companionship and, in some cases, a measure of economic support; their children were free to search for jobs elsewhere, and the grandchildren lived under the watchful eye of a relative who was often "as strict . . . and as kind as she knew how to be." (Jones, 1985, p. 228)

Church and religion are a second dominating theme in the history of African American child welfare. As mentioned previously, the church not only provided spiritual teaching and support, but also served an important social welfare function in funding and supporting child care institutions such as orphanages and kindergartens, in teaching morals and values, and in instilling hope into children. Children living in and attending these facilities, as well as others in the community, benefited from the teaching and modeling of these values.

Perhaps the most predominant theme is the one of social betterment and the obligation to contribute to the "uplifting of the race" by sacrificing and teaching the generations of the future. This theme was pervasive and was evident in every organization and function in the Black community. While the services directly benefited children and families, teachings were always future-oriented.

What can be learned from the lessons of the past? First, the field of child welfare needs to build on the tradition of mutual aid and extended family by honoring and supporting kinship care as a viable alternative to foster care placement. Care by kin reflects the rich tradition of extended family networks in African American communities (Billingsley, 1968; Martin & Martin, 1978; Stack, 1974). Kinship care, as implied by its name, refers to the placement, formal or informal, of children and youth in the homes of family members and relatives. The Child Welfare League of America (CWLA) Kinship Care Policy and Practice Committee defines kinship care as "the full-time nurturing and protection of children who must be separated from their parents by relatives, members of their tribes or clans, godparents, stepparents or other adults who have a kinship bond with a child" (1994, p. 2).

The number of children served in kinship care has skyrocketed in the past decade, in part because of the steep rise in the number of children in care, a decline in the number of traditional foster homes available, and the emphasis on keeping families together as a result of the Adoption Assistance and Child Welfare Act of 1980 (P.L. 96–272; Hegar, 1999). Despite its popularity, kinship policy and practice suffer from many unanswered, controversial issues that have serious implications for the care of African American children. These issues include selection of caretakers, certification, supervision, payment, and issues of permanency (Hegar, 1999). Payment, for example, is especially significant to African American families living on a very limited income. The addition of a monthly payment may affect the family's ability to care for another member. Certification and licensing may also be issues. Foster care regulations are well defined in terms of the amount of living and sleeping space that must be available for a child to be placed in the home. Some relative homes may not meet these standards, but would otherwise offer a safe nurturing environment to a child.

While kinship care references a distinct child welfare service, another tradition from the past relates to a broader issue, that is, the philosophy undergirding program development and organization. The first child welfare–related services were developed, organized, and operated by a group of volunteers, primarily women, who were operating from an empowerment perspective by recognizing and trying to address need. These groups had structural and organizational significance that should be adapted to enhance contemporary outcomes for children. For example, many of the persons involved in developing and managing early child welfare programs were not professionally trained.

They had dedication, commitment, and concern for the welfare of children. Today's challenge becomes finding ways to involve indigenous community members in a meaningful way in socializing and developing young children. The family support movement offers a model for creating African American–centered programs. Family support principles include the following:

- Staff and families work together in relationships based on equality and respect.
- Staff enhance families' capacity to support the growth and development of all family members—adults, youth, and children.
- Families are resources to their own members, other families, programs, and communities.
- Programs affirm and strengthen families' cultural, racial, and linguistic identities and enhance their ability to function in a multicultural society.
- Programs are embedded in their communities and contribute to the community-building process.
- Programs advocate with families for services and systems that are fair, responsive, and accountable to the families served.
- Practitioners work with families to mobilize formal and informal resources to support family development.
- Programs are flexible and continually responsive to emerging family and community issues.
- Principles of family support are modeled in all program activities, including planning, governance, and administration. (Allen, Brown, & Finlay, 1992).

African American child welfare agencies must actively recruit, train, and develop indigenous leaders from the community who possess the commitment, drive, and dedication to improving the welfare of children. Family support principles present a framework that values the contribution of indigenous workers, respects racial and cultural diversity, and builds on the strengths of families rather than pathology. Historically, the early survival of children in need was largely dependent on African American women, many of whom were not formally trained, but were dedicated to the survival and betterment of children. The future of contemporary child welfare services for Black children will also depend on actively listening to the voice of this dedicated group of women.

References

Allen, M. L., Brown, P., & Finlay, B. (1992). *Helping children by strengthening families.* Washington, DC: Children's Defense Fund.

Billingsley, A. (1968). *Black families in White America.* Englewood Cliff, NJ: Prentice Hall.

Billingsley, A., & Giovannoni, J. M. (1972). *Children of the storm: Black children and American child welfare.* Atlanta: Harcourt Brace Jovanovich.

Child Welfare League of America. (1994). *Kinship care: A natural bridge.* Washington, DC: Author.

DuBois, W. E. B. (1909). *Efforts for social betterment among Negro Americans.* Atlanta, GA: Atlanta University Press.

Haynes, B. (1919). Lincoln House: Its work for Colored Americans. *The Standard, 6,* 122–124.

Hegar, R. (1999). Kinship foster care in context. In M. Hegar & R. Scannapieco (Eds.), *Kinship foster care: Policy, practice and research.* New York: Oxford University Press.

Johnson, A. (1994). Eartha Mary Magdalene White (1876–1974). In. D. Hine, E. Brown, & R. Terborg-Penn (Eds.), *Black women in America: A historical encyclopedia* (pp. 1256–1257). Bloomington: Indiana University Press.

Jones, J. (1985). *Labor of love, labor of sorrow: Black women, work and the family, from slavery to the present.* New York: Random House.

Lasch-Quinn, E. (1993). *Black neighbors: Race and the limits of reform in the American settlement house movement, 1890–1945.* Chapel Hill: University of North Carolina Press.

Martin, E. P., & Martin, J. M. (1978). *The Black extended family.* Chicago: University of Chicago Press.

Peebles-Wilkins, W. (1995). Janie Porter Barrett and the Virginia Industrial School for Colored Girls: Community response to the needs of African American children. In E. P. Smith & L. A. Merkel-Holguin (Eds.), *A history of child welfare* (pp. 135–153). New Brunswick, ME: Transaction Publishers.

Ross, E. L. (1978). *Black heritage in social welfare, 1860–1930.* Metuchen, NJ: Scarecrow Press.

Stack, C. (1974). *All our kin: Strategies for survival in the Black community.* New York: Harper & Row.

Stadum, B. (1995). The dilemma in saving children from child labor: Reform and casework at odds with families' needs, 1900–1938. In E. P. Smith & L. A. Merkel-Holguin (Eds.), *A history of child welfare* (pp. 21–43). New Brunswick, ME: Transaction Publishers.

CHAPTER 16

Traditional Helping Roles of Older African American Women
The Concept of Self-Help

Dorothy S. Ruiz

Many of the pioneers in social work and social welfare, as noted in previous chapters, were themselves mothers, sisters, daughters, and wives. While not all were biological mothers, their personal tenacity, vision, labor, and commitment produced programs, services, and a legacy of kinship care that has become fundamental to the survival of the African American community. Steeped in the tradition of caregiving and mutually reciprocal support networks, African American women have developed a tradition of keeping their families, communities, and churches alive, nurtured, and thriving.

Older African American women have played very important helping roles within their extended and fictive family networks and communities. As caregivers for their children, grandchildren, nieces, nephews, and a host of fictive kin, older African American women, particularly grandmothers, set the standards for appropriate behavior. It is often the grandmother who provides direction and advice on education, sexual conduct, respect for self and others, religious practices, and love. In addition to caregiving and advising, African American grandmothers have provided social and emotional support to family members, communicated important social values to offspring, and assisted in the birthing of babies. The helping roles of older women, however, have not been limited to family and household responsibilities; these women also held important leadership positions within the church and other areas of community life.

Often viewed as strong and resourceful, African American grandmothers are important figures in the stability and survival of their families. From slavery to the present, older Black women, namely grandmothers, have been pivotal forces in the socialization of children and the stabilization of their families and communities. The strength and resilience of African American women are embedded in their ability to endure the harshness of slavery and oppression, their ability to perform multiple roles, their love of family, and their strong religious beliefs. African American grandmothers are the backbone of the family. Frazier (1939) described them as the "guardian of the generations." Although grandmothers have continued their helping roles as guardians and caregivers in contemporary American society, they are now confronted with new and challenging responsibilities as the twenty-first century begins.

The Precolonial African Family

In his work, *The Negro in the Making of America,* Quarles (1964) describes the traditional West African family as a kinship group numbering in the hundreds. The dominant figure in the extended family community was the patriarch, who had a number of functions: peacemaker, judge, administrator, and keeper of the purse. Blassingame (1972) noted that women also played important roles in the patriarchal family structure. They made clothes, served as warriors, did the marketing, and worked in the fields alongside their husbands. The care and training of the children was primarily the responsibility of the women. As a result, deep bonds of affection developed between mothers and their children. However, "regardless of the meaningful roles of women in precolonial Africa, the authority pattern was patriarchal" (Staples, 1976, p. 115). The family unit in precolonial African society was highly structured, rigidly patriarchal, and very important. Women were described as uncommonly graceful, alert, modest, bashful, and chaste. Their duties were to weave calico cloth and make earthenware; the men made tools and weapons (Blassingame, 1972). The roles of women in precolonial Africa were important, but different from their roles in American slavery (Ladner, 1971).

The Slave Family and the Role of Mothers in the Socialization of Children

The African mother became a dominant and important figure in the family within the American slave system and was characterized as a devoted nurse and mother (Frazier, 1939). Considered the mistress of the cabin and the head of the house, the mother had a more fundamental interest in the children than the father, and "as a worker and free agent, except where the master's will was concerned, she developed a spirit of independence and a keen sense of her personal rights" (Frazier, 1939, p. 47). Essentially, her wishes in family matters were paramount. Neither tradition nor economic necessity had instilled in her the spirit of subordination to masculine authority. In spite of the most demanding conditions of the slave system, African American mothers remained the most important and reliable figures in the family. Emancipation only solidified her spirit of self-sufficiency, which slavery had taught (Frazier, 1939).

It became apparent that the structure and function of the African family would change radically under the system of slavery; however, the importance of the family remained unchanged (Staples, 1976). The relationship between mother and child was important throughout all of Africa, and the institution of slavery "acted to reinforce the close bond that had already existed between mother and child" (Ladner, 1971, p. 17). "The institution of the family was an important asset in the perilous era of slavery" (Staples, 1976, p. 117), and the family was the most durable survival mechanism for American slaves. The strong bond between mother and child was accompanied by a great amount of respect for both parents by their children. Mothers in the community of slaves were held in high esteem by their children; fathers were loved and respected as well, not only for their physical strength, but also for their courage and compassion (Blassingame, 1972). Extolling the virtues of the family, Blassingame (1972) wrote:

> Although it was frequently broken, the slave family provided an important buffer, a refuge from the rigors of slavery. While the slave father could rarely protect the members of his family from abuse, he could often gain their love and respect in other ways. In his family, the slave not only learned how to avoid the blows of the master, but also drew on the love and sympathy of its members to raise his spirits. The family was an important survival mechanism. (p. 103)

The two most serious drawbacks to the father's status in the family were "his inability to protect his wife from sexual advances of whites and the physical abuse of his master" (Blassingame, 1972, p. 88). His inability to prevent the sale of his wife and children was also an example of his powerlessness. Essentially, the restriction of primary group relationships and the separation of families were among the most destructive aspects of American slavery.

The destructive nature of slavery was also seen in its impact on the welfare of women. The hardship placed on women who had to work in the fields and take care of their own children as well as the master's children and his family is only a small part of the demanding responsibilities that they experienced. In *Darkwater*, DuBois (1920/1969) wrote, "The crushing weight of slavery fell on black women. Under it there was no legal marriage, no legal family, no legal control over children" (p. 169). Advertisements like the following show the destructive nature of slavery on family relationships and at the same time illustrate the importance of women to family cohesion:

> One hundred dollars reward will be given for two fellows, Abram and Frank. Abram has a wife at Colonel Stewarts in Liberty County, and a mother at Thunderbolt, and a sister in Savannah. (DuBois, 1920/1969, p. 169)

DuBois questioned whether "any race of women could have brought its fineness up through so devilish a fire" (1920/1969, p. 171). Frazier (1939) asserted that it was because of the conditions imposed by the slave system that the mother emerged as the most dependable and most important member of the family. Sociologist and National Urban League researcher Charles S. Johnson (1934) believed that the role of the African American mother was "more important than in the familiar white American group" (p. 177). The primacy of the mother's role was enhanced because of the need for children to remain with their mothers. Generally, the father's role in the family was more incidental because he could be sold very easily, therefore making his stay within the home more transient. However, it should be noted that the father's role was certainly not unimportant.

Frazier (1939) believed that the African American female, in addition to being the mistress of the cabin and head of the family, had a more fundamental interest in her children than the father did. And, although the cruelties of slave life were an impediment to the healthy functioning of the family, many of the traditional functions of the family were maintained. Among these was the rearing of children. In slave communities, the parents helped their children understand their oppressed position, taught them values unlike those that their masters tried to instill in them, and gave them a basis for positive self-esteem (Blassingame, 1972). In addition to teaching their children how to survive oppression, slave parents taught their children important spiritual values. Such values included having a sense of morality, being honest, leading Christian lives, and refraining from stealing and lying. Furthermore, these children were taught ways to stay alive and to avoid physical abuse. They were taught to obey their masters and to "hold their tongues around white folks" (Blassingame, 1972, p. 99). Mothers also instilled in their children the presence of a "Supreme Being that takes care of them during their trials" (Blassingame, 1972, p. 99). The teaching of religious values was both fundamental and unifying in the slave community. Furthermore, the family unit served as one of the most important survival mechanisms for the slave. The family provided "companionship, love, empathy for suffering, cooperation with other blacks, fulfillment of gratification, ways to avoid punishment, and ways to maintain positive self-esteem" (Blassingame, 1972, pp. 78–79). Through the separations and hardships, the slave mother remained loyal and devoted to her children. The strong attachment that mothers showed for their children could be compared to the "deep affection between husbands and wives" (Frazier, 1939, p. 78). The struggle for existence strengthened family ties, and even after Emancipation, the bonds remained strong between mothers and their children (Staples, 1976).

Helping Roles of Grandmothers in the Slave Family

The role of older women in the slave community was also outstanding. Powdermaker (1969) found that the typical household consisted of grandparents, nieces, nephews, adopted children, and others who were not related even by adoption. Older women, usually grandmothers, gave the family its unity, coherence, wisdom, and sense of values. In his book, *The Negro in the United States,* Frazier (1939) described African American grandmothers' importance to their families by saying:

> The Negro grandmother's importance is due to the fact not only that she has been the "oldest head" in a maternal family organization but also to her position as "granny" or midwife among a simple peasant folk. As the repository of old wisdom concerning the inscrutable ways of nature, the grandmother has been depended upon by mothers to ease the pains of childbirth and ward off the dangers

> of ill luck. Children acknowledge their indebtedness to her for assuring them, during the crisis of birth, a safe entrance into the world. Even grown men and women refer to her as a second mother and sometimes show the same deference and respect for her that they accord their own mothers. (p. 117)

The grandmother's presence and influence regarding the welfare of the Black family has been established. Powdermaker (1969) noted that grandmothers were present in many households and were likely to have more influence than mothers did in a child's life, although the natural mother maintained the authority. Powdermaker further reported that where an elderly woman is head of a household that includes married daughters, she carries authority with the children; even where her position is less dominant, she is likely to take over responsibility for their welfare and behavior. Most women were as eager for grandchildren as for children, often for the same reasons. Blassingame (1972) state that "grandparents . . . loomed large in the life of the slave child—they frequently prepared tidbits for the children, and grandfathers often told them stories about their lives in Africa" (p. 95). Grandmothers had a pivotal role in the plantation economy during slavery and were respected highly by both the slaves and masters. Frazier (1939) reported that the grandmother "kept secrets and was seen as loyal and affectionate by the master," and she was "the defender of the family honor" (p. 114). She became an irreplaceable member in the family, for she fulfilled a number of different role responsibilities. Among these were confidante, advisor, authority on first babies, cook, wet-nurse, and seamstress. The loyalty and reverence accorded the grandmother by extended family, as well as by the master and his family, was inscrutable.

In general, the social conditions for Blacks in America did not change appreciably after Emancipation, and it was often the grandmother who "kept the generations together" (Frazier, 1939, p. 116), while mothers worked and many fathers set out to find their lost children and wives. Within the context of an oppressive society, Black women were forced to accept total responsibility for their families and work outside the home.

Grandmothers displayed enormous devotion and love for their families. The following passage taken from Frazier's 1939 work depicts the energy, courage, and devotion of a nearly 70-year-old grandmother:

> During the Civil War an old slave and his wife attempted to escape from a plantation near Savannah but were caught and returned to their master. While the old man was receiving five hundred lashes as punishment, his wife collected his children and grandchildren, to the number of twenty-two, in a neighboring marsh, preparatory to another attempt that night. They found a flatboat which had been rejected as unseaworthy, got on board—still under the old woman's orders—drifted forty miles down the river to the lines of the Union army. An officer who was on board the gunboat that picked them up said that "when the 'flat' touched the side of the vessel, the grandmother rose to her full height with her grandchild in her arms, and said only 'My God! are we free?'" (p. 114)

The courage displayed by the woman represents the commitment that grandmothers have for their families. Grandmothers worked hard and suffered quietly while taking great pride in carrying a heavy burden. Frazier wrote in 1939 that "each generation of women, following in the footsteps of their mothers, has borne a large share of the support of the younger generation. Today, in the rural sections of the South, especially on the remnants of the old plantation, one finds households where old grandmothers rule their daughters and grandchildren with matriarchal authority" (p. 113).

Postbellum Roles and Older Women

Economic growth, rampant racial violence, and accompanying race reform, along with northern and western migration, characterized the period from 1898 to 1920. During this time, Black women worked primarily as unpaid domestic workers in their own homes and in their communities. Much of their unpaid service was in the church, a service of much pride for these women (Malson, Mudimbe, Boyi, O'Barr, & Wyer, 1988). Although major social and economic changes were occurring, the racial climate for African Americans was steadily worsening (Malson et al., 1988). In spite of the racial problems, however, Black women experienced some degree of economic progress in cities such as the District of Columbia. Although they were often employed as domestics and washerwomen, they received higher pay and more prestigious positions in private homes, cleaning office buildings, and as unskilled and semiskilled workers in commercial laundries. In general, however, African American women workers had fewer opportunities than Black men to occupy high-paying and more prestigious positions. Because of racism, there were few white-collar positions for Blacks in the labor force, and because of sexism, many of the top-level positions reserved for Blacks in the District of Columbia were occupied by Black men. During this time, prominent Black men such as Frederick Douglass, George Edmund Haynes, and Lawrence Oxley occupied the top clerical and political positions reserved for Blacks in the federal government. Black women, with similar if not superior educational training, (for example, Mary Church Terrell), were not considered for such positions (Malson et al., 1988). Nonetheless, according to the census reports for the District of Columbia, in 1890, approximately 55 percent of African American women were employed in paying positions. By 1910, this figure had increased to 60 percent, but by 1930, the same figure had dropped to about 53 percent. Many expressed concern about the employment of Black mothers, especially the uneducated and nonprofessional women. To some, this was an indication of lack of racial progress and family stability. Yet others believed that "[t]he race needs wives to stay at home, being supported by their husbands, so that they can spend time with the training of their children" (Malson et al., 1988, p. 164). This view, perhaps unrealistic, represented the ideal for many Blacks. The 1920 census revealed that some 50 percent of all married women in the District of Columbia were employed. And most Black working women in the District in 1920 were either single, widowed, or married with no spouse or children in the home. Perhaps the intentions were honorable, but for many husbands it was not reasonable to oppose the employment of their wives when their family's survival was dependent on their financial contributions.

The late nineteenth and early twentieth centuries were ripe for reform, and women played a critical role (Vaz, 1995). A number of violent and disturbing social factors such as lynchings and race riots set the stage for racial reform work during the late nineteenth century. In addition to the overt violence of racism, Blacks were still economically, politically, and socially disadvantaged, and many conditions had not changed drastically since slavery. Black children were less likely than White children to attend school because of work in the field, and they were six times more likely to be illiterate than their White counterparts (Vaz, 1995).

The emerging social problems forced action and reaction among reformers. These leaders, often lacking financial resources and political support, drew upon the values of self-help and racial solidarity. Out of these efforts came the Afro-American League/Council (1890), the National Association of Colored Women (1896), and the Niagara Movement (1905). In 1908, the National Association for the Advancement of Colored People (NAACP) was founded in response to racial injustice. The participation of Black women was evident during the early years of the NAACP. Ida B. Wells-Barnett of Chicago and Mary Church Terrell of Washington, DC, were the only two women representing the Black community at first. By 1910, however, the Black female presence was more evident and continued to expand. Many Black women played a significant role in connecting the NAACP to the Black community, ultimately leading to a Black-headed NAACP (Vaz, 1995). Black women helped the NAACP to become the advancement organization for the race. The consciousness of Black women helped to raise the level of sensitivity within the NAACP (Vaz, 1995).

The steady, yet small movement of Blacks to Northern cities that began after the Civil War more than doubled from 41,378 persons between 1870 and 1890 to 107,796 by 1900. A total of 200,000 Blacks migrated to the North and West between 1890 and 1910 (Osofsky, 1964). By the beginning of the twentieth century, the migration of southern Blacks to the North and West was an established fact. The new immigrants to the urban areas joined the movement to improve Black life. Urban reformers were primarily interested in finding jobs and good homes, health, businesses and unions, and protection of domestic workers from exploitation (Osofsky, 1964). Black women played a major role in these efforts.

Out of her concern for new Black female migrants to New York, Victoria Earle Matthews, the youngest daughter of a Georgia slave, organized the White Rose Industrial Association to provide lodging and meals for women until they found work. The objective of the organization was to protect girls from the dangers of the city. To this end, young women who came to the city were escorted to their place of employment or to the White Rose Working Girls' Home. The White Rose Home became a settlement house as well as a temporary lodging place for young female migrants. There were classes in domestic training and race history and an extensive library of books on Black life. The White Rose Home continued to operate even after Victoria Matthews's death in 1907. Black women played major roles in a variety of organizations between 1898 and 1920.

Changes in African American Family Structure

Within the last four decades, a number of structural changes have occurred in African American family life. In his discussion of the diversity in family structure in African American communities, Billingsley (1992) noted that from 1865 to 1965, the African American family was characterized by a high degree of stability; the central focus of the traditional family was the nuclear family unit, consisting of the mother, the father, and their children. The decline in two-parent families began after the 1960s at a time when it became difficult for Black men to maintain decent wages as blue-collar workers in the industrial sector. At the beginning of the 1960s, 78 percent of all Black families were headed by a married couple, followed by 64 percent in 1970, 48 percent in 1980, and 39 percent in 1990 (Billingsley, 1992). Given the social and structural problems that African Americans faced, this downward trend in two-parent families is likely to continue, and grandmother-maintained households will likely increase as well.

Billingsley (1992) further noted that in 1980, for the first time since slavery, a majority of African Americans lived in single-parent families. The nuclear and extended family forms, that were adopted after slavery as adaptive mechanisms are in a rapid state of decline, declared Billingsley. Post-industrialization has resulted in a number of alternative family structures, and grandmothers raising grandchildren alone is among the most obvious. The grandmother-headed family is an adaptive strategy for meeting the basic needs of its members, given the situation that they face in contemporary society (Billingsley, 1992). Technological changes since the 1950s and, more recently, the crack cocaine epidemic, HIV/AIDS epidemic, and the incarcerations of young African American mothers have all contributed to the restructuring of the African American family. Grandmothers have been thrust into caregiving roles that have a foundation in African and African American tradition, but in contemporary society are described as unfamiliar and nontraditional and as roles that threaten their morale and increase their role confusion (Emick & Hayslip, 1996; Hayslip, Shore, Henderson, & Lambert, 1998).

Increase in Grandparent-Maintained Families

According to the U.S. Bureau of the Census (1997), since 1970 there has been a 77 percent increase in the number of households headed by grandparents. In 1970, 2.2 million or 3.2 percent of American children lived in a home maintained by a grandparent. This number had increased to 3.9 million or 5.5 percent by 1977 (Casper & Bryson, 1998; U.S. Bureau of the Census, 1998; Velkoff & Lawson, 1998), and by 1998, it had risen to 4 million or 6 percent of all children under age 18 (U.S. Bureau of the Census, 1998). The greatest increase was among children with only one parent present in the household. This pattern, grandchildren living in households maintained by grandparents with only mother present, increased by 118 percent from 1970 to 1997 (Casper & Bryson, 1998; U.S. Bureau of the Census, 1997). Since 1990, however, the greatest growth has been in the number of grandchildren living with their grandparents only, with neither parent present (Casper & Bryson, 1998; U.S. Bureau of the Census, 1998). The increase in households headed by African American grandmothers is especially noteworthy. In 1992, 12 percent of African American children lived in the home of their grandparents, in comparison to 4 percent of White and six percent of Hispanic children (U.S. Bureau of the Census, 1992).

Contemporary Helping Roles and Family Relationships of Grandmothers: Problems and Challenges in the Twenty-First Century

A number of reasons for grandparents acting as parents to their grandchildren are discussed in the extant literature. Authors cite such reasons as drug abuse, incarcerations, divorce, desertion, death of parent, child abuse, unemployment, teenage pregnancy, and HIV/AIDS (Barnhill, 1996; Burnette, 1997; Caliandro & Hughes, 1998; Emick & Hayslip, 1996; Hayslip et al., 1998; Kee, 1997; LeBlanc, London, & Aneshensel, 1997; Longino & Earle, 1996; Minkler & Roe, 1996; Pruchno & Johnson, 1996; Sands & Goldberg-Glen, 1996;). These problems are leaving a devastating impact on African American families and communities, and they are likely to get worse in the new millennium.

According to the American Association of Retired Persons (AARP; 1994), African American grandparents, grandmothers in particular, are more likely to be surrogate parents than are White or Hispanic grandparents, and the number one reason is drug abuse. The cocaine epidemic, incarcerations, and HIV/AIDS are all interrelated and will continue to cause serious problems for African American families and communities. Many grandmothers are not prepared to deal with the problems of children with special needs.

New problems for grandmothers present new and challenging role responsibilities. Whereas many grandmothers welcome the role of grandparenthood, others view it as an untimely burden. Economic, physical, emotional, and educational problems accompany their new parenting responsibilities. A small group of studies have investigated the psychological, social, and economic problems and needs of grandparents who are primary caregivers for their grandchildren (Burton & DeVries, 1993; Kelly, 1993; Minkler & Roe, 1993, 1996). In their study of surrogate parenting, Burton and DeVries (1993) reported that African American grandparents, in general, see their role as necessary for the survival of the family. This role assumption reflects the strengths of grandmothers and the resiliency and adaptability of African American families (Billingsley, 1992). As the historical record indicates, it is not uncommon for African American grandmothers to place the needs of the family above their own.

Although African American families have traditionally been characterized as extended family networks with much cooperation and support, some contemporary studies show that African American grandmothers are not receiving consistent and reliable support from family members (Burton, 1992). Other studies show a rich support network

(Minkler & Roe, 1993); however, social isolation is seen among some of the younger grandmothers who are experiencing role conflict caused by being employed and having child care responsibilities (Minkler & Roe, 1993). Other psychosocial responses include feelings of guilt and shame because of the drug or alcohol use by their children.

In their study of African American grandmothers, Minkler and Roe (1996) have identified consequences of surrogate parenting in the areas of health problems, economic difficulties, and the lack of government support. A number of health problems, such as depression, insomnia, hypertension, back and stomach pain, and other problems associated with the physical and emotional demands of child care have been reported by clinicians (Miller, 1991; Minkler & Roe, 1996). In a study of grandmothers raising grandchildren as a result of the crack cocaine epidemic, Minkler and Roe (1996) found that grandmothers tended to minimize the severity of their own health problems in an effort to show that they were capable of taking care of their grandchildren. Some studies have reported declining health after grandparents become surrogate parents, while other studies have found changes in social behaviors, such as increases in cigarette smoking and alcohol consumption (Burton, 1992; Minkler & Roe, 1996; Minkler, Roe, & Price, 1992).

The health problems of African American grandmother caregivers are often exacerbated by financial problems. African American women have traditionally occupied low-wage jobs, often without good retirement benefits. As reported by Minkler and Roe (1996), grandparents must sometimes spend savings or make other sacrifices in an effort to adjust to the role of parenting their grandchildren. Yet, grandparent caregivers do not receive the type of financial support that foster care providers receive (Minkler & Roe, 1996). They are also denied such benefits as psychological counseling and clothing allowances, which are available to foster care providers. Although their traditional helping roles are still intact, African American grandmothers have some specific problems and needs with regard to health, economic, and social issues requiring additional program, policy, and research considerations.

Programs and Interventions to Support Grandparent Caregivers

The last few years have seen an increase in interest in the phenomenon of grandparent caregiving in the United States with a concomitant increase in the number of community interventions and service programs to assist grandparent caregivers. In an effort to stimulate the development of program ideas, the Brookdale Grandparent Information Center was established at the Berkeley Center on Aging at the University of California in 1991 with a grant from the Brookdale Foundation Group. The focus of this initiative is on grandparents who are primary caregivers for their grandchildren. The initiative is designed to survey the extent and nature of services for grandparent caregivers across the country. In 1993, The Brookdale Foundation also provided support for the establishment of the AARP Grandparent Information Center, which provides resources and information on the array of issues and concerns of custodial grandparents. In addition, the Brookdale Foundation initiated the Relatives as Parents Program (RAPP) in 1996.

The RAPP is designed to encourage and promote the creation or expansion of services for grandparents and other relatives who have taken on the responsibility of surrogate parenting because the biological parents are unable or unwilling to do so. Presently, there are 60 local programs and 20 state agencies that participate in the RAPP Network and provide extensive services to relative caregivers in 28 different states.

Grandparent Support Group. The Grandparent Information Center of the AARP is a resource for custodial grandparents as well. In conjunction with national and community agencies, it offers information and referral assistance. The AARP Center serves as a starting point for learning where to get assistance with legal concerns, financial resources, child care, medical issues, schools, social concerns, and emotional issues of both child and grandparent caregiver. The Center also develops publications, conducts public awareness campaigns, and provides assistance to grandparent groups and agencies.

Support Groups for Grandparent Caregivers. The support group is the most common form of community intervention to assist the grandparent caregiver. Some 300 support groups are operated in different communities throughout the United States. Support groups are designed to provide opportunities for members to share feelings while giving and receiving informational support about resources and methods for coping with the new caregiving role (Minkler, 1994). Support groups may be organized and headed by the grandparents themselves, or they may be sponsored and headed by churches, schools, social service agencies, or another organization. Most often, support groups do not have funds to finance their activities.

Comprehensive Programs. The Brookdale Foundation has identified approximately 24 comprehensive programs. With a paid staff and funding, these comprehensive programs offer services such as parenting classes, supportive services for children in the care of relatives, counseling, peer training, respite care, and legislative advocacy on the rights of grandparents raising grandchildren (Minkler, 1994). Comprehensive programs are also designed to address some of the more unique problems regarding a particular population. For example, Aid to Imprisoned Mothers (AIM) offers transportation to women's prisons, allowing the grandmothers and grandchildren in their care an opportunity to visit the imprisoned mother in an effort to maintain family relationships (Minkler, 1994). Grandparents as Second Parents (GASP) is a telephone support service for relatives who are caregivers. Most are caring for grandchildren because of a parent's problems with crack cocaine. Project GUIDE is a Detroit-based program responding to drug abuse problems. The program is designed to provide intensive training to grandparent caregivers, as well as social and cultural events.

Conclusion

From the time of slavery to the present, sisters, daughters, wives, and grandmothers or older African American women have played major roles as helpers and caregivers within Black family networks. During slavery, women were the dominant figures in the Black family. As the late nineteenth and early twentieth centuries approached, African American women increased their presence in the higher paying urban economic workforce. At a time when racial conflicts were escalating, Black women joined racial reform movements to combat discrimination. Approximately 100 years after slavery, major demographic and socioeconomic trends began to take place in the African American family. And, over the past three decades, the African American family has seen a decline in the two-parent family structure. Presently, many single-parent households are maintained by grandmothers alone. The traditional roles of grandmothers have changed from helpers to primary caregivers to their grandchildren, whose parents are either not able or not willing to take care of them. The last three decades have witnessed a major shift in the roles of grandparents because of the crack cocaine epidemic, the HIV/AIDS epidemic, and the incarcerations of young adult mothers. These three major social and public health problems have devastated many families, and they have placed an enormous amount of burden on older women who may not be prepared economically, physically, or emotionally to care for their grandchildren.

To date, there is very little research on the problems of African American grandmothers raising their grandchildren and great-grandchildren. Not much is known about the demographic characteristics of this population. Previous studies have not included African American grandparents in significant numbers. Studies that have focused exclusively on African American grandparents are small and qualitative in nature. Although qualitative studies make important contributions, empirical studies are needed so that broader generalizations may be made. Although not new in practice, the research and policy emphasis on surrogate parenting among grandmothers is relatively new and open to exploration. Some additional issues that may be considered by social scientists include the impact of raising grandchildren on physical and psychological health, the educational needs of African American grandmothers, the impact of incarcerations of adult children on grandmother caregivers, and the impact of HIV/AIDS and drug abuse on caregiving. In addition to research, community interventions, such as the ones mentioned earlier (support groups and services for children), are useful resources for grandmother caregivers. Policy recommendations are also needed so that African American grandparents may benefit from legislation regarding their particular problems. To ensure strong and healthy families, it is necessary to know more about the daily lives of African American grandparents. The empowerment tradition upon which these grandmothers rely warrants a more thorough examination in order to be used as a model for future practice and policy development.

This research was supported by the National Institutes of Health, National Institute on Aging, Behavior and Physiology in Aging. Grant #2 T32 AG00029.

References

American Association of Retired Persons. (1994). *Grandparent-headed households and their grandchildren.* Grandparent Information Center Fact Sheet.

Barnhill, S. (1996). Three generations at risk: The imprisoned women, their children, and the grandmother caregiver. *Generations*, *20*(1), 39.

Billingsley, A. (1992). *Climbing Jacob's ladder: The enduring legacy of African American families.* New York: Simon & Schuster.

Blassingame, J. W. (1972). *The slave community: Plantation life in the Antebellum South.* New York: Oxford University Press.

Burnette, D. (1997). Grandparents raising grandchildren in the inner city. *Families and Society*, *78*(5), 489–499.

Burton, L. M. (1992). Black grandparents rearing children of drug-addicted parents: Stressors, outcomes, and social service needs. *The Gerontologist*, *32*(6), 744–751.

Burton, L. M., & DeVries, C. (1993). Challenges and rewards: African American grandparents as surrogate parents. *Generations*, *17*, 51–54.

Caliandro, G., & Hughes, C. (1998). The experience of being a grandmother who is the primary caregiver for her HIV-positive grandchildren. *Nursing Research*, *47*(2), 107–113.

Casper, L. M., & Bryson, K. R. (1998). *Co-resident grandparents and their grandchildren: Grandparent-maintained families.* U.S. Bureau of the Census, Population Division, Fertility and Family Statistics Branch.

DuBois, W. E. B. (1969). *Darkwater: Voices from within the veil.* New York: Schocken Books. (Original work published 1920)

Emick, M., & Hayslip, B. (1996). Custodial grandparenting: New roles for middle aged and older adults. *International Journal of Aging and Human Development*, *43*(2), 135–154.

Frazier, E. F. (1939). *The Negro family in the United States.* Chicago: University of Chicago Press.

Hayslip, B., Shore, R., Henderson C., & Lambert, P. (1998). Custodial grandparenting and the impact of grandchildren with problems on role satisfaction and role meaning. *Journal of Gerontology: Social Sciences*, *53B*(3), S164–S173.

Johnson, C. S. (1934). *Shadow of the plantation.* Chicago: University of Chicago Press.

Kee, D. M. (1997). *Grandparents as caregivers for adolescent grandchildren.* Master's thesis, California State University, Long Beach.

Kelly, S. J. (1993). Caregiver stress in grandparents raising grandchildren. *Image: Journal of Nursing Scholarship*, *25*(4), 331–337.

Ladner, J. (1971). *Tomorrow's tomorrow.* New York: Anchor Books.

LeBlanc, A., London, A., & Aneshensel, C. (1997). The physical costs of AIDS caregiving. *Social Science and Medicine*, *45*(6), 915–923.

Longino, C., & Earle, J. (1996). Who are the grandparents at century's end? *Generations*, *20*(1), p. 13.

Malson, M., Mudimbe-Boyi, E., O'Barr, J., & Wyer, M. (1988). *Black women in America.* Chicago: University of Chicago Press.

Miller, D. (1991, November). *The "grandparents who care" support project of San Francisco.* Paper presented at the Annual Scientific Meeting of the Gerontological Society of America, San Francisco, CA.

Minkler, M. (1994). Grandparents as parents: The American experience. *Aging International, 2*(1), 4–28.

Minkler, M., & Roe, K. (1993). *Grandmothers as caregivers: Raising children of the crack cocaine epidemic.* Newbury Park, CA: Sage.

Minkler, M., & Roe, K. (1996). Grandparents as surrogate parents. *Generation, 20*, 34–38.

Minkler, M., Roe, K., & Price, M. (1992). The physical and emotional health of grandmothers raising grandchildren in the crack cocaine epidemic. *The Gerontologist, 32*, 752–760.

Osofsky, G. (1964). *The making of a ghetto.* New York: Harper Torchbooks.

Powdermaker, H. (1969). *After freedom: A cultural study in the deep South.* New York: Atheneum.

Pruchno, R., & Johnson, K. (1996). Research on grandparenting: Review of current studies and future needs. *Generations, 20*(1), 65.

Quarles, B. (1964). *The Negro in the making of America.* London: Collier-Macmillan.

Sands, R. G., & Goldberg-Glen, R. S. (1996). *The impact of surrogate parenting on grandparents: Stress, well-being, and life satisfaction.* AARP Andrus Foundation Final Report. Research Information Center, 601 E. Street NW, Room B3-221, Washington, DC 20049.

Staples. R. (1976). *Introduction to sociology.* New York. McGraw-Hill Book Company.

U.S. Bureau of the Census. (1992, March). Marital status and living arrangements, 1990 Census of the population. Current population reports, population characteristics. (Series P-20, No. 468). Washington, DC: U.S. Government Printing Office.

U.S. Bureau of the Census. (1997, March). 1970 and 1980 censuses and 1990 and 1997 current population surveys. In *Marital status and living arrangements* (March 1994, Table A-6). Washington, DC: U.S. Government Printing Office.

U.S. Bureau of the Census (1998, March). Current population reports. In *Marital status and living arrangements* (Series P-20, No. 574). Washington, DC: U.S. Government Printing Office.

Vaz, K. M. (1995). *Black women in America.* Newbury Park, CA: Sage Publications.

Velkoff, V. A., & Lawson, V. A. (1998). *Gender and aging.* International Programs Center, U.S. Department of Commerce, Economics and Statistics Administration, Bureau of the Census, December 1998.

Index

Abbott, Edith, 36, 38, 40, 41
Frazier and, 191
on Haynes, 45
Abraham Lincoln Center, Chicago, 168, 173
Addams, Jane, 126
Frazier and, 191
B. H. Haynes and, 38, 40, 41
NAACP and, 194
Terrell and, 159
Ades, Bernard, 174
Adoption Assistance and Child Welfare Act of 1980, 211
Africa—Continent of the Future (G. Haynes), 120
African American longshoremen study (Frazier), 192–193, 196
African American–owned businesses, 76
African American social welfare movement, xi
African American women, 12
African Communities League (ACL), xvi, 76
See also Universal Negro Improvement Association (UNIA)
African Methodist Episcopal Church women, 25
African Redemption Fund, 79
Afro-American (term), 7
Afro-American League/Council, 221
Afrocentricity, 77, 113
Agricultural College For Women (England), 61
Aid to Imprisoned Mothers (AIM), 225
Alabama State Federation of Colored Women's Clubs, 66
Alabama Women's Hall of Fame, 56
Allen, Richard, 19
Allen A.M.E. Church, Philadelphia, 25
Allen-Meares, P., xii
All-Philadelphia Conference on Social Work, 24
Allport, Gordon, 160
Alpha Kappa Alpha Sorority, 119
Alpha Phi Alpha Fraternity, 140, 141
Alpha Suffrage Club, xvi, 94
American Association of Retired Persons (AARP), 223
Grandparent Information Center, 225
American Association of Social Workers (AASW), 142, 169–170
American-Danish Foundation, 192
American Dilemma, An (Myrdal), 194
American Federation of Labor, 164
American Institute of Social Service, 183
American Joint Distribution Committee, 173
American Sociological Association, 189
Amos, James E., 82–83
Anderson, Edwin H., 139
Anthony, Susan B., 61, 159
Anti-Lynching Society (London), 92
Armfield, Felix L., xvi
Armstrong, Samuel Chapman, 19–20
Armstrong Association of Philadelphia, xv, 19–20
Bureau of Information, 23
extended philanthropy, 20–21
injustice correction by, 28–29
professional empowerment, 30
program flexibility, 29
as social service agency, 25
social work contributions, 22–24
strengths model, 28
Associated Charities, Washington, DC, 183, 185
Colored Department of, 180
Associated Negro Press, 165, 169
Associates in Negro Folk Education, 139–140

Association for the Protection of Colored Women, Philadelphia, 23
Atlanta, Neighborhood Union of, 144–145
Atlanta Community Chest, 208
Atlanta University, School of Social Work, 24, 105, 116, 143, 194
  Conferences, 207–208
  Frazier and, 189, 190, 191
"Aunt Lindy: A Story Founded on Real Life" (Matthews), 3
"Awakening of the Afro-American Woman, The" (Matthews), 7

Baldwin, Ruth Standish, 37, 39, 50
Ballentine, Anna T., 59
Baltimore Afro-American, 197–198
Baltzell, E. Digby, 18
Barnett, Charles Aked, 88
Barnett, Claude, 169
Barnett, Ferdinand L., 80, 88, 90, 93
Barrett, Janie Porter, xvi, 67, 209
  on parole officers, 131
  starts Virginia Industrial School for Colored Girls, 126–127
  See also Virginia Industrial School for Colored Girls
Barrett Learning Center, Hanover County, VA, 123, 125
Basis of Racial Adjustment, The (Woofter), 194–195
Beckett, Marcella, 24
Ben J. Sopkins Apron Factory, 165–167
Benjamin, Syrene Elizabeth Thompson, 26
Bent-Goodley, Tricia, xvi
Berkeley Center on Aging, 224–225
Bethlehem Center, Nashville, 118
Bethlehem House Settlement, Nashville, 116
Bethune, Mary McLeod, 106, 140
Bickett, Fannie Yarborough (Mrs. T. W.), 102, 107–108
Billingsley, A., 26, 203, 222
Binney, Charles C., 20
Bishop Tuttle Memorial Training School of Social Work, St. Augustine's College, Raleigh, NC, 143
  G.E. Haynes and, 116
  Oxley and, 99, 104, 105
  Richards and, 107
Black Belt Diamonds: Gems from the Speeches, Addresses and Talks of B. T. Washington (Matthews), 3
Black Bourgeoisie (Frazier), 189
Black Boy of Atlanta, The (Ross Haynes), 120
Black Empowerment (Solomon), xiv
Black Muslims, 82
Black Star Line Steamship Corporation, 78, 81–82
Black Women in United States History, 56
Blair Bill (against lynch law), 92
Blassingame, J. W., 216, 217, 219
Boaz, Sophia, 38, 39
Bost, Mrs. W. Thomas, 107–108
Bowen, Louise deKoven, 37, 40, 41
Bowen, Mrs. J. W. E., 208
Boy Scouts, 210
Boys' Improvement Club, Jacksonville, FL, 206
Brawley, B. G., 120
Breckinridge, Sophonisba, 40, 41, 43
  B. H. Haynes and, 36, 37–39, 44
Bronze Booklet Series, 140
Brookdale Grandparent Information Center, 224–225
Brooklyn Literary Group, 62
Brookwood Labor College, 164
Brophy, Mrs. T. W., 41
Brotherhood of Sleeping Car Porters, Educational Department of, 164
Brown, Charlotte Hawkins, 107, 108
Brown, Henry, 58
Bryson, Lyman, 140
Bunce, Gertrude, 208
Burch, Mrs. George, 208
Bureau for Colored Children (The Bureau), xv, 19, 26–27
  professional empowerment, 30
  program flexibility, 29
  strengths model, 28
Bureau of Labor Statistics, Division of Negro Labor, 101
Bureau of Social Service, Goldsboro, NC, 103
Burman, S., xii
Burton, L. M., 223
Burwell, N. Yolanda, xvi, 102, 107

Calhoun Colored School and Social Settlement, 118, 204–205
Capacity building
  Garvey on, 77
  See also Institution building
Caretakers, child welfare, 211
Carlton-LaNey, Iris B., xv, xvi
Carnegie, Andrew, 138
Carnegie Foundation, 139, 140
Carrie Steele Orphan Home, 125, 204, 207
Carrie Steele-Pitts Home, 125
Carstens, C. C., 126, 131
Carter, Lewis, 25
Certification of child welfare services, 211
Chambers, C. A., 125
Chandler, Susan Kerr, xvii
Charities, 183
Charity Organization Society
  Baltimore Friendly Visitor program, 180
  community building, 75
  of New York, 183
Chesapeake and Ohio Railroad, 89
Chestnut, Charles, 9
Chicago Defender Press, 169
Chicago Relief Administration, 167

Chicago School of Civics and Philanthropy, 36, 37, 38, 164
Chicago Women's Club, 92
Child Welfare League of America, 126
  Kinship Care Policy and Practice Committee, 211
Child welfare services
  African American, 204–206
  combined facilities, 207
  development of, xiii, 203–213
  early twentieth century, 203–204
  Edwards and, xvii, 164–165, 171, 173–174
  homes for wayward children, 209–210
  homes for working girls, 209
  kindergartens, 207–209
  organizational responses to, xiii
  orphanages, 206–207
  reform, xvi
  services, xvii
  Terrell on, 159
  women's roles in, xiii
  See also Older African American women; Virginia Industrial School for Colored Girls
Church, Luisa Ayres, 153
Church, Robert Reed, 153–154
Churches and church organizations, Negro, 119
  child welfare services and, 204, 210–211
  older African American women and, 215
Cleghorn, Kate, 194
Cleveland, NUL and, 144
Clinton, Marie Louise, 107
Coleman, Maude B., 107
Colleges, child welfare services and, 205
Collins, Caleb Alexander, 179
Collins, Mary Jane Driver, 179
Collins, Sarah Sinclair, 27
Colored Big Sister Home for Girls, Kansas City, MO, 125
"Colored Offenders and the Police Courts" (Fernandis), 180
"Colored Serenader, The," Oxley as, 100
Colored Settlement of Washington, DC, 180
Colored Social Settlement, Washington, DC, 180–182, 183, 185
Colored Woman in a White World, A (Terrell), 153, 159
Colored Women's League (CWL), 5
  of Washington, DC, 155
Columbian Exposition, Chicago (1893), 89–90
Columbia University, 114
Combined facilities for children and aged people, 207
Commercial Club, Nashville, 116
Committee of Forty, National Negro Congress, 93
Community building, 75
Community Charities Chest Committee, 125
Community of African American women, 12
Community organization
  in disenfranchised communities, 71
  functional, 77
  Oxley promotion of, 104
  principles of, 22
Community practice, social and economic development model of, 77
Comprehensive programs for grandparent caregiver support, 225
Congress of American Women, 169–170, 173, 175
Congress of Industrial Organizations, 145
Consciousness raising, 76
Conservative *versus* liberal political agendas, 67–68
Conservator (newspaper), 89
Constitution (Atlanta newspaper), 197, 198
Contact hypothesis, 160
Convict Lease System, Georgia, 159
Cook, Sharon Warren, xvii
Coolidge, Calvin, 56
Cooper, Anna Julia, 155
Cooperative Women's Civic League, Baltimore, 186
Coppin, Levi J., 20, 25
Coppin, Melissa E. Thompson, 25, 26, 27
Cotton States and International Exposition, Women's Auxiliary to the Negro Department of, 6
Council of Social Work Education, 174
Council on Colored Work, YWCA, 117
Course of African Philosophy, The (Garvey), 77
Creditt, W. A., 20
Critical consciousness, 71
Crono, E., 82
Cullen, Countee, 119
Curah, Huguette A., xvii

Dancy, John C., 145
Daniel, S., 128
Darkwater (DuBois), 217
Davis, A. F., 184
Davis, Ann, 65
Davis, Arthur, 194
"A Day at Lincoln House, Wednesday, May 26, 1970" (Haynes), 46–47
Delta Sigma Theta Sorority, 156
Denmark, Frazier's study of cooperative movements in, 192
Detroit Urban League, 23, 145–146
DeVries, C., 223
Dickerson, J. Edward, 20
Dickerson, Joyce G., xv
District of Columbia. *See* Washington, DC
District of Columbia v. John Thompson (1950), 160
Division of Work Among Negroes, North Carolina State Board of Charities and Public Welfare, 101–102
  social research, 104–105
  social work education, 105–106
  social work profession and, 107

Dodge, Grace, 11
Douglass, Frederick, 90, 154, 220
Drake, St. Clair, 193
Draper, T., 80
Drug abuse, 223
Project GUIDE (Detroit), 225
DuBois, W. E. B., 18
Frazier and, 191
on Garvey, 76, 82
Terrell and, 159
Wells-Barnett and, 93
on women during slavery, 217
Dunbar, Paul Laurence, 11
Durham Fact-Finding Conference, 139
Durham School, Philadelphia, 22

East Nashville Fire of 1916, 116, 118, 120
Ecological perspective of UNIA & ACL, 76
Education
child welfare services and, 204–205
Fernandis on, 184–185
Edwards, Anna, 163
Edwards, Anna Bell, 163
Edwards, Bell, 164
Edwards, Horace, 163
Edwards, Thelma, 163, 169
Edwards, Thyra J., xvii, 163–177
child welfare and study abroad, 164–165
final years, 172–174
journalistic work, 169
lecture tours, 169–170
as model social worker, 174–175
organizing Black women, 165–167
personal life, 171–172
relief work, 167–168
social work education, 163–164
Spanish Civil War and, 170–171
world tours, 168–169
Elderly advocacy, Oxley and, 100, 101
Elfland Home for Girls, 107
Elizabeth Ross Haynes Club, 120
Elizabeth Russell Plantation Settlement, xvi, 62, 65–66
Elliott, Mary A., 59
Emlen, John T., 19–20, 21, 22, 23
Empowerment tradition, xiv
extended family model of, xv
Fernandis and, 182
Garvey and, 76
Oxley and, 99–100
patience in, 148
Philadelphia, 30
practice dimensions, 115
practice principles for organizing with women of color, 12
Wells-Barnett and, 88, 90
See also Racial uplift; Self-help
Encyclopedia of Social Work, 189
Erlich, J., 68, 69
Ethiopia, Peace Movement of, 82
Ethnic communities, social work practice in, 69–71
Evans, Anne M., 67
Extended family model of empowerment, xv, 113, 211

Family structure
changes in, 222
contemporary helping roles and family relationships, 223–224
grandparent as head in, 222–223
during slavery, 216–218
Family support programs, 181–182, 211–212
Fanon, Frantz, 195
Father Divine, 82
Fathers' role during slavery, 217–218
Federal Security Agency, Subversive Personnel Committee, 173
Federated Press, 169
Federation of Colored Women's Clubs, 206
Fellowship Program, National Urban League, 118
Female Benevolent Society, Philadelphia, 92
Feminist issues, Terrell and, 157–158
Fernandis, John, 180
Fernandis, Sarah Collins, xvii, 179–188
career, 185–186
Colored Social Settlement and, 180–182
on education, 184–185
historical significance of, 183–184
neighborhood network building, 182–183
Fields, Mamie Garvin, 156
Fisk Preparatory School, Nashville, Tenn., 36, 58
Fisk University, Nashville, Tenn., 36, 114, 116, 118
Ford, Henry, 145
Forten, James, 19
Fortune, T. Thomas, 3, 80
Fort Valley High and Industrial School, Georgia, 192
Forum, 197
Foster care
regulations, 211
WCA, 26
Foundation of Religion and Labor, 170
Franklin, Benjamin, 18
Frazier, E. Franklin, xvii, 24, 113, 189–201
on grandmothers, 216, 218–219, 220
on mothers' role during slavery, 217, 218
psychology of race hatred, 195–198, 199
racial justice commitment, 193–195
socialism of, 191–193
social work and, 190–191
Frazier, W. W., 20
Frederick Douglass Center Women's Club, 94
Free Speech and Headlight, The (newspaper), 89, 90–91
Friends of Mrs. Ella Sachs Plotz, 140

Frisell, N. B., 20
"Functions of Leadership" (Wells-Barnett), 89

Gamble, D., 77, 81
Garvey, Amy Jacques, 79
Garvey, Marcus, xiv, xvi
- aims and objectives, 78–79
- Black Star Line Steamship Corporation, 81–82
- charisma, 82
- ecological perspective of, 76
- functional community organizing, 77
- *See also* Universal Negro Improvement Association (UNIA)

Garveyism, 77–78
Garvey Movement, 77–78
Garvey's Voice, 79
Gate City Kindergarten, Atlanta, 208
Gender, African American social work and, 113
Giddings, P., 59, 157
Gilkerson, M. E., 106
Giovannoni, J. M., 26, 203
"Girls' Home Responsibilities" (M. M. Washington), 67
Gitlin, Murray, 173
Glueck, Bernard, 194
Gordon, L., 114, 117
"Go-To-High School, Go-To-College" radio broadcast, 140–141
Gottleib, P., 144
Grammer, C. E., 20
Grandmothers
- contemporary helping roles and family relationships of, 223–224
- as heads of households, 222–223
- slavery role of, 218–220
- *See also* Older African American women

Grandparent Information Center, American Association of Retired Persons (AARP), 225
Grandparents as Second Parents (GASP), 225
Grant, Claudia, 24, 27
Grass roots efforts, Matthews's, 13
Graves, Mrs. A., 208
Graves, William, 39, 40–41, 43
Great Depression
- African American employment and, 146
- African American migration and, 138–139
- Oxley and, 106

Great Migration, 18
- *See also* Migration, African American

Grossman, J., 42
Grossman, J. R., 144
Guillen, Nicholas, 170

Hamilton, T., 157
Hampton Institute, 19, 127, 179
Harlan, L. R., 58, 59, 61
Harris, Abram, 147
Harris, Ada B. Carter, 26
Harrison, Benjamin, 154
Hart, Hastings, 126, 128
Harvey, Aminifu, xvi
Haynes, Birdye Henrietta, xv, 35–53, 114, 115
- career overview, 35–37
- formal duties, 46–47
- handling gangs, 45–46
- health, 48
- "Home and Babies" program, 210
- informal duties, 47
- at Lincoln House, 43–48
- resignation, 47–48
- Rosenwald and, 37–39
- support system, 50
- Wendell Phillips Settlement and, 39–43
- White reformers' attitudes towards, 49–50

Haynes, Elizabeth Ross, xvi, 50, 114–115
- affluence of, 58
- involving clients as participants, 119
- philanthropy, 117–118
- publications, 120
- social service work, 116–117
- teaching, education, and skill development commitments, 118–119

Haynes, George Edmund, xii, xvi, 35, 36, 39, 114–115, 220
- and his sister, 50
- on his sister's administrative work, 45
- on his sister's employment, 43–44
- involving clients as participants, 119
- NLUCAN and, 37, 116
- publications, 120
- teaching, education, and skill development commitments, 118

Hemingway, T., xiv
Henry Street Settlement, New York City, 44
Herndon, Mr. and Mrs. A. F., 208
Hiatt, James S., 20
Hine, Darlene Clark, 56, 60, 87
HIV/AIDS, 223
Hodges, Vanessa G., xvii
Holloway, Cecelia, 117
Holt, Olivia, 48
Home and school visitors, 22
Home for the Aged and Infirm Colored Persons, Philadelphia, Penna., 19
Homes for wayward children, 209–210
Homes for working girls, 209
Hoover, J. Edgar, 82
Hope, John, 198
Hope, Lugenia Burns, 145, 208
Hopkins, Wayne L., 25
Hopper, Franklin, 140
Housing restrictions, African American, 17–18, 42
Howard, Mrs. David T., 208
Howard University Socialist Club, 191
Hubert, James, 44
Hughes, Langston, 119, 170
Hull House, 38, 42

Ida B. Wells Club(s), 5, 92, 94
"Ideal Home for a Girl, An" (M. M. Washington), 67
Illinois Children's Home and Aid Society, 36, 38
Illinois Emergency Relief Commission, 167
Immigrants, 80, 184
Immigration Act of 1917, 18
Incarcerations, 223
Industrial Home for (Wayward) Colored Girls, 127
Infant mortality, 204
Injustice, correction of, 28–29
Institution building, 100
See also Capacity building
Intellectual biography, xii
"Intermittent Husbands and Lax Family Ties" (Fernandis), 180
International Congress of Women (1904), 67
International Council of Women of the Darker Races, 67–68
International Labor Congress (1944), 173
International Ladies Garment Workers Union (ILGWU), 165–167
International League for Peace and Freedom, 159
International People's College, Elsinore, Denmark, 164

Jacks, J. W., 5
Jail, child welfare and, 124, 127
Jefferson, Lucy C., 66
W. H. Jefferson Funeral Home (Miss.), 66
Jenks, Mrs. William F., 20
Jennifer, William, 107
Jim Crow Laws, 159
Johnson, A., xii
Johnson, Charles S., 37, 139, 140, 198, 217
Johnson, Kate Burr, 105, 107–108
Johnson, William R., 106
Joint Emergency Relief Commission, 167
Jones, Absalom, 19
Jones, Eugene Kinckle, xiv, xvi–xvii, 36, 44, 137–152
empowerment-based practice guidelines, 146–149
Haynes and, 47, 50, 137
historical outreach, 139–143
on leadership development, 148
on local knowledge, 149
as member of "Talented Tenth," 147
as NUL executive secretary, 138–139
on patience for empowerment, 148
pushing NUL agenda, 143–146
on racial prejudice, 148–149
radio broadcasts, 140–141
on social research, 147
on trained Negro social workers, 147
Journalism
Matthews and, 3
Wells-Barnett and, 89
Julius Rosenwald Fellowship, 36
Juvenile court system, 124, 127

Keller, Gertrude, 104
Kelley, Florence, 36, 48, 191, 193
Kellor, Frances, 10
Kennedy, John F., 101
Keyser, Frances Reynolds, 11
Kindergartens, 207–209
Kinship care services, 211
Knights of Labor, 146
Knights of Pythias, 205
Koerin, B., 112
Kusmer, K. L., 144
Kyle, Constance, 170

Lafon, Thomy, 206
Lake County Children's Home, xvii
Larkin, John, 106
Lathrop, Julia, 38
Laura B. Spellman Rockefeller Memorial Fund, 101, 140
Leadership
development of, 148
Matthews's, 13
of settlement leaders, 70–71
Wells-Barnett on, 89, 96
League of Cook County Clubs of Chicago Women, 94
League of Women Voters, National, 185–186
League on Urban Conditions Among Negroes. *See* National League on Urban Conditions Among Negroes (NLUCAN)
Lee, Porter, 194
"Let's Confer Together" (Ruffin), 5
Lewis, J. W., 40
Liberation, Wells-Barnett on, 95
Licensing child welfare services, 211
Light House of New York Association for the Blind, 46
Lincoln Center, Chicago, 168, 173
Lincoln House Settlement, New York City, xv, 14, 139
Haynes and, 35, 36, 43–48
"Home and Babies" component, 210
Lincoln University (Penn.), 22
Lindeman, Eduard, 161, 191, 193
Lindsay, Inabel Burns, 147, 195
Little Mother's League, Durham School, Philadelphia, 22–23
Local knowledge, Jones on, 149
Locke, A., 112
Locust Street Settlement, Child Welfare Department, 127, 210, 209
Lodges, child welfare services and, 205
Lowndes County, Alabama, 119
Loyal Union. *See* Women's Loyal Union

Lynch law, 221
  Blair Bill against, 92
  Matthews and, 4
  Terrell and, 154
  Wells-Barnett and, 87, 90–92
Lynch Law in America (Wells-Barnett), 92
Lynch Law in Georgia (Wells-Barnett), 92
Lyons, Maritcha, 4

Manly, Alex L., 21
Martin, Elmer P., xvii, 75, 113, 175
Martin, Joanne M., xvii, 75, 113, 175
Martin, T., 77, 82–83
"Martyred Negro Soldiers" button, 94
Masons, child welfare services and, 205, 206
Matthews, Larmartine, 2, 7
Matthews, Victoria Earle, xv, 1–16, 209
  African American women and, 12
  community empowerment and, 7–8, 12–13
  empowerment tradition and, 12
  journalist, 3
  leadership and legacy, 11, 13
  as national organizer and leader, 5–7
  recognizing racism, 14
  slavery, 2
  traveler's aid, 9–11, 118, 221–222
  vision of, 13
  White Rose Mission and, xiii, 8–9
  women's clubs movement and, 3–4
  Women's Loyal Union and, 4–5
Matthews, William, 2
McCrea, Roswell, 120
McCrory, Mary Jackson, 108
McDougald, Elise, 49
McDowell, Calvin, 90
McKay, Claude, 80, 170
McKinney, Susan, 4
McMurry, L. O., 89
Messenger, The, 49, 191
Midwest, employment in, 18
Migration, African American, xv, 17, 18, 29, 221–222
  Garveyism and, 80
  NUL newcomers' dance, 119
  NUL support services, 118, 137–138
  Progressive Era, 14
  reasons for, 111–112
  Southern poverty and, 64
  tensions over, 144
  M. Washington on, 57
  See also Traveler's aid
Milnor Street Nursery, Jacksonville, FL, 206
Minkler, M., 224
Mob Rule in New Orleans (Wells-Barnett), 92
"Modern Woman, The" (Terrell), 156–157
Moore, E. W., 20
Moorehouse, Hattie, 7
Moorish Americans, 82
"Moral Standards of the Alleys, The" (Fernandis), 180
Morton-Jones, Verina, 44
Moss, Thomas, 90, 154
Mothers' clubs
  child welfare services and, 205
  NACW and, 158
Mothers' Congress, 159
"Mother's Relation to the Teacher" (M. M. Washington), 67
Mothers' role during slavery, 216–218
Mt. Meigs Reformatory for Juvenile Law-Breakers, xvi, 66
Mt. Meigs Rescue Home for Girls, xvi, 66
Mowbray, Paul, 116
Murray, James, 58
Murray, Lucy, 58
Mutual aid
  child welfare and, 124, 210–211
  See also Self-help
Myrdal, Gunnar, 138, 194
Nashville Negro Board of Trade, 116
National Afro-American Council, 93
National American Women's Suffrage Association, 158, 159
National Association for the Advancement of Colored People (NAACP), xvi, 194, 221
  self-help and, 112
  Wells-Barnett and, 93
National Association of Charities and Corrections, xvii
National Association of Child Welfare, 130
National Association of Colored Graduate Nurses, 142
National Association of Colored Women (NACW), xiii, 3, 221
  child welfare and, 124, 206
  E. R. Haynes and, 117
  M. M. Washington and, 67
  merger with NFAAW, 6–7
  self-help and, 112
  Terrell and, 155
  Wells-Barnett and, 92–93
National Bar Association, 142
National Colored Press Association, 89
National Colored Women's Association, 88
National Colored Women's Congress (1895), 6
National Committee on Urban Conditions of Negroes, 39
National Conference of Charities and Corrections, 183
National Conference of Social Work (NCSW), 141–142, 143, 193–194
National Equal Rights League (NERL), 93
National Federation of Afro-American Women (NFAAW), 3, 6–7, 66, 155

National League for the Protection of Colored Women in New York City and Philadelphia, 10–11
National League of Women Voters, 185–186
National League on Urban Conditions Among Negroes (NLUCAN), xiii, 23, 37, 116
  See also National Urban League
National Maritime Union, 173
National Medical Association, 142
National Negro Congress (1909), 93
National Negro Congress, Women's Section, 169–170
National Notes (NACW), 67
National Urban League (NUL), xii, 50
  community building, 75
  Department of Research and Investigation, 147
  Fellowship Program, 118, 143
  G. Haynes and, 115, 116
  Jones and, 138, 139
  NCSW and, 193–194
  Neighborhood Union of Atlanta and, 144–145
  newcomers' dance, 119
  self-help and, 112
  Wendell Phillips Settlement House and, 43
National Youth Administration, 22
Nationhood, Garvey on, 77
Negro at Work in New York City, The (G. Haynes), 120
Negroes in Domestic Service in the United States (Ross Haynes), 117, 120
Negro Factories Corporation, 81
Negro Family in the United States, The (Frazier), 189
Negro Fellowship League and Reading Room, xvi, 80, 94
Negro history commemorations, 66
Negro in the Making of America, The (Quarles), 216
Negro in the United States, The (Frazier), 189, 218–219
"Negro's Opportunity Today, The" (Jones), 141
Negro World, 79, 80
Neighborhood Covenant, 205
Neighborhood Union of Atlanta, 144–145
New Currents of Thought Among Negroes in America (Frazier), 191, 1890
New Era Club, 205–206
Newman, D., 101
New York School of Philanthropy, 114, 140
New York School of Social Work, 179, 190
New York State Conference of Charities and Corrections, 141
Niagara Movement, 93, 221
North, employment in, 18
  See also Migration, African American
North Carolina Federation of Colored Women, 107
North Carolina Public Welfare Institutes for Negroes, 105, 107
North Carolina State Board of Charities and Public Welfare, 108n1, 108n2
  Division of Work Among Negroes, 101–102
  social research, 104–105
  social work education, 105–106
  social work profession and, 107
Notable Black Women, 55–56
Nurses. *See* Universal African Black Cross Nurses

Obedience, Wells-Barnett on, 96
Oberlin College, 154, 159, 160
Odd Fellows, child welfare services and, 205
Ohio State University, 140
Older African American women, xvii, 215–228
  contemporary helping roles and family relationships, 223–224
  family structure changes and, 222
  grandparent caregiver support, 224–225
  grandparent-maintained families, 222–223
  postbellum roles, 220–222
  in precolonial African family, 216
  role during slavery, 218–220
Old Folks and Orphans' Home, Memphis, TN, 207
Old folks' homes, xv
Old Ladies and Orphans' Home, Memphis, TN, 207
Opportunity, 146
Organized leisure, xv
Orphanages, 206–207
"Out of Work: A Study of Employment Agencies" (Kellor), 10
Ovington, Mary White, 36
  Colored Social Settlement, Washington, DC and, 183, 184
  Haynes and, 44, 50
  NAACP and, 194
Owen, Chandler, 80, 191
Oxley, Alice Agatha, 100
Oxley, Lawrence A., xvi, 99–110, 220
  Division of Work Among Negroes, 101–102
  personal side of, 100–101
  self-help and, 102–104
  social research, 104–105
  social work education, 105–106
  social work practice and, 106–108
Oxley, Mamie Elizabeth Hill, 100
Oxley, William J. B., 100

Pan-Africanism, 76, 78
Parris, Guichard, 115
"Pathology of Race Prejudice, The" (Frazier), 197

Patterson, Mary Jane, 155
Paul, J. Rodman, 20
Payments, child welfare services, 211
Peace Movement of Ethiopia, 82
Peebles-Wilkins, Wilma, xvi, 112
Penn, I. Garland, 90
Pennsylvania, slavery in, 18
People's Voice, The (newspaper), 173
Perkins, Frances, 100
Permanency of child welfare services, 211
Perry, Fredericka Douglass Sprague, 125
Phelps, Winthrop, 7
Phelps Stokes Fund, 140
Philadelphia, Penn., 18, 19, 21, 25
Philadelphia Colored Directory, 23
Philadelphia Negro, The (DuBois), 18
Philadelphia Training School for Social Workers, 22
Philanthropists, child welfare services and, 206
Phillips, Henry L., 20
Phillips, Karl F., 146
Pickens, W., 76, 82
Pou, Edward, 106
Poverty, African American, xiv, 64
Powdermaker, H., 219
Powell, Adam Clayton, Jr., 173
Praxis, Matthews, understanding of, 13
Preparatory School for Colored Youth, 154
Prison Congress of the United States, 92
Prison reform, 66
Progressive Era (1898–1918), xiii, 113, 156, 183–184
"Progress of Colored Women, The" (Terrell), 158
Project GUIDE, Detroit, 225
Psychology of race hatred, Frazier on, 195–198
Public Welfare League (Tenn.), 116
Public Works Administration, Housing Division of, 167

Quakers, 58
Quarles, B., 216

Race first, 77
Race man, 115
Race pride, 112–113
Race riots, 221
Race woman, 115
"Racial Adjustments Through Neighborhood Groups" (F. B. Washington), 24
Racial justice, Frazier and, 193–195
Racial prejudice
  in child welfare services, 203–204
  Frazier's study of, 196–197
  Jones on, 148–149
  social work profession and, xiii
  Terrell and, 153, 161
Racial uplift, 112–113
  child welfare services and, 211
  Colored Women's League (CWL) and, 155
  See also Empowerment tradition; Self-help
Radio broadcasts, 140–141
Randolph, A. Phillip, 80, 164, 191
Rape, lynching and, 91
Reconciliation, Wells-Barnett on, 96
"Red Record, A: Tabulated Statistics and Alleged Causes of Lynchings in the United States, 1892-1893-1894" (Wells-Barnett), 91
Reform schools, 124, 127
Reid, Ira de A., 147
Relatives as Parents Program (RAPP), Brookdale Grandparent Information Center, 224–225
"Retention of Miss Haynes at Wendell Phillips, Stipend for Colored Girls School of Civics" (Graves), 40–41
Rich, Anna, 10, 11
Richards, Bertha, 107
Richardson, Abigail L., 22–23
Rivera, F., 69
Robeson, Paul, 170
Robinson, J. A., 107
Robinson, J. G., 107
Robinson, William, 191
Rockefeller, J. D., 138
Roe, K., 224
Rogers, J. A., 80
Roosevelt, Franklin D., 100, 106, 167
Rosenwald, Julius, 37–39, 41, 43, 138
Ross Haynes, Elizabeth. *See* Haynes, Elizabeth Ross
Rothman, J., 68
Royal College for the Blind, 61
Ruffin, Josephine St. Pierre, 4, 66, 205–206
Ruiz, Dorothy S., xvii
Russell, Hattie, 102
Russell Sage Foundation, Child Welfare Department, 123, 126, 128

Sabbath, Tawana Ford, xv, 17–33
Sadler, Frank, 40, 41
St. Augustine's College, Raleigh, NC, Bishop Tuttle Memorial Training School of Social Work, 143
  G. E. Haynes and, 116
  Oxley and, 99, 104, 105
  Richards and, 107
Scattergood, J. Henry, 20
Schiefflin, William J., 20
Schomberg, Arthur A., 139
School attendance, compulsory, 203
School of Public Welfare, University of Chapel Hill, NC, 108n1
Schools, child welfare services and, 204–205
Scoville, Samuel, Jr., 20
Secret organizations, child welfare services and, 205
Segregation, xiii
  Alabama, 62–63, 64
  child welfare and, 124

Segregation *(continued)*
Fernandis's work and, 183–184
Frazier's response to, 193–195
Haynes and, 49–50
Oxley and, 100, 105–106
professional, 142
self-help and, 103
Terrell's fight against, 160
in welfare work, 102
Self-efficacy, Garvey on, 77, 81
Self-help
African American migration and, 112
child welfare and, 124
Colored Women's League (CWL) and, 155
Division of Work Among Negroes, NC, 101–102
Oxley and, 99–100, 102–104
See also Empowerment tradition; Racial uplift
Self-reliance, Garvey on, 77
Settlement houses, xv
community building, 75
Philadelphia, 24–25
See also specific settlement houses
Sexism
employment and, 220
social work profession and, xiii–xiv
Terrell and, 153, 157–158
Sexual exploitation of African American women, xiii–xiv, 64
Matthews and, 7–8
Shelby County, Tenn. lynch laws, 90
Shepard, James E., 106
Simon, B., 75, 76, 115, 119, 144, 148
Sims, George, 44, 47
Slavery, 2, 18, 216–218
Small, Sam, 197, 198
Small groups group building, 13
Smith, Anna, 2
Smith, Caroline, 2
Smith, E. E., 103
Smith, J., 55–56
Smith, Stephen, 19
Smith, Victoria Earle, 2
Smith, William, 2
Social and economic development model of community practice, 77
Social debt, African American, 113
Social research, 104–105, 147
Social responsibility, Terrell and, 161
Social Service, 183
Social Work, 115
Social workers
African American, 49
among African Americans, 103–104
Social work profession
African American social welfare movement, xi
assimilationist practice, xvii
development, 17, 111–114
Edwards as model for, 174–175
family support approach, 181–182
Jones's empowerment-based guidelines, 146–149
M. M. Washington and, 69–71
in North Carolina, xvi, 106–108
Philadelphia, 27
pioneers, xiv–xv
Terrell and, 160–161
Wells-Barnett and, 95–96
Solomon, Barbara, xiv
South
employment in, 18
psychology of race hatred in, 196
Southeastern Federation of Colored Women, 66
Southern Horrors: Lynch Law in All Its Phases (Wells-Barnett), 4, 91
Soviet Russia Today, 169
Spanish Civil War, 170–171
Spanish Relief Campaign, 171
Spaulding, C. C., 106
Steele, Carrie, 125, 207
Steward, Gustavus Adolphus, 198, 199
Stewart, Henry, 90
Stone, Mary L., 11
Sumner, Walter T., 39, 40, 41
Supervision, child welfare services, 211
Support groups, grandparent caregiver, 225

Taylor, Graham, 36, 38
Terrell, Mary Church, xvii, 2, 153–162
affluence of, 58
on child welfare, 124–125, 206
Colored Women's League and, 5, 155
leverage of, 160
NAACP and, 221
NACW and, 6–7, 157–158
political savvy, 158–159
racism/sexism and, 153–155
social work practice and, 160–161
women's clubs movement and, 4, 155–157
Terrell, Robert, 154
Third Ward Women's Political Club, Chicago, 94
Thomas, J. O., 198
Thompson, K., 68
Tilghman, A. E., 2
Tindley, Charles A., 20
Townes, E. M., 87, 95
Town Night School, Tuskegee, Ala., xvi, 62, 63–65
Traveler's aid, 9–11, 118, 221–222
See also Migration, African American
Trend of the Races, The (G. Haynes), 120
Tropman, J., 68
Trotter, William, 93
Tuskegee, Ala. poverty, 64
Tuskegee Institute, 19, 56, 60–61
Tuskegee Spirit, 61

Tuskegee Woman's Club, xv–xvi, 62–63
Elizabeth Russell Plantation Settlement and, 65
Town Night School and, 63
Twain, Mark, 61
Two Million Negro Women at Work (Ross Haynes), 120
Tyler, George, 82

Unionism, 145–146, 164
United Charities, Chicago, 38
Universal African Black Cross Nurses, xvi, 80–81
Universal African Legion, 80
Universal African Motor Corps, 80
Universal Negro Improvement Association (UNIA), xiii, xvi, 75–85
aims and objectives, 78–79
decline of, 82–83
funding, 81–82
leadership, 82
membership and dues, 79–80
organizations within, 80–81
preamble, 78
University of California, Berkeley Center on Aging, 224–225
University of Chapel Hill, NC, School of Public Welfare, 108n1
University of Chicago, 114
School of Social Administration, 140
University of Pennsylvania School of Social and Health Work, 22
University of Pittsburgh, 140
Unsung Heroes (Ross Haynes), 120
Up from Slavery (Washington), 61
Urban League
Detroit, 23
Philadelphia, 21, 25
See also National Urban League (NUL)
U.S. Department of Agriculture, Women's Rural Organization, 67
U.S. Department of Commerce, Negro Affairs Office, 146
U.S. Department of Labor
Oxley and, 100–101, 106
Women in Industry Service, 120
U.S. Employment Service, 101
U.S. Public Health Service, Women's Advisory Council, 186

"Value of Race Literature, The" (Matthews), 5
Van Kleeck, Mary, 117–118, 191, 194
Victimization of African American women, 7–8
Victoria, Queen (England), 61
Virginia, women fund managers and, 127–128
Virginia Federation of Women's Clubs, 123, 125
Virginia Industrial School for Colored Girls, xvi, 123–135, 209–210
admissions and intake, 128–129
discharge, 131–132
founding, 127–128
parole, 130–131
preparation, 129–130
response to, 132
turned over to state, 125
Virginia State Board of Welfare, 128
Virginia Union University, 141
Vision, Matthews's, 13
Voice of Iola, 89–90
See also Wells-Barnett, Ida Bell
Voluntary associations
child welfare and, 124
Fernandis and, 182
women and, 220

Waites, Cheryl, xv
Wald, Lillian, 36, 43, 44, 48, 126
Haynes and, 46
Walker, A., 87
Walker, C. J., 80, 206
Walton, Elizabeth, 44
Washington, Baker, 59
Washington, Booker T., xv, 9, 11
accomodationist philosophy, 37
on Alabama poverty, 64
Frazier on, 191–192
M. M. Washington and, 56, 58, 59–60
National Afro-American Council and, 93
Terrell and, 159
Up from Slavery, 61
Washington, Davidson, 59
Washington, DC
Associated Charities, 180, 183, 185
Colored Settlement of, 180
Colored Social Settlement, 180–182, 183, 185
Colored Women's League (CWL), 155
women's opportunities in , 220
Washington, Forrester B., 23–24, 104, 106–107, 140, 145
Washington, George, 206
Washington, John H., 61
Washington, Josephine Turpin, 2
Washington, Laura Murray, 59
Washington, Margaret Murray, xv–xvi, 6, 55–73
B. T. Washington and, 59–60
early life, 58
Elizabeth Russell Plantation Settlement and, 65–66
organizing Southern rural women, 61–62
as role model, 57
rural leadership road, 57–60
social work practice and, 69–71
state and national work of, 66–68
Town Night School and, 63–65
as Tuskegee's third First Lady, 60–61
Tuskegee Woman's Club and, 62–63

Washington, Portia, 59
Wayward children, homes for, 209–210
WCA. *See* Women's Christian Alliance (WCA)
Weaver Orphan Home, Hampton, VA, 127
Weil, M., 75, 77, 81
Welfare Federation of Philadelphia, 23
Wells-Barnett, Ida Bell, xiv, xvi, 87–98
 anti-lynching crusade, 90–92
 club organizer, 92–95
 Garvey and, 80
 on liberation, 95
 NAACP and, 221
 on obedience, 96
 on reconciliation, 96
 social work practice and, 95–96
 sues Chesapeake and Ohio Railroad, 89
 on White reformers, 49
 as womanist race leader, 88–90
 women's clubs movement and, 4
Wendell Phillips Settlement House, Chicago, xv
 Haynes and, 35, 36, 39–43
 racism on board of, 42
Wharton Center, 24
"What Professional Training Means to the Social Worker" (F. B. Washington), 24
Wheatley, Phillis, 9
"When Shall a Girl Be Permitted to Receive Her First Company" (M. M. Washington), 67
White, D., 155, 157, 159
White, Eartha Mary Magdelene, 206
White attitudes
 about Southern poverty, 64
 of reformers, 49–50
White Rose Home for Working Girls, xv, 11, 13, 14, 209, 221–222
White Rose Mission and Industrial Association, xiii, 8, 11, 14, 209, 221
White Rose Traveler's Aid Society, 9–10
Williams, Talcott, 20
Wilson, W. J., 17
Womanism, 87, 114
Womanist Christian Ethic, xvi, 95
Woman's Era (Boston), 3, 5, 6, 14, 92
Woman's Era Club of Boston, 3, 5
Woman Today, The, 169
Women, older. *See* Older African American women
Women's Christian Alliance (WCA), xv
 Philadelphia, 19, 25–27
 professional empowerment, 30
 program flexibility, 29
 strengths model, 28
Women's Civic League, "Colored" branch, 186
Women's clubs movement
 child welfare services and, 205–206
 community building, 75
 criticism of, 157
 E. R. Haynes and, 117
 Matthews and, 3–4
 in North Carolina, 108n1
 Terrell and, xvii, 155–156
 Wells-Barnett and, 92–95
Women's Forum, Chicago, 94
Women's Home Missionary Society, Boston, 179–180
Women's League of Women, Tuskegee, Ala., 62
Women's Liberal Club, Bristol, England, 61
Women's Loyal Union, 4–5, 9
Women's Rural Organization, U.S. Department of Agriculture, 67
Women's suffrage movement, xvi, 4, 94, 158, 159
Wood, L. Hollingsworth, 139
Wood, Mrs. L. Hollingsworth, 140
Woodson, Carter G., 66
Woofter, Thomas, 194–195
Working girls, homes for, 209
Working Women's Conference, Philadelphia, 22
Works Progress Administration, 22
World Fellowship of Faiths, 159
World Peace Echo, 79
World's Christian Endeavors Convention, 7
World's Fair, Chicago (1893), 89–90
World systems theory, 175
Wright, Richard R., Jr. (AME bishop, b. 1878), 19, 20, 21
Wright, Richard Robert (banker, 1855–1947), 120

Young Men's Christian Association (YMCA), 117, 190
Young Women's Christian Association (YWCA), 11, 117
Youth programs, 40
 See also Child welfare services

African American Leadership
An Empowerment Tradition in Social Welfare History

Cover design by Metadog Design Group

Cover art by Paul Nzalamba
Paul Nzalamba, a native of Uganda, expresses his cultural heritage as well as his personal experiences through his art. Nzalamba's work is characterized by an exotic and rhythmic use of vibrant color and form. Much of his subject matter has its roots in the scenes, people, and animals of his upbringing and is expressive of a man who cares a great deal about people, their strengths, struggles, and beauty.

Paul Nzalamba, P. O. Box 65036, Los Angeles, CA 90065

Interior design and composition by Cynthia Stock, Electronic Quill

Typeset in Berkeley

Printed by Victor Graphics, Inc.